Secrets of Inferno

In the Footsteps of Dante and Dan Brown

by Dan Burstein
and Arne de Keijzer

THE
STORY PLANT

The Story Plant
Studio Digital CT, LLC
PO Box 4331
Stamford, CT 06907

Jacket design by Barbara Aronica-Buck

Print ISBN-13: 978-1-61188-082-3
E-book ISBN-13: 978-1-61188-081-6

Visit our website at www.TheStoryPlant.com

First Story Plant e-book edition: August 2013
First Story Plant printing: September 2013

Printed in the United States of America

0 9 8 7 6 5 4 3 2 1

For
Julie, my Beatrice…Woman of my dreams and dream of my real
life every single day,
and
David, who like the ancient Jewish King in Dante's *Paradiso*,
knows how to rid the world of Goliaths and write philosophy
and poetry.
—Dan Burstein

For
Helen and Hannah, with love.
"Alas, how scant is speech."
—Arne de Keijzer

"Then she opened up a book of poems
And handed it to me
Written by an Italian poet
From the thirteenth century.
And every one of them words rang true…"

—Bob Dylan, "Tangled Up in Blue"

Contents

Editor's Note 13

Introduction: *Secrets of Inferno: In the Footsteps of Dante and Dan Brown* 15

Section 1:
Dante for the Twenty-first Century

Welcome to My Dante Spring
  By Dan Burstein, Creator, author, and coeditor of the Secrets series 25

Dan Brown and the Case of the Wrong Dante
  By Teodolinda Barolini, Da Ponte Professor of Italian, Columbia University 39

Damnation vs. Demography: Contrasting *Infernos* of Dante and Dan Brown
  By Alison Cornish, Professor of Italian, Romance Languages, and Literatures department, University of Michigan 49

Dante as Humanist, Radical Reformer, and Old Testament-Style Prophet
  An Interview with Steven Botterill, Associate Professor of Italian Studies, University of California, Berkeley 57

Letting the Genre out of the Bottle: Dan Brown's *Inferno* as Modern Parody
  By Glenn W. Erickson, Professor of Philosophy, Universidade Federal do Rio Grande do Norte (Brazil) 67

Preposterous but Not Absurd: Dan Brown's *Inferno* Embraces More of Dante's Perspective Than You Might Think
  By Giuseppe Mazzotta, Sterling Professor of Humanities for Italian, Yale University 77

Why Everyone Who Reads Dan Brown's *Inferno* Could Benefit from Reading Dante's *Inferno*—and All of the *Divine Comedy*
  By William Cook, Distinguished Teaching Professor of History (Emeritus), State University of New York, Geneseo 83

Dante to Washington: Gridlock, Partisanship, and Factionalism are Deadly Sins and Will Land You in the Inferno
  By Dan Burstein, Creator, author, and coeditor of the Secrets series 88

Beneath the Veil: Parallel Universes and *Inferno* Resonances
  By Dan Burstein, Creator, author, and coeditor of the Secrets series 95

Section 2:
Bold New World

An Overview of Dan Brown's Arguments on Population Control,
Technology, and Transhumanism
By Arne de Keijzer, coauthor and coeditor of the Secrets *series* 111
Demografiction
*By Joel E. Cohen, Abby Rockefeller Mauzé Professor of Populations at
The Rockefeller University and Professor of Populations at the Earth
Institute of Columbia University* 122
"You Simply Have to Be Insane to Think that You Can Just
Continue to Grow Forever on a Finite Planet"
*An Interview With Paul Ehrlich, Bing Professor of Population Studies,
Stanford University, president of Stanford's Center for Conservation
Biology, and author of* The Population Bomb 127
The End of the World Isn't as Likely as Humans Fighting Back
*An Interview With Jamais Cascio, Distinguished Fellow, Institute
for the Future and Senior Fellow, Institute for Ethics and Emerging
Technologies* 134
I Am Not Zobrist
*An Interview With Laurie Garrett, Senior Fellow for Global Health,
Council on Foreign Relations and author of* The Coming Plague 145
Transhumanism and the Promise of the Future
*An Interview With Natasha Vita-More, Chairman, Board
of Directors of Humanity+ and author of the "Transhumanist
Manifesto"* 151
"Whether You Think the Future Makes Sense or It Doesn't, It is
Here. Get Used to It."
*An Interview With David Orban, Futurist, CEO of Dotsub,
and former chairman of Humanity+* 161
Nothing Is Going to Be the Same
*An Interview With Gregory Stock, Biophysicist, biotech entrepreneur,
and founding director of the Program on Medicine, Technology and
Society at UCLA's School of Medicine* 169

Section 3
Dan Brown Decoded

Dan Brown, the Infernal Novelist
  By David A. Shugarts, Investigative reporter, author of Secrets of the
  Widow's Son, *and contributing editor to the Secrets series* 183
"I Need Another Clue"
  By Cheryl Helm, Dan Brown codes and puzzles expert 206

Section 4
The Dante Baedeker

Firenze: a Dante Travel Journey
  By Dan Burstein, Creator, author, and coeditor of the Secrets *series* 217
The Firenze Folio
  By Julie O'Connor, Fine art photographer and photojournalist 230
The Props of Dan Brown: Three Churches of World Significance
  *By William Cook, Distinguished Teaching Professor of History
  (Emeritus), State University of New York, Geneseo* 247
Dolci: Musings and Meditations on Dante and Dan Brown
  By Dan Burstein, Creator, author, and coeditor of the Secrets *series* 252

Acknowledgments 287
Contributors 289

Editor's Note

Secrets of Inferno: In the Footsteps of Dante and Dan Brown follows the same format as that of our earlier books in the *Secrets* series: *Secrets of the Code, Secrets of Angels & Demons, Secrets of Mary Magdalene, Secrets of 24, Secrets of the Lost Symbol,* and *Secrets of the Tattooed Girl.* *Secrets of Inferno* combines original writing by Dan Burstein, Arne de Keijzer, and David Shugarts (the *Secrets* team), as well as contributed essays and interviews by more than a dozen experts and specialists whose professional life and work are in fields that include Dante studies, population and demography, medicine, and futurism. Our choice of experts parallels the issues explored in Dan Brown's *Inferno.* These include Dante, the *Divine Comedy,* and the history of the city of Florence, the impact of an expanding world population, the human enhancement philosophy embodied in transhumanism, and humankind's increasing ability to play god with our own evolution through our increasingly sophisticated technology and science.

When presenting a contributed essay or interview, we have generally taken care to distinguish our editor's voice from the authors' contributions by setting our introductory comments in italics. The text that follows is in the original voice of the author or interviewee. In the case of interviews, questions posed by the editors are in bold. Words, sentence fragments, or explanatory notes that appear in brackets are ours; those in parentheses are those of the author.

Page numbers, when cited, refer to the original US hardcover edition of Dan Brown's *Inferno* as published in May 2013. These reference points may be different in other languages and other editions. When referring to Dan Brown's earlier books we often use their abbreviations: *DVC* (*The Da Vinci Code*), *A&D* (*Angels & Demons*), and *TLS* (*The Lost Symbol*).

Each of the scholars and experts who have contributed commentaries to our book have their own preferred ways to refer to Dante's great poem and other matters explored in this book (i.e., when and where to capitalize Heaven and Hell, paradise and purgatory). Dante's own original title was the one-word *Commedia*; *Divina* was added by Boccaccio after Dante's death. In this book we use *Commedia* as a synonym for *Divine Comedy*, and vice versa.

Different English translations of the *Divine Comedy* exist, among them those of Henry Wadsworth Longfellow, John Ciardi, Charles Singleton, John Sinclair, Allen Mandelbaum, and, most recently Clive James. As those versed in the world of Dante know, each of these translations has its own strengths and weaknesses. We have used different translations in different places in this book. Our scholars each use their preferred translation—and sometimes their own. Contributors also use various styles in referring to Cantos, titles, footnotes, and other conventions; we did not attempt to standardize them here, so please forgive a small tower of Babel in our formatting and style conventions.

In giving our readers the insights of our contributors, we have faced monumental space constraints and have thus had to leave things out that we would have otherwise liked to use. We want to thank all the authors, interviewees and experts who contributed to *Secrets of Inferno*. We urge our readers to buy the books, explore the websites of our experts, and pursue the multitude of ideas referred to within these pages. For background on our contributors, see the back of the book.

Secrets of Inferno is a book of critical commentary on Dan Brown's novel, *Inferno*, and many other subjects. Our work is completely independent from and unauthorized by Dan Brown. As might be obvious in a work of critical commentary, the plot of *Inferno* is discussed and dissected at various points in these pages, so please be forewarned by this "spoiler alert" if you have not yet read the novel.

One final thought: If you have never read Dante, or if you have not read *Divine Comedy* in a long time, we strongly suggest you make the journey now. Intriguing and contemporary as Dan Brown's *Inferno* is, Dante is in a class by himself when it comes to the pleasures of poetry, literature, and the life of the mind.

Introduction

Secrets of Inferno:
In the Footsteps of Dante and Dan Brown

Just a decade ago, it seemed that you couldn't get on an airplane or a subway or sit in a café without seeing someone (more likely a number of people) reading Dan Brown's *The Da Vinci Code*. It was at the top of the *New York Times* bestseller list and on its way to becoming one of the bestselling books of all time. We were intrigued and curious ourselves. How much in *Da Vinci Code* was fact? How much was fiction? Which parts were which?

The more we explored and read the background materials—the same books, artworks, legends, and esoterica that Dan Brown had pored over in the course of creating his story—the more we found our family and friends interested in what we were learning. At a holiday party in 2003, we inquired of the head buyer for Barnes & Noble if she thought there would be a market for a book that would analyze fact and fiction in *The Da Vinci Code*. On the spot, she offered to buy 50,000 copies for her stores.

Armed with that enthusiastic support, we decided to put together an unauthorized companion book that would pursue what seemed to us a set of provocative and important issues raised by *The Da Vinci Code* (or *DVC* as we call it). We didn't want the book to be just our opinions. So we sought out world-class experts in every area of knowledge touched by Dan Brown's mega selling book—theology, history, art, codes, the historical Jesus and the historical Mary Magdalene, the real-life Gnostics, Leonardo da Vinci, architecture, science, mathematics, the Knights Templar, the Vatican and the Papacy, the so-called Priory of Sion—to help us.

We fully understood that *DVC* was a work of fiction and of pop culture. We disregarded Dan Brown's preamble asserting that, "all descriptions of artwork, architecture, documents, and secret rituals in this novel are accurate." (He continues to put similar statements at the front of all his books, including *Inferno*, the most recent: "All artwork, literature, science, and historical references in this novel are real"). We understood that he had braided strands of fact and fiction into an incredible adventure tale that took Robert Langdon and Sophie Neveu through Paris, London, and points beyond, at a whirlwind pace. Along the way, while keeping readers turning every page and eager to go on reading into the night past every short, cliffhanging chapter to the next one, Brown had managed to work in a stunning collection of intriguing bits of religion, art, history, and culture. This was a great late night suspense story and a great beach/poolside read.

Yet we saw it as much more than that. The book caused many people to think, argue, and debate. It drove readers into bookstores and to the Web. In the middle of our increasingly vulgar and dumbed-down pop culture, here was a book that made people hungry to know more and even to go out and find answers for themselves in response to the questions that nagged at them when they closed the book.

Our book, *Secrets of the Code*, ended up as a mega bestseller in its own right. It was translated into more than thirty languages, sold several million copies, and showed up on bestseller lists all over the world, from the *New York Times* to *Le Monde*. Over the years that followed, we did similar unauthorized guidebooks to Dan Brown's other novels, including *Angels & Demons* (*A&D*), *The Lost Symbol* (*TLS*), and now, *Inferno*. We also branched out and did guidebooks to other pop culture phenomena, including other novelists (Stieg Larsson) and TV shows (*24*).

What we have learned from a decade of doing these books is that works of pop culture are great ecosystems in which to promote thought and discussion about important ideas, trends, and issues worthy of being discussed in the global public square. Dan Brown, in particular, has a unique gift for making these ideas, trends, and issues accessible and fun to learn about. No matter how maddening he may be from a literary point of view—the dialogue is often cringe-inducing, the characters are generally made of flimsy cardboard, the suspensions of disbelief he asks of his readers are extraordinary—somehow, he works it so you want to keep reading.

What's more, the reader can effortlessly tour important works of visual art, architecture, and literature, as well as plunge into esoteric episodes of history, without having to do anything other than tag along at Robert Langdon's ridiculous pace. (We have checked the action in all his books and they have all turned out to be based on fundamentally impossible timelines, but never mind!)

With *Inferno*, Brown has given us an extraordinary gift on multiple levels.

First and foremost for us, there is the story of the great late thirteenth and early fourteenth century poet-author Dante Alighieri, the creator of the *Divine Comedy* (also known in these pages by its Italian name, the *Commedia*). The *Divine Comedy* is composed of three parts—*Inferno*, *Purgatorio*, and *Paradiso*. As Dan Brown's title implies, he has drawn most of his use of Dante from the *Inferno* section, whereas our book treats Dante more holistically.

Dan Brown is one in a very long line of authors and creative artists in many fields who have been fascinated by Dante and who have used or been inspired by parts of *Divine Comedy* in their works. Brown tells us himself in his *Inferno* that, "In the seven centuries since its publication, Dante's enduring vision of hell had inspired tributes, translations, and variations by some of history's greatest minds. Longfellow, Chaucer, Marx, Milton, Balzac, Borges ... had all written pieces based on Dante ... Monteverdi, Liszt, Wagner, Tchaikovsky, and Puccini composed pieces based on Dante's work ... Even the modern world of video games and iPad apps had no shortage of Dante-related offerings."

To that list, Brown could have added Boccaccio (Dante's first major fan, who urged that the book Dante had called his "Comedy" be preceded by the word, "Divine"), Botticelli, Blake, Delacroix, Rodin, Gogol, T.S. Eliot, Ezra Pound, James Joyce, Samuel Beckett, Malcolm Lowry, Primo Levi, Dorothy L. Sayers, Salvador Dali, and many, many more. Even Chinese artist and activist Ai Weiwei has now joined the list of Dantistas with his 2013 foray into pop/rap/heavy metal generating a music album called *The Divine Comedy*. Indeed, while Dante has gone into serious eclipse in modern high school and university education (where *Divine Comedy* was once required reading for an educated person), Dante enjoyed a banner year in 2013.

Even before the publication of *Inferno*, Matthew Weiner, the creator of the hit TV show *Mad Men*, decided to launch the 2013 season with a two-hour opening episode in which protagonist Don Draper, in the seeming paradise of Hawaii, is seen reading the 1960s John Ciardi translation of *Divine Comedy*, and narrating Dante's famous opening lines about coming to be lost in a dark forest in the middle of his life. Each of the ensuing 2013 episodes of *Mad Men* had a direct connection to Dante's rings of hell, as Don seemed to be descending deeper week by week. The season ended on the prospect of Don having hit bottom, entering psychological purgatory, atoning for his sins, and trying to start a new life.

As *Mad Men* showed, Hollywood has historically done its bit to keep Dante alive in pop culture. From the stunning ten minute choreography of life in the Inferno contained within the 1935 Spencer Tracy film *Dante's Inferno* to David Fincher's *Se7en* (and at least one film critic's) theory that numerous scenes in *Easy Rider* are modeled on Gustave Doré's illustrations of *Divine Comedy*, many have tried to capture Dante on film. Yet no one has truly succeeded. Dan Brown and Sony will get their chance when they turn Brown's 2013 *Inferno* into a big budget movie, currently scheduled for release in December 2015.

The Dante of Dan Brown's *Inferno* may have very little in common with the fourteenth century poet and his creative output. Several of our Dante commentators will tell you as much in the following pages (see pieces by Barolini, Botterill, Cook, and Cornish, for example), although at least two of our distinguished academics find that Brown has come up with an intriguing postmodern recasting of Dante's work (see Erickson and Mazzotta).

For us, however, Brown's novel, despite its limitations, has given our contemporary culture a wonderful chance to have a new discussion and to learn about Dante, the *Divine Comedy*, Florence, and all the big ideas connected to Dante's amazingly rich treasure house of intellect. If, in spite of Dan Brown's sometimes clunky prose style and characters as weightless as Dante's "shades" in the underworld, you are led to want to know more about Dante, you have come to the right place.

Here is a chance to think about good and evil—and how the meaning of those words has changed over the years—fate and free will, science and religion, knowledge and mystery, male and female, the real and the imagined, mortality and immortality. Plus, political science, visual art, language and literature, philosophy and history, the Bible and the Greek and Roman classics, Florence and its endless supply of Renaissance geniuses and its beautiful art, and of course, poetry.

Brown only skims the surface of Dante's treasures. But that's OK. He has invited all his readers to this Dante party, and we have responded in this book by bringing together academic Dante specialists from leading universities, with scientists, philosophers, ethicists, medical researchers, futurists, and members of our own *Secrets* team to comment on Brown's use of Dante and the many other issues that underlie the plot of *Inferno*.

Brown doesn't stop at Dante and Florence of the fourteenth century. His *Inferno* also calls attention to a series of twenty-first century issues he wants to explore. These include overpopulation of the planet, potential responses to the challenges of resource shortages and survival in an overpopulated world, the contemporary movement known as transhumanism, and the growing community of scientists, technologists, and societal thinkers who are interested in and working on the power of technology to self-evolve the human species in ways that have never before been possible.

Let's specify at the outset that we disagree with the way Brown chose to frame some of these issues. To our way of thinking, Brown has revivified 1970s and '80s Neo-Malthusian concerns about the so-called "population bomb." Ironically, *Inferno* comes at just the time when most of the regions of the developed world—North America, Europe, and Japan—are facing very low birth rates and population growth statistics. Some countries even have negative population growth. In Italy, where Brown's evil villain-turned-am-biguous-hero Zobrist has been working to perfect his sterilizing virus, the birth rate is near historic lows. The total population has grown only very modestly from fifty-eight million in 2000 to an estimated sixty-one million today. More Italian politicians, economists, and sociologists are concerned with their country's "birth dearth" than with curbing population growth. Speaking of Japan's population decline, Dr. Shoichiro Toyoda, former Chairman of Toyota Motor Corporation, once quipped that if current trends continue, there will be no Japanese left a thousand years from now.

Although China's record of three decades of enforced one-child policies troubles every Western humanist, the political leadership in Beijing has achieved what was previously thought impossible. China has brought its population growth under control. Today's Chinese birth rate is only modestly higher than Italy's.

Worldwide, a series of advances in agriculture and medicine have allowed total world population to continue growing significantly, without the apocalyptic battle (at least, not yet) over resources that was predicted to be happening about now. Even very poor countries have experienced meaningful improvements in nutrition, health, and infant mortality rates over the last forty years. So far, the worst-case scenarios have not obtained and many experts would argue that the world of 2013-14 is better fed and healthier than most experts would have predicted a generation or two ago.

Of course, some important populations continue to grow. Africa, India, West Asia, the Middle East, and parts of Latin America are all continuing to grow far faster than the rest of the world. We are emphatically *not* arguing that population has disappeared as an issue. But more than focusing on exactly how many billions of people the world can bear—as Brown does—we think the key issue is developing the ideas and solutions that will continue to make life livable and manageable for everyone on the planet. There can be no question that nations and societies all over the world must develop more thoughtful and sustainable policies, as well as new technologies and new ways to distribute resources. Whether it is our very survival as a species that is at stake or "only" the quality of our lives in the future, we must face up urgently to the realities of climate change, sea level change, new (and old) toxins and pollutants, new (and old) viruses and diseases, and the growing list of dwindling and harder-to-extract energy and mineral resources. It's these types of issues on which global emphasis should be put—not on figuring out how to "thin the herd" as Zobrist wants to do, and especially not by forcibly reducing populations.

Overall, the issue of the "population explosion" is less of a worry on the long list of potential global crises than it was three or four decades ago. (Our esteemed contributor, Paul Erlich, author of the 1968 book, *The Population Bomb*—whose work is cited by Dan Brown in *Inferno*—disputes the latter statement, so please see his essay for some countervailing thoughts.) In these pages, you will hear from a variety of experts on population, viruses, and the future of the planet, each of whom weighs in with his or her own point of view on the story Brown has spun.

Brown's *Inferno* introduces many readers for the first time to the transhumanist movement. We have brought several leading thinkers from that movement into the pages of *Secrets of Inferno* as well. But it seems to us that Brown sets up a false logic chain by making Zobrist and Sienna, who are committed population warriors, the spokespeople for transhumanism and the technologies that are leading us in the direction of self-evolution.

In our experience, the people most interested in transhumanism and in the power of new technology to solve global problems and enhance the capabilities and lifespans of *Homo sapiens* are generally *not* terribly troubled by population trends. Certainly, they are not troubled in the way Zobrist is. And most scientists, engineers, and medical researchers trying to get us to see why we should not overly fetter the development of powerful new technologies are desirous of *more* freedom for their research. They are *not* trying to restrict the freedom of other people to bear children as they choose.

Trying to think about the real issues involved with the survival of our species, its evolution, and future enhancement is grist for the most interesting mill of philosophy, ethics, morality, science, politics, and futurist speculation. Dante would have relished this discussion and he would have had very strong opinions about it. He's the one, after all, who coined the term *transhumanism*.

It's too bad that Dan Brown does not use *Inferno* to stimulate more of this debate. But in a way, he has already done it. One of the key points of his 2009 novel, *The Lost Symbol*, was that the great sages of history have always known that humans are "as gods." The secret writings of the wise people of many societies over the last several thousand years (termed by Brown in *TLS* the "Ancient Mysteries") all reflect this fundamental idea of humankind as its own godly force. Within human society, we have always had the vision we need to be as gods; in the twenty-first century we have the technology as well. Not only can we shape our own destiny, we must do so. We must take responsibility for creating the future we wish to have. This is true whether we are speaking about ourselves as individuals, our societies and governments, or even our species. This idea—particularly cogently expressed in Brown's work in *TLS*—is actually somewhat akin to Dante's commentaries on free will and the responsibilities of leaders for the outcomes obtained by their societies.

Whether you loved Dan Brown's *Inferno* and couldn't put it down, or you are a Brown critic or skeptic, *Secrets of Inferno* will hopefully take you further—beyond the Pillars of Hercules, beyond the known world—to consider and contemplate the fascinating stew of art and ideas that Robert Langdon and Sienna Brooks could only whisk by at breakneck speeds.

T.S. Eliot once observed that, "Dante and Shakespeare divide the world between them. There is no third." Fortunately, modern society does not suffer for a lack of venues in which to reflect on Shakespeare. But for Dante, that is not the case. Brown has brought Dante back to the top of the bestseller list and invited us to explore Dante's world. And that's the main reason for creating *Secrets of Inferno* and sharing it with interested readers.

— Dan Burstein and Arne de Keijzer
July 2013

Section 1

Dante for the Twenty-first Century

Welcome to My Dante Spring

BY DAN BURSTEIN

Creator, author, and coeditor of the *Secrets* series

"The novel will be set in Europe, in the most fascinating place I've ever been," Dan Brown said.

That was May of 2010. He was speaking obliquely about *Inferno*, which he was then in the middle of writing. For those of us in the Dan Brown-watching business, the game was afoot. What city was he talking about? Fellow watchers started talking and tweeting. I guessed Istanbul, for three reasons: (1) It would be just like Dan Brown to create a teachable moment by saying he was writing about "Europe" when he really meant Turkey, since most Americans don't think of that majority-Islamic country as being in Europe. In fact, Istanbul has as much (or more) claim to being European than most other European cities. For centuries after the fall of Rome it was the capital of the Holy Roman Empire and the wealthiest and most beautiful city in Europe. (2) Some simple Googling turned up a Dan Brown visit to Istanbul in December 2009, complete with a talk on science and religion sponsored by the US Consulate. (3) Istanbul is, indeed, a fascinating city.

I turned out to be wrong, of course. The main setting for *Inferno* is Florence. And I would tend to agree with Brown's assessment that Florence is the most fascinating place in Europe. Perhaps I get the consolation prize, because Istanbul, with its fabulous Hagia Sophia church/mosque/museum and its rich multicultural history at the crossroads of civilizations is the third and final destination of Robert Langdon's quest in *Inferno*, after he has been to Florence and Venice.

When Dan Brown and his publisher officially told the world in early 2013 that the next Robert Langdon adventure would be set in Florence and would revolve around Dante, the poet of the *Divine Comedy*, I was almost catapulted to intellectual Paradiso.

Dante has always been a hero and an interest of mine, and Florence one of my favorite places. But I had not read the *Divine Comedy* in over forty years.

I was contemplating my upcoming sixtieth birthday and finding myself increasingly tempted to return to writing poetry, as I had as a teenager and young adult. In particular, I was thinking of working in some new genres of poetry, and I thought that Dante, master innovator of the poetic form and the Italian language itself, could be an inspiration. I relished the opportunity to reread the *Divine Comedy* and immerse myself, even if only briefly, in the world of Dante. I knew there was a lot to be gained from revisiting the classics with the benefit of new perspective in life. And I also knew that the experience of revisiting Dante would help prepare me to write something meaningful about Dan Brown's new book.

***

So began what I call my "Dante Spring." I would reread the *Divine Comedy* (the Mandelbaum and Ciardi translations, and some of the Henry Wadsworth Longfellow version, and then Clive James when his translation appeared in April, just a month before Brown's *Inferno*). I explored over one hundred books with critical commentaries on Dante. These ranged from Eric Auerbach's seminal early twentieth century modernist work, *Dante: Poet of the Secular World*, to Harriet Rubin's innovative 2004 book, *Dante in Love*. I would, of course, discover an incredible wealth of Dante scholarship on the web. I made near daily visits to "Digital Dante," hosted by Columbia University, and "Danteworlds," hosted at the University of Texas at Austin.

After familiarizing myself with who was doing what in contemporary Dante scholarship, I sought out the most interesting Dante specialists and asked them to contribute to this book. As a result, you will find a number of the world's leading Dante scholars represented in the pages of *Secrets of Inferno*: Teodolinda Barolini, Steven Botterill, William Cook, Alison Cornish, Giuseppe Mazzotta, and more.

My family and I visited Florence (recounted in the travel report on "Firenze" in Section 4 of this book) and other places relevant to Dante. In Florence, I came face to face with Dante in the form of a depiction of him possibly by his friend Giotto, the greatest painter of the 1300s. This image is part of a large tableau on the walls of the Bargello Museum. The Dante portrait detail also appeared on a poster that had come into my family's life when I was a child at the time of the 700th anniversary of Dante's birth. The poster is still with me today and is a personal totem of sorts, symbolizing Dante as a constant force in my life.

In Bologna on a gorgeous April afternoon, I experienced a seminal moment: I visited a friend whose apartment terrace looks directly out at the city's famous two towers that had inspired Dante's first poem. It isn't clear whether Dante actually attended the University of Bologna, which was already a two-hundred-year-old institution when Dante was a young man and served as one of only a handful of major centers of formal education in medieval Europe. Historians do think he visited what is now called Santo Stefano, today a complex of seven churches and religious buildings that includes a cloister courtyard featuring pillars with gargoyle-like capitols that date back a thousand years and perhaps longer. These depict people doing penance and being humbled by weighty boulders on their backs. I knew from my recent rereading of the *Commedia* that Dante describes this exact scene in his visit to *Purgatorio*.

As I made my rounds commuting to my business life during the week and running errands on weekends, I listened (twice) to the twenty-four-lecture audio course on the *Divine Comedy* done a decade ago by The Teaching Company, featuring professors William Cook (whom I recruited to write for this book) and Ronald Herzman.

***

I also explored from a fresh perspective some of the writers and artists most important to me in my life to learn more about their own interests in Dante and connections to him: James Joyce, Samuel Beckett, T.S. Eliot, William Blake, and Auguste Rodin in particular.

I found a commentary about the existential novelist and play-wright Samuel Beckett who is said to have died with a copy of the *Commedia* at his bedside. Apparently, throughout his writing career he had taken the slothful Belacqua from Dante's *Purgatorio* as his own alter-ego. According to one critic, Beckett's interest in "waiting" as a fundamental factor in human existence—expressed so brilliantly in *Waiting for Godot*—mirrors a subtheme of the early parts of *Purgatorio* where Belacqua appears.

For my entire adult life I have had a pair of bookends that are replicas of Auguste Rodin's monumental sculptural work, The Thinker. These were given to me by my father, who in turn received them from his father as a Bar Mitzvah gift in 1928. So these have been in my family for eighty-five years. But I never knew—and I don't think my father ever knew—that this iconic physical image glorifying humanism and rationalism was intended (most art historians agree) by Rodin to be modeled on Dante.

Enormously captivated by the *Divine Comedy*, Rodin spent twenty years of his life working on scenes from the poem. Several of his most famous sculptures are based on episodes recounted in the *Commedia*, including The Kiss and the Gates of Hell. By pure synchronous accident I happened across a documentary film tracing the efforts of B. Gerald Cantor (founder of the financial firm, Cantor Fitzgerald) and his wife Iris to recast in bronze Rodin's Gates of Hell, which had previously only been cast in plaster. The film documented the Cantors' passion for bringing Rodin's work back to life, as well as Rodin's passion for recreating Dante's world in 3D.

On Bloomsday (June 16, the annual celebration of James Joyce's *Ulysses*), I reread parts of Joyce's great modernist novel. *Ulysses* very obviously, and in great detail, parallels Homer's *Odyssey* in walking through a day in the life of the fictional Leopold Bloom in Dublin in 1904. (Dan Brown, as we shall see later, uses some similar techniques to create plot points in his *Inferno* that mirror episodes and events in Dante's *Inferno*).

I thought about how much Joyce, who exiled himself from his native and much beloved Ireland, drew on Dante's experience as an exile from his much-beloved Florence. Dante writes in the *Commedia* about how the "art" of living in exile is just that—an art form—and references a number of other historical experiences of exile, especially the Biblical experience of the Jews in Exodus. Joyce, who called Dante his "spiritual food," said he loved Dante almost as much as he loved the Bible.

Now, in my Bloomsday rereading of *Ulysses*, I realized for the first time that several passages parallel not only the *Odyssey* but also the *Divine Comedy*. The Aeolus episode in Joyce's *Ulysses* is drawn from the story of Odysseus's visit to Aeolus, the god of wind. One of Odysseus's men commits a forbidden act and opens the bag of wind they have been given; this then blows them seriously off-course. The parallel Aeolus episode of *Ulysses* takes place in the offices of the *Freeman*, a newspaper. Here the theme of wind is represented by the windy rhetoric used in the media and in the discussions of those who work at the paper. Within the episode, I now discovered, there are multiple references and even direct quotations from the sequence when Dante encounters Paolo and Francesca in *Inferno*. These are the two adulterous lovers who are condemned to be locked permanently in an embrace they cannot consummate and to be buffeted forever by Hell's fierce winds. Wind becomes the common theme connecting not just Homer but Dante to Joyce's story.

It was also during my Bloomsday musings that I realized what I had previously missed in multiple readings of the *Divine Comedy*: Dante sees a great identity between himself and the character he has created for his Ulysses. Dante is guilty himself of all the "sins" for which Ulysses is condemned, especially daring to go where no one else has gone, to break the boundaries self-imposed on humans by the conventions of society, to explore the unknown and obtain new and sometimes forbidden knowledge. Appropriately enough for Bloomsday, I read Harold Bloom's 1994 book, *The Western Canon*, which devotes a major chapter to Dante. Among other profound insights, Bloom nails Dante's "extraordinary audacity" and his amazing inventiveness, which combine to deliver "the most original version of Ulysses that we have." And the voice of this Ulysses, who seeks to "break all bounds and risk the unknown" is "dangerously close" to Dante's, says Bloom.

***

At times it seemed as if there was some divine plan to make Dante and the *Divine Comedy* suddenly more contemporary and relevant to my life in the spring of 2013. When Pope Benedict resigned at the end of February, for example, experts on the papacy immediately launched into weeks of media discussion on the implications of the resignation. One morning I awoke to an Op-Ed piece in the *New York Times* recalling that the last voluntary resignation of a pope had been 700 years earlier, when Pope Celestine V stepped aside. This was the very papal resignation—I knew from all the recent reading I had been doing—that infuriated Dante, and triggered his condemnation of those who try to stay "neutral" in the great moral conflicts of their era. (In *Inferno*, Dante sees Celestine, and says, "I saw and recognized the shade of him / Who by his cowardice made the great refusal").

Celestine's resignation led to the selection of Boniface VIII, Dante's archenemy, as Pope. Boniface's tenure, in turn, led to the schism in the Church and the establishment of the Avignon papacy. Dante is bitterly critical of Celestine for not defending the papacy against Boniface and for what he believes are Boniface's crimes against the spiritual essence of Christianity. Dan Brown draws on Dante's withering indictment of the "neutrals" for the epigraph against neutrality that appears in his *Inferno*. This idea becomes something of a mantra for Brown throughout his novel.

Even television was suddenly alive with the spirit of Dante every week, beginning with the April 2013 season opener of *Mad Men*. Matthew Weiner, the show's creator, had apparently decided months earlier to adopt Dante's *Inferno* as the *leitmotif* for the season. The first episode began with *Mad Men*'s chief protagonist, Don Draper, and Don's young wife Megan, relaxing in swimsuits and sunglasses on the beach in Hawaii in 1968. Megan has a tropical-looking cocktail in hand; Don is reading *Inferno*. In a stentorian voice-over, actor John Hamm, who plays Don, intones Dante's 700-year-old words that are still among the most memorable lines ever written:

> Midway in our life's journey, I went astray
> from the straight road and woke to find myself
> alone in a dark wood . . .

Like Dante, Don finds himself in the "dark wood" of moral and midlife crises. Each week, for the rest of the season, Don's behavior tested another ring of Dante's Hell as he committed all manner of sins and kept falling and falling downward—just like the show's opening graphic montage—toward the darkest reaches of Hell. From the *Wall Street Journal* to the *Huffington Post*, critics who knew Dante weighed in week by week to explain the allusions in each episode. When Matthew Weiner went on Terry Gross's NPR show, *Fresh Air*, he discussed his own interest in Dante and why he had used the *Inferno* as the subtext for Don Draper's life in the particularly hellish year of 1968. By the season's end, we were left believing that Don had hit bottom and will now seek the path of redemption. Perhaps the 2014 season will take Don into Purgatory and beyond.

During those very days I was in Italy during the spring of 2013, the Italian government had run into near total paralysis and gridlock. Facing urgent economic issues and high unemployment, weeks had gone by with the future leadership of the country unsettled. Even for a country that has experienced frequent complications forming coalition governments, the divisions were absolutely unprecedented in modern times. Meanwhile, back at home, the Republican-led US House of Representatives was voting for the thirty-seventh time to overturn Obamacare, which had already been passed, signed into law, and upheld by the Supreme Court.

As I read these typical news stories from our times, I thought about Dante. He was a crusader against partisanship and factionalism in politics, as I show in my essay further on in this book,

"Dante to Washington: Gridlock, Partisanship, and Factionalism are Deadly Sins and will Land You in the Inferno." He criticized partisanship out of his own bitter experiences in the civil wars of the Guelphs vs. Ghibellines and of the Black vs. White Guelph factions. He blasted the then-current Florentine practice of one faction passing a law in October, and then losing power to a rival faction who would press to overturn that same law in November. This passage of *Divine Comedy* reminded me of American politics and the Obamacare debate.

***

In the weeks of the Dante Spring just before the publication of *Inferno*, web speculation was running high on what Dan Brown would do with the body of esoterica that surrounds Dante. Although I don't put too much store in such theories, I thought it might be valuable to review some of this material. So, I made my way through Walter Arensberg's 1921 monograph on the *Cryptography of Dante*, in which the author, a wealthy art collector and devoted Dantista, sought to highlight complex codes, numerology patterns, acrostics and hidden symbols in the *Divine Comedy*. ("Perfect for Dan Brown!" I thought).

Similarly, I found a copy of René Guénon's 1925 study, *The Esoterism of Dante*. Guénon links Dante to just about every secret society and mystical group Dan Brown has ever shown interest in—Templars, Rosecrucians, Cathars, and Freemasons, among others. ("Perfect for Dan Brown!" I thought, again). I read the accounts of the first publication of *Divine Comedy* after Dante's death, and the legend that holds that the last few cantos could not be found for many months. Eventually, one of Dante's sons had a dream in which his father appeared and showed him the spot where he had hidden the last cantos in the wall of the house. ("Perfect for Dan Brown!" I thought, once again).

There is some real credibility to be given to the idea that Dante learned a lot from French troubadours and their tradition of romantic courtly love songs—and that his presentation of the story of Beatrice fits well into this context. The association to the

French troubadours could well have connected Dante to the Templars. He was bitterly critical of the pope and the emperor who together conspired to round up, torture, and massacre the Templars in France in 1307. It appears his exile may have taken him to Paris in this time period, where he could have witnessed or at least heard first hand about the show trials and torture of the Templars. All of these anecdotes are perfect for Dan Brown, and fascinating to contemplate in and of themselves.

In the end, Brown chose to use exactly none of this material about possible links between Dante and mystical sects or secret societies in his *Inferno*. Perhaps he has suffered too much criticism for having appeared to endorse the Priory of Sion hoax in *Da Vinci Code*; perhaps he was disappointed that his *Lost Symbol*, detailing the rich history of Freemasonry among the founding fathers of the United States, never caught on as *DVC* had (although it did sell millions of copies). Maybe he simply tired of being the secret society guy and had too much work to do on the transhumanist/population bomb part of his plot to bother with the esoteric Dante. In any event, I was happy to have gained some exposure to the more "alternative" theories about Dante, and equally happy to leave them largely aside in this book.

***

Most of Dante's purpose in writing the *Divine Comedy* is to address the major issues of religion, morality, politics, and philosophy. But one of the true joys of rereading Dante at this stage of my life was discovering how wide his knowledge is and how innovative his thinking was for an age we label "dark." On one of our days in Florence, we went to the Uffizi, one of the world's great art museums. If you set out to follow the actual design of the collection through the labyrinthine galleries, the first room you come to presents several different images of Madonnas by Cimabue, Duccio, and Giotto, among others. In this room, you can see the different techniques developed by these three great painters, all of whom lived fairly close in time to each other but had surprisingly different styles. It was evident to me that while all of these are treasures, Giotto's artistic approach was the most brilliant and the closest to what we now know as the Renaissance style. In the *Divine Comedy*, Dante embraces Giotto as the apostle of the new, even indicating his preference for Giotto over Cimabue, who had been considered the master painter of his era until then, and was no doubt still revered as such by much of Florence at the time Dante wrote.

Dante is unafraid to go with his very well honed instincts and pick winners and losers. Giotto is but one example. He also esteems Thomas Aquinas at a time just before the canonization of St. Thomas and while the Thomas legacy was still under attack in some quarters of the church. St. Bernard is also a key figure in *Paradiso*. He too would not have been a consensus choice to play that role if the choice were made by the leading lights of the church in Dante's time.

Whether it is the pagan Romans whom Dante admires and creates special places for in the afterlife, or the ancient sages of Jewish history whom he places in Heaven, or the ideas of the Islamic philosopher Averroes, who was Aristotle's champion in medieval times, Dante is unafraid to recognize and promote the intellectual insights of those he identifies with, even though they might be considered heretics or at least troubling nonbelievers by others. And this is in a time when the institution of the Inquisition has already been established and the danger of being charged with heresy is not to be taken lightly.

***

While thinking about Dante and the concept we might call "diversity" today, I reached out to Professor Teodolinda Barolini, a Dante scholar at Columbia University, whom I hoped to enlist to contribute to this book. Barolini interested me because she had written about how unique Dante is for his time in thinking differently about women, Jews, Muslims, homosexuality, and much else. I also liked the fact that in 2010, when *Dante's Inferno*, the video game, appeared, she was willing to talk to the media about the problems with the game and to do so in non-academic terms.

The video game turned Beatrice into the "prototypical damsel in distress," Barolini told *Entertainment Weekly*. The whole idea of the *Divine Comedy* is that it is Beatrice who is supposed to be saving Dante. But in the video game, it is he who saves her. Barolini also objected to turning Dante into a crusader in the game, when in real life, he was not a participant in the Crusades at all.

I guessed that if Professor Barolini was willing to enter the realm of pop culture by taking on this game, she would be willing to comment on another kind of pop culture phenomenon—Dan Brown's *Inferno*. Ultimately, she agreed to do so and her essay, "Dan Brown and the Case of the Wrong Dante," appears later in this Section. But along the way, we had an extensive discussion of Dante, diversity, and what she called Dante's "medieval multiculturalism." She sent me her brilliant essay, "Dante's Sympathy for the Other," which proved to be the most thought-provoking of all the commentaries I read during my Dante Spring. We were on the phone one day, and the last thing she mentioned was that she was thinking about writing a piece on Dante and science.

***

After my call with Professor Barolini, I found myself thinking: Science? Dante? Really? Like everything else in my Dante Spring, a new idea is an invitation to do a little digging, and as I did, I started turning up a number of papers and chapters from books that suggest Dante was very far ahead of the curve when it came to what passed for science in the early fourteenth century.

I found a 2005 article in the *Guardian* reporting on a scientist who believes that Dante shows unique insight into the physical experience of flying, as well as the principles of inertia and invariance when, in Canto XVII of *Inferno*, he describes descending from one circle of Hell to the next by climbing on the back of the winged monster Geryon and flying through the chasms between the circles. I also found a 2011 *Boston Globe* article reporting on the ideas of a professor at Mount Holyoke on what Dante did *not* know—and how Galileo developed some of his key ideas in theoretical mathematics by analyzing and critiquing Dante's measurements and proportions ascribed to the geography of Hell in *Inferno*.

But Dante knows a lot about natural science, geometry, and astronomy. He knows the earth is spherical and he understands much about the earth's relationship to the sun, the time zones, and the overall extent of the universe. Armed with the works of Greek and Roman scholars, rather than weighed down by too much medieval nonsense, he is able to intuit aspects of the revolutions in astronomy that the work of Copernicus and Galileo will trigger over the next two centuries. Some poetically inclined contemporary physicists even see inklings of quantum theory in Dante's description of what he experiences as he travels through the Empyrean zone at the conclusion of *Paradiso*.

If you find great wisdom and intellectual depth in Dante, as I obviously do, it becomes easy to promote him to modernist hero. I know, of course, that no matter how far ahead of his time he may appear to be, he is still a poet of the thirteenth and early fourteenth centuries. He is therefore still subject to many of the biases, prejudices, fears, strictures, superstitions, and generally retrograde thinking of a Europe dominated by Crusades, Inquisitions, civil wars, and battles between popes and emperors. But when you think about the raw, wild, passion of his ambition in writing the *Divine Comedy*—and how successful he was in fulfilling that ambition—you come to understand him as one of the most towering and inventive forces in the history of the written word.

Although his great work is a great poem, with extremely intricately structured rhyme (*terza rima*, the interlocking three-line rhyme scheme that is for Dante what iambic pentameter is for Shakespeare), it is actually also the first modernist novel. Scholars will distinguish between Dante-the-Poet who is the author of the *Commedia* and Dante-the-Pilgrim who is its main character. But the fact is that no author before, and none for a long time after, dared to write such a huge epic story in the first person. Homer has his Odysseus, Virgil has his Aeneas, but Dante is author, narrator, and action hero all at once. And what action!

In a time of narrowly scripted religious belief, this Tuscan genius, exiled from his native place, with no religious, political, or noble standing, claims to have ventured to the afterlife and returned, having seen the face of God. He carries out his own independent judicial review to determine who to place in Hell and who elevate to Heaven. Unlike Shakespeare, who studiously avoided writing about contemporary figures or issues except in the most veiled manner, Dante condemns recent popes, emperors, and high officials to Hell, while seeing fit to save and honor a cast of pagans and other unorthodox characters. He provides the most concrete, detailed vision of the geography of the *Inferno*, *Purgatorio*, and *Paradiso* ever made explicit. And however fanciful this metaphorical topography is, Dante's fantasy becomes the collective standard vision of Catholic believers for centuries afterwards. He addresses major loopholes in the theology of the day about how Limbo functions and about how the process of purgation works. He creates a brand new area of the afterlife for the neutrals, never discussed in any Biblical or religious text. He admits publicly there is no good or logical answer about salvation and redemption for people who subscribe to different belief systems and have never known Christianity.

Above all, Dante takes the woman that he most admired, who was his own personal poetic embodiment of beauty, grace, and love, and puts her—A woman! A contemporary lay person! A personal acquaintance!—in the exalted echelons of Heaven.

Dante, the exile, lived long enough to see his work praised and embraced by many people and to obtain a certain sense of success and vindication. What is truly amazing, considering how new, audacious and boundary-breaking the *Commedia* was, is how rapidly it took hold all across Italy and Europe. Just half a century after his death, Dante was known as the great Florentine poet and was already being translated into other languages and being used as a basis for the vernacular tales of other great storytellers, such as

Boccaccio and Chaucer. And, all of that took place in what was still a dark age, before the printing press and before the Renaissance flowering of humanism.

William Cook, one of our contributors, likes to tell his students that after you have read the *Divine Comedy*, you are now prepared to read the *Divine Comedy*. He means, of course, that there is so much in Dante's incredible multidimensional story that you need to read it more than once even to begin to appreciate its depth.

As my Dante Spring came to an end, I had not only learned much more about Dante and the *Divine Comedy* than I had expected at the beginning, I was also prepared to understand Dan Brown's *Inferno* much better than I would have otherwise.

Dan Brown and
the Case of the Wrong Dante

BY TEODOLINDA BAROLINI
Da Ponte Professor of Italian, Columbia University

Let me begin with a personal note. This is the first Dan Brown novel that I have read. I accepted the invitation to think about Brown's *Inferno* because I have spent my life studying the "real" *Inferno*, by Dante Alighieri. As a scholar I have an interest in making sure that information about Dante is accurate (Mr. Brown graciously included our website, Digital Dante at Columbia University, in his acknowledgments). I figure I owe something—if not to the public that reads Mr. Brown's novels then certainly to Dante, who has given me a lifetime of intellectual pleasure.

In Brown's book, Professor Robert Langdon is pitted against an adversary who is a Dante fanatic. Bertrand Zobrist, a bio-chemist, is "a proponent of the Population Apocalypse Equation" (p. 177), the alleged mathematical recognition that only a mass extinction event can save our planet. Based on the conviction that the fourteenth century Black Death conferred long-term socio-economic benefits on Europe by having "thinned the human herd" (p. 177), Zobrist has worked out his own scheme to save humanity by unleashing a virus. With a young doctor whom he meets in a Florentine hospital (Sienna Brooks), where he awakens with his head full of terrifying infernal visions, Langdon is on a desperate quest to decipher the clues that Zobrist has left behind, hoping to prevent the release of the virus.

Beginning with a projected image of Botticelli's map of Dante's *Inferno*, various clues lifted (and twisted) from Dante's *Divine Comedy* direct Langdon to extraordinary works of art and architectural monuments in Florence, Venice, and Istanbul. The eastward directionality of the quest ("St. Mark's was so eastern in style that guidebooks often suggested it as a viable alternative to visiting Turkish mosques" (p. 324); Istanbul is called the "way-station between two worlds" where West meets East) suggests a reversal of the human itinerary from its cradle in Mesopotamia. Reversals are programmatic in Brown's *Inferno*, as they are in the original: "*Dante's* Inferno. *The finale. The center of the earth. Where gravity inverts itself. Where up becomes down*" (p. 409).

The principle of reversal, "where up becomes down," governs the plot, and makes this not your typical thriller: here the crime succeeds (and is perhaps not even a crime). Langdon does not succeed in stopping the dispersal of the virus (which he ultimately learns will not kill but randomly cause sterility in one-third the human population). Nor is his failure viewed as a bad thing, since at the end of the book "a breed of new thinkers" will tackle the crisis. These new thinkers—Zobrist's follower Sienna Brooks ends up working with the World Health Organization—belong to the transhumanist movement. Transhumanism, which is to Langdon's "old-fashioned" Darwinism what Darwinism is to Dante's Catholicism ("Bertrand's rare insight into genetics did not come as a flash of divine inspiration" (p.453)), believes "that we as humans have a moral obligation to *participate* in our evolutionary process" (p. 453).

Following the principle of reversal, Brown's *Inferno* really has no villain; in fact, it has an anti-villain. The book's two Dante enthusiasts—Zobrist and Langdon—end up not diametrically opposed, but morally convergent. The book's epigraph, "The darkest places in hell are reserved for those who maintain their neutrality in times of moral crisis," turns out to be Zobrist's credo (163 and 319). By the Epilogue it has become Langdon's credo as well: "*The darkest places in hell are reserved for those who maintain their neutrality in times of moral crisis. For Langdon, the meaning of these words had never felt so clear: In dangerous times, there is no sin greater than inaction.*" Moreover, Langdon confirms in the Epilogue that Zobrist taught him to think about overpopulation, and acknowledges that he was previously in denial: "Langdon knew that he himself, like millions, was guilty of this. When it came to the circumstances of the world, denial had become a global pandemic. Langdon promised himself that he would never forget this."

Dante too was committed to cutting through denial, and wrote the *Divine Comedy* (*Inferno* is the first of the three parts of the *Divine Comedy*, followed by *Purgatorio* and *Paradiso*) as a poem that he hoped would "save the world" in moral terms—as Sienna Brooks the transhumanist wants to "save the world" in biogenetic terms ("Then I met Bertrand—a beautiful, brilliant man who told me not only that saving the world was *possible* . . . but that doing so was a moral imperative" (p. 436)). Brown has meditated on the psychology of denial, pernicious among the best and the brightest ("Langdon recalled a recent Web-tracking study of students at some Ivy League universities which revealed that even highly intellectual users displayed an instinctual tendency toward denial" (p. 214)) and has given considerable thought—as Dante did—to the use of entertainment (etymologically, that which holds our attention) for didactic purposes: "According to the study, the vast majority of university students, after clicking on a depressing news article about arctic ice melt or species extinction, would quickly exit that page in favor of something trivial that purged their minds of fear; favorite choices included sports highlights, funny cat videos, and celebrity gossip" (p. 215).

In his *Inferno*, Brown has imitated Dante in writing entertainingly for didactic purposes, as a means of circumventing readers' denial. The use of Dante in Brown's *Inferno* is thus programmatic, sutured into its DNA through the deep didacticism that is "hidden" under the entertaining clues that are intended to offer a cryptographer's paradise of delight. Brown is following in the path laid out by Dante's address to the reader cited on p. 253: "O you possessed of sturdy intellects, observe the teaching that is hidden here beneath the veil of verses so obscure" (*Inf.* 9.61-63).[1] The imitation here is not just at the surface level—Langdon reads these verses

---

[1] I applaud Brown for using Allen Mandelbaum's translation of the Divine Comedy, which Langdon considers "dazzling" (228). Many years ago I persuaded Allen to allow his translation to join Longfellow's on the Digital Dante website. I wish he were still with us to enjoy this reference.

and learns that he must probe the symbols—but at a deeper level: under the veil of the cryptographic thriller Brown intends to save us by teaching us about overpopulation and the transhumanist movement.

A key part of the fascination of the *Divine Comedy* for Brown is the great art that it inspired: "Throughout all of history, with the sole exception perhaps of Holy Scripture, no single work of writing, art, music, or literature has inspired more tributes, imitations, variations, and annotations than the *Divine Comedy*" (p. 83). He mentioned in one interview that he had never before dealt with a great work of literary art, as compared to visual art, and we get the impression that he has now checked "Great Literary Work of Art" off his list.

At the core of this book, and perhaps of all of Brown's books, is a complex dynamic between mass culture and elite culture, and its author's astute self-fashioning with respect to that dynamic. He is happy to exploit mass culture, but at heart he considers himself an exponent of elite culture. This dynamic is similarly present in his relationship to the tourism industry, which his books both depend upon and contribute to, while at the same time making it clear that he is no typical tourist: the acknowledgments of Brown's *Inferno* are a paean to the kind of rarified access that in the past was afforded only to scholars who had spent their lives toiling on specific manuscripts or paintings. All of these secret places are open to Dan Brown, no doubt given red carpet treatment at all the museums and libraries of Europe (with the exception of the Vatican, of whose animosity he is quite proud; see p. 269). He uses his access both to promote a voyeuristic desire on the part of his readers and to remind them that he is special, that he belongs to a vanishing elite displaced by mass tourism.

So, what grade shall we give Brown as a Dante user? Given his commitment to erudition and his obvious intelligence, he should have done better. He does a decent job of harvesting clues from a wide range of texts that include *Purgatorio* (The Seven Ps), *Paradiso* (the reference to the Florentine Baptistery in Canto 25), and even Dante's youthful *Vita Nuova* (Zobrist proclaims his love for

Sienna in language from this text on p. 320). However, there are errors, such as the bizarre and meaningless distinction Langdon makes between "formal Italian" on the one hand and the so-called "vernacular" or "language of the people" of the other (82). The word "vernacular" refers to Italian as opposed to Latin, not to a less formal Italian. The Italian vernacular encompasses a full gamut of stylistic registers: it can be both high and formal and low and ple-beian, as Dante explained in his treatise *On Vernacular Eloquence* and demonstrated in his *Divine Comedy*.

Another error is Langdon's statement that "Treachery is one of the Seven Deadly Sins—the worst of them, actually—punished in the ninth and final ring of hell" (p. 276). Treachery is indeed punished in the ninth and final ring of Dante's hell, but Dante's hell is not structured according to the Seven Deadly Sins, and the Seven Deadly Sins do not include treachery. Rather, it is Dan-te's purgatory that is structured according to the Seven Deadly Sins, more accurately called Seven Deadly Vices, because pride, envy, anger, sloth, avarice, gluttony, and lust are *inclinations to sin*, rather than the sin itself, and purgatory is the realm where those sinful inclinations are rooted out of us. Hell is where sinful acts for which one has not repented are eternally punished, and Dan-te classifies those sinful acts according to Aristotle's *Nicomachean Ethics* (*Inferno* 11). The discussion of "saligia" (p. 58) indicates that Brown knows that the Seven Deadly Sins do not include treachery and suggests that he got confused by the discrepancy between the moral order of *Inferno* and that of *Purgatorio*.

More troubling than such errors is Brown's resistance to the essence and deep logic of Dante's poem: Brown's relentless insis-tence on terror and misery leads him to characterize the souls of purgatory as "naked figures trudg[ing] upward in misery" (249). And yet the overriding emotion of purgatory is hope, and all parts of the *Divine Comedy*—even the *Inferno*—are stunningly beauti-ful, psychologically riveting, and illusionistically compelling. There would be no way to know any of this from a reading of Brown's book. Even though illusionism is a theme of Brown's book, given that the Consortium is in the business of making illusions, Brown does not convey Dante's greatness as the ultimate illusionist. He does not acknowledge that the provost's claim "The best illusions involve as much of the real world as possible" (p. 367) is verifiable throughout the *Divine Comedy*, which may well be the most successful virtual reality in history.

Many pages are devoted to Botticelli's map of hell, Brown insisting always on its forbidding qualities, its grimness (I have never seen students respond to this map as grim), while the brilliance of Botticelli's map lies in its precise spatial rendering of the possible world that Dante renders in words. Far from forbidding, it is *attractive*—it makes us want to pull out microscopes to examine all the little tiny figures that are perfectly executed in their perfect virtual reality.

Brown doesn't seem to have grasped the lesson that the centuries-old tradition of illustrating the *Divine Comedy* offers. Illustrators are drawn to the *Commedia* for its *realism*, topographical but especially psychological. In a Western literary tradition devoted to mimesis (art as representation of reality), Dante took realism to a new level. And, his realism takes the form not only of virtual renderings of the landscape of the otherworld, but of deep psychological insights into the souls whom he meets along the path. The staying power of the *Divine Comedy*, the reason there is a market for translations and that we teach it today, is that its realism is in the service of psychological penetration. Generations of readers have been dazzled by what they learn from its pages—for good and for ill—of the human spirit. This is why the illustrators of the *Divine Comedy* do not limit themselves to illustrating the otherworld topography. Rather, many of the most famous illustrations and paintings depict the souls' stories of *their past lives on earth*: Francesca holds the book she was reading when she and Paolo kissed; Ugolino and his sons are in the tower where he died without consoling them.

At the end of his book Brown shows that he does respond to the humanist energy of Dante's poem, apparently contradicting much of what he has said about the *Divine Comedy* heretofore: "Dante's poem, Langdon was now reminded, was not so much about the misery of hell as it was about the power of the human spirit to endure any challenge, no matter how daunting" (Epilogue). The *Divine Comedy* as an intellectual and indeed "transhumanizing" quest, in the sense of Dante's coinage *trasumanar* in *Par.* 1.70 and as distilled in his Ulysses' "yearning in desire / To follow knowledge, like a sinking star, / Beyond the utmost bound of human thought" (*Inf.* 26; citation from Tennyson's *Ulysses*), thus seems to be Brown's true reference point.

Brown also perhaps shows awareness of Dante's lack of orthodoxy in his epigraph on the dangers of neutrality. Dante's invention of a space in the vestibule of hell for neutral souls who "lived without disgrace and without praise" (*Inf.* 3.36), and are consequently rejected by both heaven and hell, is utterly unorthodox: it makes no theological sense to despise a lack of commitment to evil. This unorthodox idea reflects Dante's own zeal to commit, a spirit of action versus inaction that trumps orthodox theology, and leads him to create a category of cowards who are not received in hell, since "even the wicked cannot glory in them" (*Inf.* 3.42). Brown deliteralizes Dante's handling of the neutrals, moving them from a vestibule to "the darkest places in hell" but he is faithful to Dante's activist spirit, which is radical in its flouting of theology in order to disparage neutrality and inaction.

So, Brown has an idea of Dante the humanist. But rather than articulate this idea, he goes to his default comfort zone and defines Dante's greatness in bogus and historically inaccurate fashion, as part of the Catholic Church's drive to force sinners into compliance: "'Dante's *Inferno* created a world of pain and suffering beyond all previous human imagination, and his writing quite literally defined our modern visions of hell,' Langdon paused. 'And believe me, the Catholic Church has much to thank Dante for. His *Inferno* terrified the faithful for centuries, and no doubt tripled Church attendance among the faithful'" (p. 84). Catholicism seems to override Brown's capacity for research and historical accuracy, triggering reflexive blinders that make him say absurd things.

The history of the relationship between the Catholic Church and Dante's *Divine Comedy* is not remotely as Brown states it. Very briefly: the *Divine Comedy* raised the hackles of the Church, and for good reason, given what Dante had to say about the corruption of the Church and many of its most prominent figures. After all, the "half-buried body pedaling its legs in wild desperation in the air" (p. 38), a recurring but decontextualized image in Brown's book, refers, in Dante's book, to a pope. The Dominican Guido Vernani called Dante a "vessel of the devil" and the Dominicans banned the poem in 1335.[2] Special and culturally new in Dante's hell are not the tortures but the Aristotelian framework of his hell and the many classical elements[3]; the tortures were old hat. It is not true that "Dante's work solidified the abstract concept of hell into a clear and terrifying vision" (p. 64); that work had been done many centuries earlier, and not just by the Bible and Greek mythology, as Brown repeats in interviews: there was a long post-biblical Christian tradition that Dante inherited.[4] It is not true that Dante invented the "modern vision of hell," as Brown has been claiming in interview after interview. If anything, he invented the modern vision of purgatory. Purgatory was a relatively recent idea in Dante's time, compared to hell or paradise.[5] Dante invented the very idea of purgatory as a mountain, and thus conditioned later religious thought, as we can see, for instance, from the title of Thomas Merton's 1948 religious autobiography *The Seven Storey Mountain.*[6]

---

[2] See Teodolinda Barolini, *The Undivine Comedy* (Princeton: Princeton U. Press, 1992), p. 6.

[3] See Teodolinda Barolini, "Medieval Multiculturalism and Dante's Theology of Hell," in *Dante and the Origins of Italian Literary Culture* (New York: Fordham U. Press, 2006), pp. 102-21.

[4] See Eileen Gardiner, trans. and ed., *Visions of Heaven and Hell Before Dante* (New York: Italica Press, 1989), Alison Morgan, *Dante and the Medieval Other World* (Cambridge: Cambridge University Press, 1990), and Alan E. Bernstein, *The Formation of Hell: Death and Retribution in the Ancient and Early Christian Worlds* (Ithaca: Cornell University Press, 1993).

[5] See Jacques Le Goff, *The Birth of Purgatory*, trans. Arthur Goldhammer (1981; Chicago: University of Chicago Press, 1984).

[6] New York, Harcourt Brace, 1948.

What Dante did was to complicate immensely the already codified vision of hell by adding psychological depth and realism that compelled his readers to sympathize with sinners. Generations of readers have sympathized with characters from *Inferno* such as Francesca, Farinata, and Ugolino. Dante further created a moral quagmire for his readers by populating Limbo, against theological orthodoxy, with great classical poets and philosophers, and by making his beloved guide Virgil one of these same classical poets destined to return to hell, to the dismay of generations of readers. He goes further, using the heaven of justice as an opportunity to question God's justice. How can it be just, he asks, to damn a perfectly virtuous man who happens to be born on the banks of the Indus, with no knowledge of Christ: "And that man dies unbaptized, without faith. / Where is this justice then that would condemn him? / Where is his sin if he does not believe?" (*Par.* 19.76-78). Dante made things less black and white, not more so, as reflected also in the fact that his social positions are frequently more tolerant than those of his contemporaries. Elsewhere, I have shown this to be the case with respect to his treatment of women, of homosexuals, and of racial "others."[7]

Dan Brown seems to intuit something of who Dante is. The idea that motivates him, that we will make a hell of earth if we don't change paths, is Dante's. What a shame, then, that Brown does not present *that* Dante to all the potential new readers who will pick up his book.

---

[7] See Teodolinda Barolini, "Dante's Sympathy for the Other, Or the Non-Stereotyping Imagination: Sexual and Racialized Others in the Commedia," *Critica del Testo 14* (2011): 177-204, and posted on the Digital Dante website.

Damnation vs. Demography: Contrasting *Infernos* of Dante and Dan Brown

BY ALISON CORNISH

Professor of Italian, Romance Languages, and Literatures department, University of Michigan

For Dan Brown, Dante is the poet of death, a master of horror, a prophet of doom. In Dan Brown's *Inferno*, the ultimate horror is a Malthusian demographic catastrophe, in which an excess of human beings will create scenarios of bodies heaped together, writhing, moaning, grasping, eating sewage, and each other. This picture is understood as "Dantesque." According to Brown's fictional expert, Robert Langdon, Dante's powerfully realistic portrayal of "pain and suffering beyond all previous human imagination" was responsible for an "uptick" (indeed a tripling, Brown alleges) in church attendance in the fourteenth century, "scaring" people into the otherwise empty pews. But the facts are otherwise: representatives of the church were the targets of Dante's most stinging depictions. The image of the sinner buried upside down with the wriggling legs that provides an important clue to Langdon is in fact a pope, in a long line of inverted popes who essentially pimped the sacraments. By contrast, in the world of Dan Brown's novel, the most objectionable behavior of clerics is the temerity of "a bunch of celibate male octogenarians to tell the world how to have sex." Although Dante depicts horrors happening to bodies, his book is really about souls. Dan Brown's *Inferno* is epidemiological; Dante's is moral.

The novel's epigraph nonetheless depicts demographic saturation as a "moral" crisis, in which those who maintain neutrality are destined for "the darkest places in hell." (In fact, Dante's "lukewarm" are actually *excluded* from entering hell proper at all, lest the damned glory over them). It is somewhat ironic that the terror of overpopulation in Brown's novel is played out in contemporary Italy that has a perilously low fertility rate. Because Dante died twenty-seven years before the Black Death hit Europe, he is not the obvious choice for the novel's theme of plague. (It was Dante's successor, Giovanni Boccaccio, who made the most famous description of the 1348 pestilence in Florence at the beginning of his *Decameron*.) Pre-plague Italy was marked not by "overpopulation, famine, and economic hardship" but by new wealth and cultural vigor—which Dante saw as the root of moral decay. The horrors of his hell are not a prophecy of impending scarcity of resources, but a pointed diagnosis of the world's present ills. The pain of hell is its truth because, as Dan Brown's character, Sienna, acknowledges, the truth is sometimes "painfully hard to accept," especially the truth about oneself.

Though Dan Brown's protagonist is not similarly embarked on a journey of moral self-discovery, when Langdon "comes to himself" after "getting lost," at the opening of the book, he seems to be saying, "Very sorry," which may be an intentional evocation of what Dante says when he cries out to the shade of Virgil appearing on the desert slope in the initial existential crisis of the poem. Dante's first word, *miserere*, spoken in Latin, not the vernacular, literally means, "have mercy on me," but, as readers of the psalm from which it is taken well understood, it really was an acknowledgement of sin: "have mercy on me *because I have sinned*": in other words, "I'm very sorry."

The gruesome "funnel of suffering" depicted in Dante's *Inferno* is actually a pitiless anatomy of sin. The punishments of this "horrible art of justice," as he calls it, are chosen not for the degree of pain they inflict on wretched human beings, but for how they aptly express what each sin is. In this poetic sense, the punishments "do justice" to the sins. Submitting uncontrollably to lust is like being buffeted about in a great storm. Thieves who disguised themselves are doomed to continual metamorphosis, detached from any identity proper to them. Sowers of discord who split familial, religious or political units, have their shade-bodies split in ways specific to their own form of violence against human bonds.

Those who believed the best possible afterlife was absence of pain are placed in dull but painless Limbo. Tyrants are steeped in blood. And so on.

Sin comes into Dan Brown's *Inferno* pointedly only in chapter 57, when Langdon realizes that the seven Ps added to the back of Dante's plaster death mask are the repeated initial letter of *peccata*, that is, sins, inscribed on Dante's forehead by an angel in *Purgatorio*. Langdon assumes that this tattoo is inflicted on all the penitents, perhaps as part of the sadistic tenor of Dante's afterlife and his medieval culture in general. In fact, even a casual reading of Dante shows that this is a special arrangement for Dante's living protagonist who, in his progress up the spiraling terraces, will not *actually* be purging any sins the way everyone else is. He will instead participate vicariously as he walks alongside the penitents, progressively erasing each mark from his forehead, but not from his soul.

In the narrow optic of Langdon, purgatory is just more punishment, an extension of hell, and therefore sad. "And sadly, this grueling, nine-ringed ascent is the only route from the depths of inferno to the glory of Paradise." Rather than an extension or outgrowth of the underground torture chamber, purgatory, in Dante's vision, is—literally and figuratively—an inversion of hell, where pain is actually for gain, time means progress, and the love of one human being for another can retire enormous debts to justice. The mountain climb does not just lead to Paradise; it erases the disfigurations of sin on human history to return at least conceptually to that pristine moment when all was well with the world.

The "mapability" of hell and purgatory is one of the things that has appealed to readers of the *Divine Comedy* from Botticelli to Dan Brown. The Garden of Eden (at the top of purgatory's mountain), the body of Satan, and the cross of the Crucifixion are all located on a single axis passing through the center of the spherical earth. Dante has created a literary map that makes time readable, since the events of man's sin, its consequences, and its redemption are all laid out in a single line. Satan appears to dominate the world from his location at the center of the physical cosmos and yet when you finally get there and grasp his hairy sides (as Virgil does at the bottom of Dante's hell in order to use Satan as a ladder), you discover that he is upside down, plunged headfirst into the earth like one of those sinners with the wriggling shins given special attention in the novel. This literally pivotal moment in the poem, when "down becomes up" is not a lesson "that you need to go up to go down" (as Langdon misremembers it in his efforts to escape from the Palazzo Vecchio), but quite the opposite: you need to go down so that you can go up. This is true of the descent via the body of Satan, and more generally true about Dante's whole journey down through hell: it is an alternate route for climbing a mountain. What is required is humility, rather than pride.

Dan Brown's cerebral Sienna is disappointed at Dante's insufficient "grasp of the physics of vector forces" when it seems that "the earth's gravity suddenly switches directions" precisely at this moment of "conversion" or "turning around" on the body of Satan at the mathematical center of the terrestrial globe. In Dante's pre-Newtonian physics, it is not the earth's gravity, but the gravity of things, the weight of objects containing the heavy element of earth, that makes them fall toward their naturally low place. According to Aristotelian physics, lighter objects—composed of more water, air, or fire—actually have a gravity that inclines them upward with respect to the heavier objects. But again, the point is psychological as well as physical. In a tradition going back at least to St. Augustine, the soul itself has weight: the more it loves earthly things the more it will sink toward the center of the earth (i.e. towards Satan). The more it loves celestial things, the more effortlessly it will levitate, as Dante's soul does in *Paradiso*, progressing through successively higher astronomical spheres.

Indeed, already in *Purgatorio*, the going gets lighter toward the top. But Professor Langdon reads purgatory, like hell, only physically. For example, he tells an eager lecture audience that in purgatory "the gluttonous must climb without food or water, thereby suffering excruciating hunger." Of course, everybody has to climb the mountain of purgatory without food or water—which, really, should not be a problem since nobody in purgatory has a body (except the exceptional visitor, Dante). The real conundrum of the gluttons's penance is that they are made to *feel* hunger, indeed to become emaciated, by the mere perfume of forbidden fruit, even though in fact they have no need of it. This is where Dante takes on the task of explaining the aerial bodies or "shades" that populate hell and purgatory. Totally irrelevant from a theological point of view, the fictive representation of souls as shades is necessary only to a poetic depiction of the afterlife of souls, not to their existence. (So when Bernard Zobrist cryptically calls himself "the shade" in his video, he is basically saying that by the time his treasure hunt is played out, he will be dead.)

But Dante takes the paradox of starving shades in *Purgatorio* as an opportunity to consider the mystery of how human souls are joined to bodies: how we desire things that our bodies do not in fact need, how suffering is not just a bodily phenomenon, but a spiritual one, and that souls can in effect "starve" if they are not fed. The food of the soul, or "bread of angels" as Dante puts it, is the subject of the *Paradiso*: a veritable wedding feast. It is a feast moreover immune to Malthusian predictions because, as Virgil explains on the terrace of envy in *Purgatorio*, while earthly goods are in finite supply, spiritual goods propagate infinitely the more partakers there are.

For Dante, salvation has to do not with the corporeal survival of an individual or of the human race, but with the eternal condition of the eternal part of people: the soul. To solve mankind's self-destructive inclination to overpopulate, Zobrist embraces the movement of "transhumanism," symbolized by "H+," that seeks technological enhancements of human beings to make them, presumably, more sustainable. Although unremarked in the novel, it is Dante who coined the term "to transhumanize," a verb he invents to name human beings' transformation into something godlike. As summed up at the end, Dante's whole journey will have been one of "going beyond the human," from time to eternity, from human to divine, as well as from Florence to "a people just and sane."

Transhumanism is the perfect vantage point from which to contrast the world of Dante with that of Dan Brown. While the word comes from Dante's *Paradiso*, the dream of using technology to transcend the weaknesses inherent in our human bodies is played out in Dante's hell, specifically in his famous retelling of the story of Ulysses (a.k.a. Odysseus). Like transhumanists, Dante's Ulysses is aware of the weaknesses of the human body, the limitations of mortality. He convinces his few remaining, somewhat decrepit companions who might be inclined to long for home, to set out on an open-ended journey into the unknown: "Do not deny to the brief vigil of your senses the experience of the world without people." A world without people, or *The World Without Us,* as the title of one recent book puts it, is the environmentalist's dream or nightmare, depending on how one views humanity's role. A "world without people" might lead, as one reviewer of that book describes it: "back to the Garden of Eden, before Adam, Eve, and the snake." Uncannily enough, to Dante's Ulysses' surprise, in the hemisphere of water where no land or people were thought to be, he and his sailors come within sight of a mountain, dark in the distance, at whose summit we as readers will later find out is, precisely, the Garden of Eden. Yet Ulysses' own voyage ends just short of this rediscovered goal, in sudden shipwreck.

From the perspective of the celestial Paradise (far, far beyond the small scratch on the globe of the earth traced by the Greek hero's ill-fated expedition) we learn that Ulysses' ambitious transgression was ultimately a repetition of the essential human sin, the original sin in Eden, which Adam himself will describe to Dante as "going beyond the sign." "Sign" here presumably means limit: an arbitrary mark, the forbidden tree placed in the garden of delights, a sign that is a prohibition. Yet to be a sign, it must also have meaning. The limits of the human condition are a sign of something; they indicate what humanity is. Humanity is defined not just by its limits, but by its ability to acknowledge those limits—for man to understand, for example, that he is neither the source of himself nor the ultimate measure of reality. Paradoxically, it is this acceptance of limits, of finitude, of mortality, of inferiority with respect to something infinitely greater, that permits Dante to complete his journey beyond the ends of the earth, beyond the physical universe, to the infinite source and goal of everything: to "transhumanize."

Signs are Dan Brown's enduring passion, as they are for Professor Langdon, his protagonist. Dante and his culture understood the world itself as a system of signs, the universe as book with one ultimate Author. It is a world teeming with significance, as well as with the pitfalls of misinterpretation. The most fundamental misreading dramatized in the *Divine Comedy* is reading *literally* as opposed to figuratively. This is what lands a lovely, gracious, aristocratic woman named Francesca in hell. She read a French romance describing a passionate adulterous liaison as if it were a recipe book, a how-to manual, a call to sin. In her rage against the consequences of her actions, she blames the book and its author, whereas most scholars would agree that Dante does not. He blames the reader.

The rise of vernacular literature in the Middle Ages, that is to say, works written down in the language people actually spoke in their everyday lives, meant many women could now be readers. Until early modern times, Latin (like Greek, Hebrew and Arabic for other cultures) was the standard language of written communication in Western Europe, and was not generally taught to women. In the fourteenth century, there were not yet two levels of Italian, one "formal" and one "vernacular" (as Professor Langdon erroneously believes). Rather there were different Italian vernaculars spoken all over Italy, which differed not only from Florence to Bologna, but allegedly from one bank of the Arno river to the other. Moreover, vernaculars were understood to be in constant flux, not fixed by a literature or a grammar designed to teach people to read that literature. Dante suggests that the idiom his great-great grandfather would have spoken in Florence would be quite different from the one spoken there in his own time. He also estimates that poetry had begun to be written down in Italian only about fifty years before his own time, when "some man wanted to say something to some woman." The "excuse" for texts to be written in the vernacular rather than Latin is often that it is for women, even when many men without much training or experience with Latin were also (or even mainly) the audience.

In addition to the popular form of lyric poetry on the theme of love (composed in the language beloved ladies could understand), there was in Dante's lifetime a large amount of literature being translated from both French and Latin. These abundant "vernacularizations" or *volgarizzamenti* are an indication of what interested the new reading public in Dante's day: French romances, to be sure, but also rhetorical treatises and summaries of Roman history that could help citizens be better public speakers, and devotional works about saints' lives, virtues and vices, Bible stories, and simplified theology that could help people be better people. This sudden explosion of material in prose made all kinds of knowledge newly available to classes of people ignorant of or not well-versed in the literate language of Latin, such as merchants, bankers, minor nobles, and their wives. This rising vernacular literacy was connected with economic growth and the leisure that accompanied it, but also with the legal basis of Italian city-states and the mercantile and financial professions that required copious record keeping.

Professor Langdon is also mistaken when he explains that, "in the fourteenth century, Italian literature was, by requirement, divided into two categories": tragedy and comedy. Although some comedies survived from Roman antiquity and were used in the teaching of Latin, written theatrical scripts did not become a vernacular literary genre in Europe until the sixteenth century. Even so, a key distinction understood in the Middle Ages was that comedy was associated with humble people, tragedy with noble ones. Dante chooses to write in the humble modern and local mode of speech (the vernacular) rather than the venerable and cosmopolitan language of Latin, of which Virgil is the supreme master. Dante's pointed definition of his own work as a comedy in contrast with Virgil's epic poem, which he labels a "tragedy," moreover suggests that he sees the greatness of pagan culture represented by Virgil as ultimately tragic, aspiring only to the status of those in Limbo ("without hope, we live in desire"). For Dante, Christian culture rereads the pagan story in the context of the good news, the joyful purpose and ending promised by Christ, thereby turning trage-dy into comedy. It is the opposite, in fact, of Ulysses' open-ended journey of exploration that ends, inevitably, in shipwreck, when joy turns into weeping. This is the truth that, as Dan Brown proposes in Italian, is "visible only through the eyes of death."

In the last chapter of Dan Brown's *Inferno*, as the protagonist prepares to head home, Langdon observes that Dante found eter-nal life, not through the salvation of his soul, but through his fame. "So long as they speak your name, you shall never die." But while Brown seems to think this conclusion is Dante's, mistaking fame for the ultimate good is in fact condemned in Dante's *Inferno*: Brunetto Latini, Dante's old mentor who taught "how man makes himself eternal" by writing books is running an endless circuit on a flaming desert with the sodomites, suggesting that living for fame is ultimately sterile. Yet sterility in the world of Dan Brown's *Infer-no* has also become a public good, readers of Dan Brown's *Inferno* have to do lots of turning upside down in order to recover the message of Dante.

Dante as Humanist, Radical Reformer, and Old Testament-Style Prophet

AN INTERVIEW WITH STEVEN BOTTERILL
Associate Professor of Italian Studies, University of California, Berkeley

Steven Botterill is the author of two books and numerous articles on Dante. His teaching covers the spectrum of Italian literature and culture from 1200 to 1500, with occasional forays into the Romantic period and modern poetry. He is completing a book entitled Dante and the Language of Community. *We interviewed Botterill on a wide range of questions that flow from reading Dan Brown's* Inferno *and looking at Dante and the* Divine Comedy *from that perspective.*

In making the Zobrist character a Dante fanatic, and in creating so many similarities between Zobrist and Dante, Dan Brown seems to be saying that the Poet and the Bioengineer share certain motivations: They are both obsessed with painting a horrifying picture of the future in order to prod us into action. Dante wants to cause us to live more moral lives to avoid the Inferno of the afterlife and Zobrist wants to get us to address what he believes is the great population bomb that will turn life on Earth into an Inferno. Is this a fair assessment as far as Dante is concerned?

Brown's identification of Dante's purpose in writing *Inferno* as having been to terrify his audience into being virtuous so as to avoid ending up in the same situation as his characters is drastically oversimplified; I think a more persuasive case can be made that *Inferno* is intended to make its readers (or listeners—the question of who the poem's first audience consisted of is more complicated than Brown seems to realize) *think*, and use their thinking as the basis for making choices of their own, rather than simply cowing them into obedience.

It's always important to remember another fact to which Brown doesn't seem to me to attribute enough importance—namely, that *Inferno* is not a poem that is complete in itself, but is the first part of a narrative trilogy, and a trilogy that begins with images of horrible punishment and endless agony, but ends with images of perfect, intense, unending bliss. The full message of *Inferno* only becomes apparent after you read *Paradiso*. And if *Inferno* scares you into being good, well, that's a start; but Dante wants you to be good for positive reasons, not just out of fear. So I think his motivation is more complex and much more humane than Zobrist's, or than Brown gives him credit for.

What do you think of Brown's portrayal of Dante and the *Divine Comedy* on an overall basis?

Dante's *Inferno* is actually a great deal *less* mysterious and terrifying than Brown makes it appear. He seems to want to make the poem itself into something as otherworldly as its subject matter, and therefore exaggerates the extent to which reading it or studying it in itself becomes a kind of supernatural experience requiring almost magical powers of understanding. But in the end it's only a poem! Langdon's lecture in Vienna is simply risible in its overdramatization of both the poem's content and its effect on its readers; his difficulty in finding a text of the poem in Florence on a Monday when the Museo della Casa di Dante is closed is, to put it mildly, implausible; and the astonishment with which he greets the discovery that somebody has memorized an (in fact fairly short) extract from the poem comes oddly from a Harvard professor of "symbology," who ought surely to know that hundreds if not thousands of people walk the earth today who have memorized the *entire Divine Comedy*. (I myself have known at least half a dozen, though I am not one myself.) There's no great harm in all this, but it does seem to me to show how far outside the mental world of either Dante or his readers Brown remains, despite the way in which he (implicitly) and his Langdon character (explicitly) lay claim to authority on the subject.

Among the italicized musings of "the shade" (i.e., Zobrist) in the opening prologue is the phrase *"Ungrateful land!"* I find no instance of Dante uttering those words, although other references on the same page of Brown's novel come right out of Dante ("dolent city," "eternal woe," etc.). Longfellow wrote a poem where he imagined Florence as an "ungrateful land"—ungrateful to Dante for all he tried to do for Florence. But what was Dante's actual attitude toward Florence in exile? Did he see it as an "ungrateful land" or did he view it in a more nuanced way?

I think there's no doubt that Dante felt a bitterness toward Florence that was very intense in the immediate aftermath of his exile but that faded with time—or perhaps it would be more accurate to say that with time Florence ceased to be his chief preoccupation. *Inferno* is very much about Florence: Hell looks (architecturally) like Florence, it's full of Florentines, many of the major characters with whom Dante-character interacts most intensively share a Florentine history and culture with Dante-poet (Farinata and Brunetto Latini are two obvious examples). And, the question of how to be a good citizen, a good member of a virtuous urban community, is at the forefront of *Inferno*, which depicts Italian cities in general, and Florence in particular, as having failed to find the right way to flourish morally (even while flourishing economically) in Dante's time. But already in *Purgatorio* the focus shifts away from Florence and the idea of the city toward Italy and ideas of larger communities (up to and including the Empire); and in *Paradiso* the focus is not on earthly cities or communities at all, but on ideal, transcendent ones: the City of God, if you like, or celestial versions of Jerusalem and Rome where the citizens are perfectly virtuous (because they are saved and enjoy the vision of God) and the communities are led by God, Jesus, and, especially perhaps, Mary. But even in *Paradiso* Dante still criticizes Florence's moral failings at some length in the episode of Cacciaguida, his own ancestor, who uses his seat among the blessed as a pulpit for a denunciation of the decline in Florentine virtue between his own distant time and

Dante's. So Dante's feelings about Florence may have become more complex, more nuanced, over time and during the writing of the *Commedia*. But he clearly never forgave, never forgot, and never stopped thinking of what happened to him in Florence in 1300-02 as the key episode in his life—and the starting point, of course, of the whole *Commedia*. That dark wood in which Dante-character goes astray is, in part, a metaphor not only for human life in general but the culture and politics of Florence in 1300 in particular.

Dan Brown says church attendance tripled after the *Commedia* began circulating, implying that he painted such a clear picture of the afterlife, that people felt compelled to go to church and to try to avoid the Inferno. But actually, I think the Church reacted negatively to the *Commedia* when it was first published and that Dante remained an exile from Florence until his death. What's the real history here? And what accounts for the relatively quick rise to popularity of the *Commedia*?

I'd be interested to know where Brown gets his figures for church attendance! The *Commedia* certainly became unusually popular, for a work of such length and complexity, in a relatively short span of time. And although most of the evidence for that popularity has to do with the response of a public that could *read* it—a small minority of the populace as a whole, of course—there's certainly some evidence that it also became popular with people who were *listening* to it, because they couldn't read. But I don't know of any evidence that the nonliterate masses headed to church in larger numbers after the poem began to circulate, or that any such increase in attendance could be attributed directly to the poem anyway. The *Commedia* became popular with a large-scale, nonliterate audience because it is a substantial, exciting, colorful, dramatic, and skillfully constructed narrative that entertains you while making you think; and because it is written in the vernacular, not in Latin, and with the freshness and drive and eloquence of the language that its nonliterate readers were using themselves. In other words, it did what Dan Brown tries to do, only better! And the literate intellectuals who liked it and worked to popularize it were, by and large, laymen, especially lawyers, who for various reasons appreciated its sustained critique of the moral corruption and political overreaching of the institutional Church. As you say, reaction from the professional clergy and ecclesiastical readers, was often rather less enthusiastic.

How did the *Commedia* become so embraced or at least enthusiastically identified with as a theological document by the Church? Didn't Dante sentence a number of Popes and other high religious officials to the Inferno? Wasn't he bitterly critical of the hypocrisy of the Church?

The *Commedia* was not officially "embraced" by the Church until long after Dante's time: arguably, not before the middle of the nineteenth century. The fourteenth century Church could see how sharply it was criticized by Dante—a mere layman, after all—who condemns Popes to Hell and saves individuals (Manfred in *Purgatorio* III) whom the Church had excommunicated; and who gives a major role in the moral and philosophical education that leads his protagonist toward divine truth to a pagan poet, Virgil (and therefore pays a huge tribute to the pre-Christian culture from which Virgil came). Moreover, Dante depicts his own character as being motivated on his path toward salvation not principally by the teachings of the Church but by the experience of love for a human being. Even further: it is a *female* human being who shows up in the later stages of Dante-character's journey as an embodiment of all the truth-telling power and spiritual authority that the male clerical hierarchy of Dante's time (and not only Dante's!) would very much have liked to arrogate entirely to itself. There's a lot in the *Commedia* that we know made many leading religious figures across the centuries very uncomfortable, even if they did appreciate its power to convey certain essentials about the Christian faith. And, when the Church did come to embrace the poem, it did so largely by claiming that Dante was completely orthodox as a religious thinker and got all his ideas about Christianity directly out of St. Thomas Aquinas—which is very, very clearly not the case.

Dante seems to be more tolerant of non-Catholic belief systems than was the prevailing thought pattern of his day. He deals with Greek and Roman pagans as great heroes; he has Jewish leaders of the Old Testament alongside Christian leaders in *Paradiso*; he seems to leave room for salvation for the man from Asia that has never heard of Jesus. How do you see Dante's attitude toward what we might call tolerance or diversity today?

There's nothing unusual for the Middle Ages about seeing the Jewish patriarchs and heroines as being saved. That was standard belief, based on the idea that, before Christ came into the world, Judaism was the vehicle through which God revealed Himself, so that exemplary Old Testament Jews were saved because they were in some way forerunners of the truth that Christ came to bring. Much more interesting, and unique to Dante, are things like the salvation of a character from Virgil's *Aeneid* (Ripheus, in *Paradiso* XX); the presence of a pagan suicide, Cato, as the warden of Ante-Purgatory (and perhaps as himself a saved soul); and the repeated warnings that salvation depends upon the unknowable mind of God and not necessarily on the pronouncements of the Church (Manfred, again). And Dante struggles throughout the poem with the question of how damnation can be just, in the case of people who live lives of virtue by their own standards and never had the opportunity to become aware of the Christian revelation in the form of the incarnate Jesus. He accepts that such people are damned; but he doesn't like it, he doesn't understand it, and he eventually decides that it can't be understood by human reason but is something we must accept on faith. He then, of course, makes such a person (Virgil) one of the principal, and one of the most sympathetic, characters in the whole poem.

In many ways, however, it's misleading to try to map modern ideas of "tolerance" or "diversity" on to Dante's mindset, and vice versa; too much has happened in the last seven centuries to make the exercise viable in anything more than a superficial way. It's true that Dante, on the whole, seems not to have shared the more virulent forms of group hatred (of Jews, of sexual nonconformists, of women, even, arguably, of Muslims) that disfigure so much religious writing by Christians in the Middle Ages. But he has fierce hatreds of his own, some of them for things that leave us unmoved, and he tolerates things that we often find intolerable. Which is to say, he lived seven hundred years ago, in a world almost unimaginably different from our own, and we should be very careful indeed about co-opting his work for political or social agendas of our own, whether "left-" or "right-wing" in political or religious terms. If he were to return to life today I suspect that he would be equally critical of the Quakers and of Opus Dei, of the ACLU, and of the Tea Party. He was always a card-carrying party of one.

Is there any chance Dante was criticizing religion more than he was seeking to find salvation in it? If I said that, as a lay person looking at religion and history, Dante seems to me to be arguing much the same case that Martin Luther argued 200 years later, how would you react to that?

No chance at all. He was a staunch and cutting critic of the institutional church and of individual members thereof; but he seems to me to have had an intense devotion to the religion that that church claimed to represent and which, in his view, it all too often traduced and betrayed. Christianity is all-important for Dante: he sees it as the truth, and as the only way to salvation (Virgil, after all, is damned). The church, however, needs to be restored to a state, which Dante identifies with the earliest phase of its history, in which it is worthy of the religion it preaches. And for him that may very well have meant adopting a quite radical stance with regard to the structures of the church as he knew it. He shows more sympathy for radical fringe movements like the Spiritual Franciscans than he does for the established institutions of the church, because they seem to him to better embody the authentic spirit of the church's founder, Jesus. And the Luther comparison seems to me very apt indeed (I'm sorry to have to tell you that you are by no means the first reader of Dante to make it!). In some ways Dante is even more radical than Luther (it's crucial always to remember that Dante was a layman, a voice from outside the halls of ecclesiastical power, one of the flock who should have been doing as he was told. Luther, of course, was an Augustinian monk, in holy orders, and to that extent an insider.). But I doubt if Dante could ever have countenanced the Reformation. It's one thing to reform the church from within, even radically; it's another entirely to, as it were, start up a church of your own. Dante would have drawn the line at that.

Isn't Dante's behavior in writing the *Commedia* in violation of some of the sins he discusses? Isn't the book wildly ambitious? Hasn't he set himself up as arbiter in chief of all sorts of historic judgments? He condemns Popes, emperors, kings, his political opponents, etc. He revises classic stories and myths. He is more critical of Dido than Aeneas is. He has placed himself at the center of the story—almost unprecedented in his day—and placed the woman he loved/admired at the very top ranks of the Christian pantheon. He, alone among people of his age, has been invited to see the inner workings of Heaven and of God. And despite whatever he learns from the example of Latini about the perils of seeking fame, he seems to be seeking fame, revenge, and immortality through his writing. Isn't this a recipe for committing a variety of sins?

Of course it is. Dante never pretends that he himself is not a sinner. He tells us what his worst sin was pride—no surprise there; and he also tells us which sins he was not much given to (envy). Of course he was interested in fame and worldly renown; of course he wants to write a poem that will outdo Virgil and rewrite the literary history of his culture to put himself at its head. But I think we have to give him credit, throughout, for honesty. He searches his own mind and heart as acutely as those of others. He shows his own younger self, Dante-character, as having been weak, foolish, wrongheaded, easily led astray (I'm very tempted to see all the major sinners in *Inferno*—Francesca, Farinata, Pier della Vigna, Brunetto Latini, Ugolino, and above all Ulysses—as alternative versions of Dante himself, people that he himself might have become if he had not loved Beatrice and through that love come to the love of God.) And although he is certainly judgmental of others, he is rarely dogmatic in his judgments: He presents us with images of human behavior, of choices made in particular circumstances, and invites us to think about why those choices deserve punishment, or reward. He almost never says, in effect, "this is wrong because I say so," or "don't do as I do, do as I say." He's much more human than that.

It might be helpful to think of his self-appointed role as akin to that of an Old Testament prophet. He seems to have felt himself in some sense chosen—perhaps only because of the intellectual and literary gifts that he must have known himself to possess, perhaps in some more direct but for us unknowable way—and therefore to have authority to speak out as he does. But the Old Testament prophets don't claim to be exempt from sin and failure of their own: indeed their message owes much of its resonance to what they share with the people to whom they feel themselves called to prophesy, rather than to their difference from them. That unrelenting conviction of rectitude is hard-earned, for Dante as for Isaiah. And it coexists, especially in *Paradiso*, with what I at least see as a genuine and equally hard-earned humility. Dante would have been a poor Christian, and a poor writer, if he had not learned humility as well as (legitimate) pride. The Christ who humbled himself unto death, even death on a cross, is just as much his exemplar as is any prophet or prelate.

How do you feel about the many theories that emphasize supposed coded messages in the *Commedia*, whether acrostics, numerology etc.? Surprisingly, Dan Brown didn't really use this angle, even though it would seem to be right up his alley. Did Dante have any secret truths he wished to convey apart from the stated ones?

If he did, I haven't found them; and if I had found them I doubt if I would tell you! In all seriousness, I think that some material of this kind can be found in the poem, but that it is easy to make much too much of it. There are some acrostics (VOM in *Paradiso*) [which to some people signifies the word for "man" embedded as an acrostic in a discussion of sin—ed.], and Dante obviously believed, to some extent, in the spiritual significance of numbers in general and certain numbers (3 and 9 especially) in particular. And there are some echoes and correspondences sustained across the length of the *Commedia* in numerical ways—occasional similarities of theme in identically-numbered cantos of each *cantica*, for instance. But it's fatally easy to exaggerate this sort of thing. One thing that's worth remembering is that most people who encountered the poem in Dante's time did not read a written text of it; they listened to it being performed. And those who did read it did so in manuscripts that were much less regularized in every way than modern printed editions—in particular, they didn't have line-numbers, so it's hard to imagine that audience being able to see exactly where they were in any given canto, as modern readers can with a glance at the margin. Which in turn means that features occurring in identically-numbered lines of different cantos may not have been as easy to identify in the fourteenth century as they are today. So any interpretation that depends on elements that weren't present in the poem as its first audiences knew it seems to me to be ruled out *a priori*. And, in the end, Dante's message(s) are, as far as I can see, not aimed at the select few—the rich, the powerful, the holy, the Dante scholars—but at everybody who has some combination of eyes to see, ears to hear, a body to live in, and a mind to use for reflection on it all.

Secret truths are not what Dante deals in: he's far too busy trying to get as many people as he can to think as clearly as they can about truths that can be understood by anyone who reflects upon the world he or she lives in. There's something liberating, perhaps even potentially democratic, about that approach, in the fourteenth century: it's no doubt another reason why the Latinate clergy often disliked what they rightly saw as a threat to their power; and it might even be another point of contact with Luther and later Reformers. To speak of these subjects in a language "understanded of the people," as the *Book of Common Prayer* says, and to show the people salvation being achieved by an ordinary man through his reflection on the ordinary experience of humanity, rather than through unreflective obedience to the instructions of his self-proclaimed spiritual betters, is a message so startling in its day that any secret message or arcane doctrine would pale in comparison.

— *Interviewed by Dan Burstein*

Letting the Genre out of the Bottle: Dan Brown's *Inferno* as Modern Parody

BY GLENN W. ERICKSON

Professor of Philosophy, Universidade Federal do Rio Grande do Norte (Brazil)

One manner of addressing the most recent Dan Brown novel, *Inferno*, is to ask what kind of novel it is. Generic labels might be attached for the purposes of promotion and distribution, but classification is also a means to appreciate literary works critically, as Aristotle does in the *Poetics*, where plot and character, thought and diction, are used to distinguish among literary genres. Here our ambition is that, by approaching the novel as "serious literature," we may come to see it as something new in the way of postmodern hybridization.

Broadly speaking, *Inferno* is suspense fiction, a thriller. More narrowly, it is detective, crime or mystery fiction. A detective, Robert Langdon, solves a crime or mystery, through a high-culture treasure hunt, and readers participate vicariously. Blurbs and reviews refer to all four of the Robert Langdon novels as "mystery thrillers" and the author has obviously enjoyed spectacular commercial success with this formula.

The nature of the novel might be defined even more closely, for the plot thickens as more ingredients are added and the concoction takes on new hues. To show how this is done, the plot may be conveniently analyzed in terms of three traditional parts.

First, the Rising Action, which runs for the first seventy-six chapters (most of which are set in Florence), covers the period in which Robert Langdon accompanies Sienna Brooks and during which his investigation points to a terrorist plot, organized by billionaire biochemist Bertrand Zobrist, to reduce populations globally. Since the mystery reveals itself as an international conspiracy, the novel becomes a conspiracy or "paranoid thriller."

Second, the climax, in chapters 77-83 (with most of this part set in Venice), spans the period in which Langdon comes in from the cold and is debriefed, and during which he learns how the conspirators, through an elaborate hoax, turned him to their purpose. Sienna Brooks is recast as a secret and double agent. During this revisionary climax, the novel changes its complexion to an "espionage thriller."

Third, the falling action, from chapters 84-103, occupies the period Langdon is in Istanbul for the final showdown. Here the detective discovers the true character of the biological threat and learns that Zobrist had already unleashed it before the time of action of the novel. These discoveries are deflationary in character. As it has turned out, there is no contemporary version of the Black Plague and the participation of the hero made no difference in the greater scheme of things.

Zobrist's biological threat, called "Inferno," turns out to be a virus designed to modify human genetic makeup and programmed to render one third of humanity sterile. The technology behind such a creation would have been expected only far in the future and "feels like science fiction" (p. 451). The action of the novel taking place in a world in which this technology has taken effect makes *Inferno* "science fiction."

Zobrist's Inferno, like the Maltese Falcon, is what is known in Hollywood as a "McGuffin": it moves the plot insofar as everyone tries to get their hands on it. Taking the form of an ovoid sack, it is more closely an "Egg McGuffin."

***

So far our inquiry into the genre of the novel has dealt with the literal sense of the text. Were the text interpreted figuratively, other genres might be suggested. The author himself indicates such an interpretation. In a prefatory note titled "Fact," he writes (p. 3):

> *Inferno* is the underworld as described in Dante
> Alighieri's epic poem the *Divine Comedy*, which
> portrays hell as an elaborately structured realm
> populated by entities known as 'shades'—bodi-
> less souls trapped between life and death.

Harry Truman once said that he did not give his opponents Hell but merely told the truth, and they thought it was Hell. By contrast, Dante gave the faithful not truth but Hell, and they thought it was truth. Hell as Dante portrays it in his own *Inferno* is not literally a place but rather a spiritual state. He uses literal descriptions to portray Hell allegorically, and Dante's *Inferno* is an allegory. Since Brown portrays Dante's Hell allegorically, his *Inferno* is also an allegory. In addition to Zobrist's Inferno, Dante's *Inferno* is an eponym (namegiver) of Brown's.

The novel is not just an allegory of a place, but also of a story. Allegories of stories include take-offs, send-ups, lampoons, burlesques, travesties, satires and the like. These often have a sarcastic edge and are meant to disparage. Yet there is also a kind of non-ridiculing literary allegory in which the old story is just recontextualized. This genre is sometimes termed "modern parody." An example is James Joyce's *Ulysses*, which recontextualizes Homer's *Odyssey* (cited in Brown's *Inferno* on p.226) in early twentieth century Dublin.

By recontextualizing Dante's *Inferno* in twenty-first century Italy and Turkey, Dan Brown has written a modern parody of the first third of the *Divine Comedy*. Nikolai Gogol had already written a modern parody of Dante's *Inferno* in the first part of his novel *Dead Souls* (mentioned in chapter 6 of Brown's *Inferno*). T. S. Eliot parodies Dante's *Inferno* along with various other literary works in *The Wasteland* (see p. 443, where Brown references the word "wasteland").

Like Eliot, Brown incorporates various visions of the otherworld into his parody beyond Dante's. Consider chapter 45, in which the central image is the Devil's Navel (Dante's Canto XXXIV), used as an analogy for having to go one way in order to go the opposite in escaping the Invisible Palace. The name Armenia is repeated fourteen times; and the phrase "No exit," six times. These are presumably allusions, respectively, to Plato's Myth of Er at the end of the *Republic*, where the Armenian soldier Er describes his journey with dead souls to the beyond, and to Jean-Paul Sartre's play *No Exit*, in which Hell is portrayed as "other people." In the same passage, Langdon went "through the looking glass" and "disappeared into the rabbit hole," allusions to the Carolinian underworld.

***

By comprehending that, at bottom, *Inferno* is a modern parody, critical appreciation of the novel changes in several respects. We can now imagine, for starters, that Dante's rhyme scheme, the *terza rima* ("third rhyme"), is represented in the novel by everything "coming in threes." Not to mention the dozens and dozens of appearances of the numerals "III" or "3," the word "third" is used eighteen times; "three," nintey-nine times; "thirty," twenty-one times; and "tri-," in the sense of three, thirty-nine times.

Taken literally, *Inferno* has its "Brown patches," those "problems" of style, grammar and fact, which so upset reviewers and cause more than a few them to feel compelled to parody, in a ridiculing manner, Brown's writing style. But taken figuratively, these are an integral part of Brown's non-ridiculing parody of the *Divine Comedy*, which was itself termed a "comedy" in the then current sense of being written in "vulgar" (or popular) Tuscan. So let us now praise Brown for not losing the common touch.

Brown's *Inferno* observes each of the three classical unities, two of them literally and all three of them figuratively. Literally it has "unity of plot" because it recounts a single action, namely, the discovery of Zobrist's Inferno, and that as a whole. Literally it has "unity of time" because the plot unfolds within the span of a single twenty-four-hour day. Yet literally it does not have "unity of place," because it unfolds in three separate locations. Figuratively, it still has unity of plot, but the single action is now Langdon's passage through Hell. Figuratively, there is once again "unity of time" but in the sense that time stands still while Langdon is in Hell. Until

Langdon's Mickey Mouse watch is returned to him (in chapter 104), Langdon is figuratively "out of time;" as in Dante. Hell is not a material reality, but a virtual state of things: things are *as if* they were real, but they are *not* real. And finally, figuratively, the novel has unity of place because all the action transpires in Hell.

Langdon is in Hell in ways corresponding to the three parts of plot outlined above. In the rising action, having been spirited away and stripped of his memory, he is hoodwinked at every turn; in the climax, he is bewildered by his own incomprehension; and in the falling action, he is confronted with the fact that his effort has been ill-conceived and ineffectual. In the parody, these conditions are symptomatic of the same underlying circumstance, namely, that Langdon is in passage through "an elaborately structured realm populated by [...] bodiless souls trapped between life and death" (cited above).

A mapping of all the episodes of Brown's *Inferno* onto similar episodes in Dante's would be a daunting task, because Brown has woven in so many interconnections. But a few examples may suggest the network of connections and parallels. Such a mapping could begin with "Langdon bolted awake, shouting" (p. 10), which links up with the beginning of Dante's Canto IV, "like one awakened by violent hands, / I leaped up with a start" (in the Ciardi translation). For another clue that Dan Brown is consciously invoking *Inferno* Canto IV here, consider that in the middle of this scene on p. 10, Brown notes that Langdon "looked down and saw an IV tugging at the skin of his forearm," with the abbreviation for this ubiquitous hospital device a direct reference to the roman numeral for this canto.

One of the hardest aspects of Brown's recontextualizing parody of Dante to comprehend is that there are correspondences between characters in the poem and the novel, making the latter a *roman à clef*, or "novel with a key." Dante the author and Dante the character are Dan Brown and Robert Langdon, respectively. Virgil's role is played, in a sense, by Zobrist, who leads Langdon through Hell by means of a series of clues. Beatrice and Santa Lucia, who arrange for Virgil to guide Dante through Hell (Canto

II) are Sienna Brooks and Elizabeth Sinskey, who successively put Langdon in contact with Zobrist's clues (cylinder seal, Vasari painting, death mask, Doge's tomb, Medusa, commemorative plaque, video).

The provost, the character without a proper name (because of the taboo associated with speaking it) and whose super yacht is the Mendacium ("the Latin word for Pseudologos—the Greek god of deception [...] who reigned over all [...] the daimones specializing in falsehoods, lies, and fabrications" (p. 344)), is the very Devil. King David, the antitype of Christ, whom Dante does not encounter in Hell because Christ had spirited him away in the harrowing of Hell (Canto III), is the David (Michelangelo's statue) whom Langdon usually goes to see whenever he is in Florence (p. 265) but does not view on this particular trip, which is his passage through Hell. The dove who saves Langdon (pp. 12, 20, 24, 68, 281, 259) is the Holy Ghost, or Primal Love (Canto III). You can't tell the players without a program.

The names of the characters have significance on a number of levels. For example, five important character names include the letters that spell out "sin" within their names. Three share the letters for "reason," while one contains Faith, Reason, and Treason. The standard list of the seven deadly sins are pride, greed, lust, envy, gluttony, wrath, and sloth (as named by Brown on p. 58). However, at various points the novel turns treachery into one of the seven deadly sins, as an equivalent to pride (see pp. 103, 215, 276). Even though this is a mistaken reading of Dante as well as the classical list of these seven sins, treachery or treason is on Dan Brown's list all the same. It seems reasonable, meanwhile, to equate wrath with anger and sloth with laziness. Given this much, then using the letters bolded below, five characters have specific deadly sins hidden in their names:

"treason" is in the name **J**on**a**tha**n** **F**erri**s**,

"greed" in the name **A**gent Brü**der**,

"envy" in **V**ay**en**tha,

"anger" in Rob**er**t L**an**gdon,

"laziness" in **Eliza**beth Sinskey.

All of these persons were at one time or other in contact with the cylinder seal on which was inscribed the acronym for the seven deadly sins: SALIGIA (p.58). There were two more characters that also came in contact with the seal, other than its designer Zobrist. One of these, Sienna Brooks, has letters in her name spelling Eros, the personification of carnal love, or lust. The other is Ignazio Busoni, a.k.a. il Duomino, who has the letters of the Latin word for gluttony, *gula* (also cited p. 58), in his name plus nickname. What is more, some, if not all, of these characters seem to embody their particular semi-anagramatic vices: Sinskey, because of her medication, is always dozing off ("laziness"), Busoni is very fat ("gula/gluttony"), Sienna has reveries of lovemaking ("lust"), Ferris is two-faced ("treason"), and so on.

Bertrand Zobrist is another character who has the letters for "reason" in his name. But there are other layers of meaning here as well: Zobrist is a Prussian name that derives from names like Ober and Obermann; these latter names, in turn, conjure up Nietzsche's *Übermensch* (a kind of "overman" or "superman") who can define the values for a world in which "God is dead" (just as Zobrist believes he can do); and in *über*, we have several of the letters contained in *superbia*, which is Latin for the sin of pride. With the inclusion of Zobrist and "pride/superbia," we can say that all seven of the traditional sins are covered by a character name, with treachery/treason added as Brown's eighth sin to cover all bases.

In Botticelli's *Map of Hell*, the deepest ditch of the eighth circle of Hell has the falsifiers; but in Zobrist's modified version of this painting, which was meant as a parting gift to Sinskey, the deepest ditch has the "clerical profiteers" (pp. 91-2), because Zobrist ses Sinskey as a gaining personal advantage from her scholarly perspectives. In a delirium in chapter 1, Langdon reads the letter "R" on one of the clerical profiteers as referring to "Robert," that is, to himself. This means subconsciously that Langdon sees himself as profiting unduly from his scholarship. Yet Langdon is the alter ego of the author Dan Brown (as Dante, the Pilgrim in Hell's pit, is for Dante the Poet of the *Inferno*), this means allegorically that

Dan Brown (qua authorial voice) also feels himself—most plausibly, one might add—to be a clerical profiteer. This makes the novel borderline "confessional literature."

One of the many similarities between Dan Brown and Robert Langdon is that they share a taste for travel writing, and perhaps portions of the novel read like travelogue because the author is touching base with his literary roots. Homer's *Odyssey* pertains to this genre, as do the first six books of the *Aeneid*, written by Virgil and inspired by the Odyssey. All three travelogues feature a descent into Hell. Odysseus speaks with Achilles, Virgil confers with his own father, and Dante converses with many personages. In Canto IV, Dante is hailed by the pagan poets Homer, Horace, Ovid, Lucan, and his guide Virgil, as one of their number. In the recontextualization, where the names of so many important artists and writers are dropped, might Dan Brown be claiming his own place in the canon even, as in Dante's case, when he is so new on the scene? The upside of belatedness (that is, coming late in literary history) is that the contemporary high-tech world affords a magnitude of fame that might compensate for its brevity. Who among the Greats has one fifth of a billion copies in print?

***

Dante's *Inferno* in its own way is a mystery thriller, investigating what is sometimes styled "the greatest mystery of them all," death. In the same vein, both Dan Brown's novel and Dante's poem are science fiction, but with a difference of contextualization. Science in the fourteenth century meant the lore of the Scholastic followers of Aristotle, from whom Dante learned the architectonics of Hell.

Zobrist, visionary genetic engineer and Dante fanatic, combines medieval and contemporary science in defending his Inferno on the grounds that it fends off Malthusian extinction as well as moral degeneration into a Dantesque Hell. The juxtaposition of these apologies, however, engenders a great deal of cognitive dissonance. For Dante, vice is sinful and morally evil. But "sin" and "moral evil" do not figure in contemporary scientific vocabulary of Zobrist, the self-styled *Übermensch* in a world where God and traditional morality are dead.

The novel is science fiction, but of what kind? Robert Langdon thinks that Zobrist's Inferno belongs to "some kind of Orwellian dystopia of the future" (p. 438); but eventually Sinskey seems to think Zobrist's solution to the problem of overpopulation could also be a good thing (p. 450). Parallel to the question whether the novel is utopian or dystopian is that of whether it is comic or tragic? Of course Brown's puckish *Inferno* is more comic, in the sense of being funnier, than Dante's gruesome version. It nearly confirms Marx's comment about history repeating itself (referenced by Brown on p. 382), with Marx's addendum that the pattern this repetition takes is often first as tragedy, then as comedy.

For Aristotle, tragedy is *about* a better class of people and comedy *about* a worse class of people, but in the fourteenth century, "tragedy" is written *for* a better class of people and "comedy" *for* a worse class. In this Aristotelian sense, Dante's and Brown's works are tragedy; in the fourteenth century sense, both are comedy (see graphics, p. 37).

In common parlance, "tragedy" means a story with a sad ending and "comedy" a story with a good ending. Dante's *Divine Comedy* is then comedy because the misery of Hell, fulfilling God's design, is good. Brown's *Inferno* could also be comedy in this sense insofar as Zobrist's Inferno is for the good. Yet the novel presents itself as neither utopia nor dystopia, but as ethically challenged.

Let us not forget that the novel is also ecological fiction—a "green yarn," as it were—its literal moral being that an ecologically motivated antinatalism *may* be worth considering. The allegorical moral of the story is, by contrast, more self-assertive. It is first stated in an epigraphic misquote of Dante, "The darkest places in Hell are reserved for those who maintain their neutrality in times of moral crisis," then repeated in the Epilogue. Here Brown departs from Dante's infernal architectonics. For whereas in Canto III of

Dante's *Inferno*, those who took no sides, either for good or for evil (to wit, the Opportunists), are not afforded any place in Hell whatsoever; Brown consigns them to its blackest reaches.

In this updated take on Damnation, it's not what we did that was so god-awful; 'twas lack of commitment screwed the pooch. "Ya gotta go all in!" Yet existential engagement, as opposed to detachment, is no proper moral criterion. In contrast to Dante Alighieri's casuistic Hell, Dan Brown's is rife with moral ambiguity. Why should recontextualization function in this manner? It just seems that, according to the novelist, in the stretch of duration separating us from the poet, the City of Hell has undergone, if not exactly "massive urban renewal," then perhaps rather "extensive gentrification."

The Lord moves in mysterious ways ... most mysterious of these, the change of heart which reshapes our stars.

Preposterous but Not Absurd:
Dan Brown's *Inferno* Embraces More of
Dante's Perspective Than You Might Think

BY GIUSEPPE MAZZOTTA
Sterling Professor of Humanities for Italian,
Yale University

It is quite an event to see how a major popular novelist of our times writes a novel that interprets and evaluates a Florentine fourteenth century poet/theologian, Dante Alighieri. Dante's *Divine Comedy*, and especially its first part, the *Inferno*, are everywhere in Dan Brown's own novel, *Inferno*. But Dante's poem is not treated either as a mere sourcebook of imaginative inventions or a supreme literary corpus from which Brown could mechanically borrow as contemporary pop fiction writers usually do with the literary tradition. Details are taken from the poem, to be sure: the seven P's, the opening tercet of the first Canto, the pilgrim's broken path, the insight that in the experience of redemption the way up is down, the sense of the neutral angels in the cosmic battle between God and Lucifer, etc. These fragmentary bits of Dante abound in Brown's book, but they are not truly essential. Instead, Dante plays a central role in Dan Brown's novel only because his poem traces a sort of imaginative and moral compass for the novel: it reveals and prefigures a secret, unique knowledge about the nature and character of our contemporary world.

Taken by itself, from what could be called a traditional philological critical perspective, Dante's poem relates a spiritual quest that a man, Dante himself, takes during the Holy Week of the year 1300 while still alive across the three realms of the beyond— *Inferno, Purgatorio,* and *Paradiso.* On the Good Friday of that year, while he has lost his way in life, Dante undertakes what turns out to be a providential journey under the assistance of three guides, the classical Roman poet Virgil, the woman the poet had loved in his youth, Beatrice, and the contemplative monk, St. Bernard of Clairvaux who prays to the Virgin Mary that the pilgrim may reach the beatific vision, which means what we usually refer to as the experience of seeing the face of God.

In the circles of Hell or, as he calls it, *Inferno*, the first section of the poem that is under the rule of Satan, the journeyman Dante confronts the reality of evil in its diabolical masquerades, deception, and self-deceptions. These range from obsessions with power, political violence by tyrants, and civil wars, to moral corruption by clerics and popes. On Easter Sunday, Dante emerges from the eternal night of Hell to the light of *Purgatorio*, an island located in the Southern hemisphere at the antipodes of Jerusalem. There he witnesses the ethical drama of the spiritual purification of souls, a sort of reconstruction of the "human" that had been utterly disfigured by the capacity for doing evil steadily displayed in the long history of human beings themselves. The pilgrim's purgatorial experience culminates with his own immersion into Lethe, the river of forgetfulness, and into Eunoe, the river that washes away the temptations of the intellect and opens it to his ultimate metaphysical quest, the vision of God. Finally, in a flight across a universe of beauty and light under the guidance of Beatrice, a flight which is represented as a space exploration through the planets of the Ptolemaic cosmological system, Dante is touched by the divine and discovers, that is, his place in the economy of creation.

This general Christian trajectory of Dante's poem is ostensibly bracketed by Dan Brown's *Inferno*. Like Dante's poem, the novel also tells a quest story. But Brown boldly displaces Dante's theological vision into the modern, secular world of technology and the new scientific, rationalist worldview technology has been increasingly shaping and disclosing. Consistently, the Dante who in the Brown novel acts as Virgil does for him in the *Divine Comedy*—as an oracle and as the visionary author of a profound allegory that inspires the plot concocted by the brilliant and mad scientist, Bertrand Zobrist—is not the poet who lived in the intellectual context of the early fourteenth century. To the contrary (but quite legitimately), Brown has cast him as the "possessed" forerunner of fifteenth and sixteenth century Florentine Renaissance and Humanism.

The mythic and yet historical names of other Florentines—Vasari, Botticelli, Machiavelli, Guicciardini, and Michelangelo—who appear as both sublime and yet demonic forces—scan the artistic and scientific achievements of Florence that remain to this day unparalleled in the history of Western thought. Theirs is an age that valorizes the sphere of immanence over and against the spurious juxtaposition between Heaven and earth and it is one that breaks down all lines of demarcation between gods and mortals. It can be said that something like Florence's systematic redrawing of borders, its questioning the place of man and woman in the ever-shifting configuration of the world, also distinguished the brilliant culture of fifth century BC Athens. In Brown's novel, the spirit of Florence and of Venice, cities where all oppositions touch one another and all apparent discordant discourses are harmonized, reappears in the Hagia Sophia in Istanbul, the remote and familiar city known as the geographic hinge of East and West, as the historical point of contact between Christians and Moslems, and as the gate of the abyss of a likely world catastrophe.

In reading Dante, as Brown does, from the high perspective of Renaissance humanism, the twenty-first century novelist has adopted a finely nuanced rhetorical move that allows him to address some of the most elusive questions of the history-shaping technology lying at the heart of his novel. The intellectual horizon of *Inferno* is defined by the overarching framework of the contemporary movement known as "Transhumanism," which lays the foundation for a new radical understanding of the "human" and promises to expand the scope of life and its possibilities. The theory envisions a sort of utopian future for human beings. The time will come when, thanks to science's discoveries that have so altered society, humans will be capable of breaking away from the laws of gravity of the earth, experiencing a physical immortality and the resurrection of the dead, and even having genetic flaws corrected.

Because *Inferno* dramatizes explicitly these concerns and judges them as efforts to bridge the distance between human beings and the gods, it is appropriate to reflect on the way Dan Brown's sense of our technological era is related to Dante's metaphysics. Are modern technology and Transhumanism the logical, literalized outcome of Dante's poetic vision in his *Divine Comedy*? Is Dante's theology, with its premises and belief in the resurrection of the dead and in the immortal state of the blessed souls in Heaven only a prefiguration of a future scientific utopia when all these metaphorical promises will turn into reality?

As a way of answering these questions, it should be pointed out how ironic it is that Dan Brown, who provides a fairly accurate portrait of the origins and aims of contemporary Transhumanism, actually skips Dante's use of the "trans-human" metaphor. In the first canto of *Paradiso* we find Dante the pilgrim in the cosmos who suddenly hears the music of the spheres and who sees a light greater than he has ever seen on earth. The experience, says the poet, is incommunicable. He writes: "*Trasumanar significar per verba/ non si poria; pero` l'essemplo basti/ a cui esperienza grazia serbi.*" (*Par.* I, 70-72) ("The passing beyond humanity cannot be set forth in words; let the example suffice, therefore, for him to whom grace reserves the experience," as translated by John D. Sinclair, where "Trasumanar" is the new Italian word coined by Dante to convey his quasi divine experience in *Paradiso*).

These lines have many implications. They display, first of all, Dante's ethics, the ethics of a poet who stretches out his imagination to the threshold of God's infinity and yet acknowledges the limits of his powers. They also stage Dante's reflection on the distance between language and experiences, words and things, which also means that for him to be human is to inhabit a world of intelligible language. The lines, in short, convey Dante's poetry of wonder about the limits and the limitlessness of being human, about the mystery and the secrets at the heart of human experiences. He wrote a poem that places the human reality of history, science, ethics, politics, art, love, and beauty within the horizon of the divine.

It would be preposterous, but probably not entirely absurd, to suggest that Dan Brown's *Inferno* embraces totally Dante's perspective. Nonetheless, he is clear in his critique of the distortions that occur within the intellectual movement of "Transhumanism" and makes these distortions the underlying moral question at the heart of his novel. A founder of the philosophy of Transhumanism, who is identified in the novel as FM-2030 (a real person by the name of Fereidoun M. Esfandiary), wrote in 1973 a *Futurist Manifesto*, which picks up and radically alters the 1909 title, *Futurist Manifesto* by F.T. Marinetti. Whereas Marinetti calls for a new visionary art that leaves behind stale mythology and the cult of abstractions, FM-2030 completely ignores the imaginative value of Futurism and twists it to predict the advent of the "brave new world" of a new scientific revolution. Dan Brown's critique admits that the organization of scientific futurologists "is made up of responsible individuals—ethically accountable scientists, futurists, visionaries—but, as in many movements, there exists a small but militant faction that believes the movement is not moving fast enough. They are apocalyptic thinkers who believe the end is coming and that someone needs to take drastic action to save the future of the species."

One of these anxious, impatient utopists is Bertrand Zobrist, the Dante lover, who ends up "playing at being God" and creating a "dystopia" as he elaborates his plot of saving the world from its unsustainable overpopulation. He seeks to sow the seeds of sterility, as it were, in order to bring about a new plague like the Black Death of 1348. With great subtlety, Dan Brown signals his moral distaste for the scientist's "culture of death" by celebrating life: he dedicates his novel to his parents and ends it with the announcement of the birth of a new baby, Catalina, to Marta. There is nothing more dantesque in the novel than this birth-detail. The whole of the *Divine Comedy* pivots on the idea of birth, on the event—ordinary and yet extraordinary—that we were all born. More than death, which overtly is what he is dealing with in his narrative, what matters to Dante is the universal fact of being born: every birth, in all its commonness, implies that history and its future can be radically altered; the future can be different from the past, because, at least potentially, each and every one of us can change the course of events.

Zobrist's intellectual brilliance, moreover, gives rise to a deeper sense of the moral predicament of human choices and contradictions. So irresistible is he that he seduces the equally brilliant Sienna Brooks. Out of love for the master she supports his scheme, although by the end, both Sienna and Langdon will each attempt to foil it for different reasons.

The ambiguity of Zobrist, his existing between the horns of scientific eminence and the dangers of sheer, suicidal madness, leads Brown to ponder and share in the ethical ground of Dante's *Divine Comedy*: The question of evil, which Dante understands as a physical, moral, and metaphysical phenomenon. For both writers, evil is unsettling because it is almost without fail masked as the good. In fact, all characters in the novel can never quite be defined because the very identity of each of them is wrapped in ambiguities. Dante's poem also makes us plunge into a land of dissimilitude where things are never what they seem. Indeed, Dante, like Brown, views "neutrality in times of moral crisis" as a despicable condition that deprives of substantial reality the angels, who chose neutrality at the time of the great war in Heaven between God and the rebel angels, such as Lucifer.

Finally, the moral condition of human beings in the face of the difficult choices between good and evil is for Dante bound to the great, inalienable gift of liberty God has given his creatures (*Purgatorio* XVI). Dan Brown, who probably has often smiled that his first name is a short form for Dante, happily wants to see that liberty preserved.

Why Everyone Who Reads Dan Brown's *Inferno* Could Benefit from Reading Dante's *Inferno*— and All of the *Divine Comedy*

BY WILLIAM COOK
Distinguished Teaching Professor of History (Emeritus),
State University of New York, Geneseo

I have been teaching Dante Alighieri's *Commedia*, a.k.a. the *Divine Comedy*, for forty years to undergraduates, interested adults, Trappist monks, and even convicted felons. Whether to travelers in Italy or members of an adult book group, my last words to all my students are always the same: Now that you have finished the *Commedia*, you have fulfilled the prerequisite for reading the *Commedia*. So start reading!

Whenever I talk about Dante either formally or in casual conversation, I invite people to read this poem. I point out that it is hard and that there is a lot they will not understand. I prepare them for the fact that the people and events of the *Commedia* are Dante's and not ours. Even people who were famous to Dante's original audience and whose stories fill many of its pages are not household names today—Brunetto Latini, Statius, Peter Damian, Emperor Frederick II, Pope Boniface VIII. Dante himself points out in *Purgatorio* 11 that fame is fleeting.

Like the pilgrim Dante, when we begin our journey with him we are dumb. We draw wrong conclusions; we seriously misread what people tell us; we declare God's judgment to be unfair. Lest you think I am speaking for myself when defining the reading of the poem as *our* journey, I am in fact doing no more than rephrasing the first of the poem's 14,211 lines: *Nel mezzo del cammin di nostra vita* (In the middle of the journey of *our* life). Note how peculiar those two last words are. Shouldn't Dante say either "my life" or "our lives"? But Dante announces to us both our differences from him and our common humanity with him.

Like Dante, we may fear to accompany him on the frightening journey. Even the first canto of *Inferno* is scary, especially the unlikely meeting of Dante with the Roman poet Virgil, who has been dead for 1319 years at the time of the meeting. In the second canto, Dante tells Virgil, at least indirectly, that such a voyage to the afterlife that Virgil is proposing is for the truly exceptional people, specifically Aeneas and St. Paul. He only agrees to go when he learns that his old flame Beatrice had left heaven to summon Virgil to take Dante on this journey/pilgrimage. Since most of us do not put ourselves in the category of Aeneas and Paul and since no one from heaven has summoned us to accompany Dante, we might just decide to put the poem away. And Canto 3 does not make it easier when Dante walks through the entrance arch to hell with its famous last line: *LASCIATE OGNI SPERANZA, VOI CH'ENTRATE* (ABANDON ALL HOPE, YOU WHO ENTER). Students read on because they have to, but for the rest of us, the invitation is uninviting.

Brown misses not only the spiritual essence of Dante's journey, he also misses the rich commentary of Dante on politics, the arts, human behavior, and much more. While Dante's journey to the Christian afterlife is by definition a spiritual/religious experience, we need to be careful to understand that it is not spiritual in the sense of unworldly or lacking concern for the world. Dante's poem clearly contains a political vision that is integral to his understand of how we should live on earth and how a well governed world allows us to focus on matters eternal because of the security and justice it offers.

Dante not only writes poetry but writes about poetry and the arts generally. People are sometimes surprised to find early in *Paradiso* that Dante the pilgrim is told to do a scientific experiment in order to understand one part of heavenly reality. Hence while the poem is religious to the core, saying that does not mean that Dante does not continue to the very end to have "worldly" concerns. To use Dante's own metaphor: as difficult as it was for Jason to snatch the golden fleece, it was even more difficult to bring it back. The *Commedia* itself is Dante bringing back to the world he still lives in what he has learned and experienced during his journey.

All of this rich fabric and texture is absent from Dan Brown's view of Dante. Through most pages of Brown's novel, Dante's great poem is basically a prop. It certainly contains mysterious statements, and for Brown some of these serve as clues that need to be decoded. Brown is sometimes clever, sometimes not. But he never invites his readers to explore this poem. Only in the epilogue on literally the last page of the book, does Brown's protagonist Robert Langdon, in three lines, suggest there is something more to the *Commedia*: "Dante's poem, Langdon was now reminded, was not so much about the misery of hell as it was about the power of the human spirit to endure any challenge, no matter how daunting." This is simply too little, too late. After essentially exploiting Dante for well over 400 pages, it is not sufficient to do your imitation of Gilda Radner's great character on *Saturday Night Live* and utter your version of her famous words, "Never mind!"

Dante's epic poem has been reduced to a good crossword puzzle. To be sure, crosswords can be clever and challenging, but Dante's poem is not a puzzle to be solved. First, Dante's poem is an invitation to take an extraordinary journey, one that will lead you to ask the most universal of questions and to focus on your own life in ways you never imagined. One could argue that Dan Brown makes us stop every so often and reevaluate what we thought we knew about his characters (e.g, What are the real motivations of Sienna Brooks and who is she working for?) or locations (What treacherous duke is associated with Hagia Sophia in Istanbul?). These moments are among the most satisfying in his *Inferno*. However, Langdon never stops to reconsider who *he* is, whereas the central theme of Dante's *Commedia* is to reawaken the pilgrim's moral conscience and teach him the way to use well what he learns in his extraordinary voyage. Dante is deeply introspective. He wakes up in a dark wood, clearly an allegory for being morally and spiritually adrift, does not know how he got there, and is unsuccessful in getting himself out of the forest. This is not only his story but that of all people who reflect; it is the human condition. The remaining ninety-nine cantos are in a real sense Dante getting back on track.

For Brown, Dante's poem is something to be manipulated and something which requires solutions. Yet Dante's poem is as much about mystery as it is accumulating knowledge. Once when teaching Dante to inmates, I asked how many of them knew that the crime they committed was wrong at the time they did it. Every hand went up. The problem was not primarily one of ignorance but of bad choosing, a matter of will rather than intellect. Although knowledge is necessary to keep our choices from being random, knowledge does not guarantee moral results.

By the end of Dante's journey through hell, his intellect is in pretty good shape. But his will is still weak—as evidenced by his lapsing into old habits when he meets his pal Casella in *Purgatorio* 2. Even before that encounter, the poet reminds his readers that if we think we understand everything, we are misleading ourselves. From journeying through hell with Dante, one would rationally conclude, for example, that even the very best of those who are not baptized Christians will do no better in the afterlife than Limbo, the first circle in hell. Furthermore, we could assume that any suicide would be condemned to the part of Circle 7 reserved for those who are violent against themselves. Yet the first character Dante the pilgrim meets in Purgatory—remember that souls in Purgatory are all on their way to heaven—is a pagan who committed suicide.

There are many surprises throughout Purgatory and Paradise. Dante meets the Roman poet Statius, who tells us that he was initially attracted to Christianity because a poem of Virgil's appeared to have been fulfilled in Christ. Yet Virgil is a resident of hell, and Statius is on his way to heaven. The Emperor Constantine, who more than once is mentioned as making mistakes that have been catastrophic to Christianity, is in heaven. So is an obscure pagan priest who is a character in Virgil's *Aeneid*. When Dante asks his guide Beatrice how this can be, she can only respond that even the citizens of heaven cannot penetrate the greatest mysteries of God.

I sometimes say to students, prefacing my remarks by joking that this is Bill Cook's oversimplification number 733 (this is late in the semester; of course): There are two kinds of people in this world—those who see life as a puzzle to be solved and those who see life as a series of mysteries to be embraced. It is clear that Dan Brown operates in the first reality. Dante, certainly not one to back away from an intellectual challenge, is ultimately in the second.

Sometimes Dante does engage in problem solving. He takes a three-part university exam in *Paradiso* from three pretty tough and tested professors: Saints Peter (faith), James (hope), and John (love). They ask difficult questions and follow ups. They require him to make distinctions. Dante quotes other apostles to them and clearly knows his Aquinas. The toughest questions are saved till the last. Once Dante has passed the intellectual part of the test, Peter asks Dante if he *possesses* faith, for it is not enough just to be able to give a good intellectual definition of faith. Furthermore, after all of this academic-sounding stuff, Dante enters into a realm outside space and time, a place of mystery that he can neither grasp nor transmit to his readers.

Hence, a prime lesson of the *Commedia* is the necessity, on the one hand, of using all human potential to understand and on the other hand, to recognize that there are limits to our understanding. On this point, as on so many other matters, Dan Brown is both un-Dantesque and ultimately anti-Dantesque. I do not know if he does not know Dante well enough or whether he simply wants to play with this poem. With either possibility, the result is the same. The reader of his *Inferno* is not encouraged to take a journey so much greater than Robert Langdon's.

In Dante's *Inferno* 5, one of the reasons that Francesca fell into a lustful relationship with her brother-in-law that cost both her life and her salvation is that she was with the wrong Paul (Paolo). When St. Augustine struggled with lust, he was led to a volume of Paul's letters that counseled not to trust lust but to turn to Christ. Thus he was converted. Francesca does not have St. Paul but instead the randy Paolo. So too, if you curl up with *Inferno*, choose the version by the right Dan, that's Dan Alighieri and not Dan Brown.

Dante to Washington: Gridlock, Partisanship, and Factionalism are Deadly Sins and Will Land You in the Inferno

BY DAN BURSTEIN
Creator, author, and coeditor of the *Secrets* series

Many scholars, including several in this volume, cringe over Dan Brown's infernal misappropriations and mischaracterizations of Dante. Clearly, key elements of the "whole" Dante are missing in action in Brown's novel. To me, Dante comes off so one dimensionally in *Inferno* that I sometimes think Brown has him confused with Savonarola, the Dominican Friar who appeared on the scene in Florence a century and a half after Dante. Savonarola was an intolerable and intolerant moral scold, who constantly, and largely for his own political purposes, urged Florentines to repent from the full flower of Renaissance humanism and predicted that without changing course, they were going to suffer in Hell for all eternity.

Like a momentarily popular charismatic far right wing figure in contemporary America, Savonarola spewed fire and brimstone as he preached. He launched the infamous "Bonfire of the Vanities"—burning precious Renaissance books and art works in the public square. He painted a picture of pervasive and extreme moral depravity and denounced many in power as morally corrupt. He nearly suffocated the Renaissance in its birthplace and at its high tide, until he himself finally fell out of favor and was burned at the stake in the Piazza della Signoria in 1498. The Dante of Dan Brown's *Inferno* seems to be this sort of character, all about sin, eternal damnation, and the narrowing chance for repentance as time presses on toward the apocalypse. Brown sets Dante up as a parallel figure to Zobrist—fellow extremists separated by seven centuries, both acting as one-man zealot bands bent on stopping the world from going to the Inferno. This is why Dante's words (mish-mashed as they are) are on Zobrist's mind in Brown's Prologue (the "dolent city," the city of "eternal woe") as he chooses to jump from the Badia tower to his death. (Suicide is not a sin Dante would have committed, and, commensurate with fourteenth century theology, he condemns most of its victims to the Inferno, although he holds considerable sympathy for certain suicides, like Cato, who is elevated to Purgatory even though he was both a pagan and a suicide).

While Dante was definitely a moralist (as Savonarola purported to be), and one who was deeply concerned with getting his fellow Florentines—and the Church itself—back on the one true moral and spiritual path, he was also much, much more than that. Brown thinks Dante's great contribution was to paint a word picture of Hell so frightening that it would cause sinners to repent and change their ways. But for me, Dante's most enduring legacy is less in religion than it is in other domains: Poetry, Language and Linguistic Theory, Psychology, Proto-Science, Philosophy, the Novel, and Political Science—to name just some key ones.

Rereading the *Divine Comedy* for the first time in four decades in the wake of Brown's *Inferno*, I was struck by how important a *political* epic it is. The *Commedia* is, in fact, a major commentary on the search for good government, the appropriate practice of political leadership and the quest to find justice in an Italy that sorely lacked it. In the current atmosphere of American partisanship, gridlock, and political scandal, Democrats as well as Republicans, the White House as well as the Congress, and even the Supreme Court, would all do well to take a refresher course on Dante. So too would most political cultures around the world.

The *Divine Comedy* seems relevant and modern today in large part because the central element of Dante's political argument is his polemic against excessive partisanship, factionalism, and gridlock. We rail against these same problems in our twenty-first century political culture, but few if any modern commentators can muster the type of poetic imagery that Dante uses to condemn those who divide people, cities, and nations into warring camps for their own political and personal gain.

Over and over again, Dante returns to the dangers of political warfare between parties, among the city-states of Italy, and between forces of the Emperor and the forces of the Pope. He was anything but an armchair theorist. Although his profession at the time of writing the *Divine Comedy* was Poet in Exile, Dante's portfolio of prior experiences included both military and political service. His personal story of politics, war, and exile, is bound up in the century-long Guelph/Ghibelline civil wars. At twenty-four, he fought with the Guelph cavalry against the Ghibellines at the Battle of Campaldino in 1289. This was a bloody battle with more than two thousand casualties that resulted in a decisive Guelph victory and restoration of Guelph power in Florence, one more episode in the long seesaw battle that dominated thirteenth century Tuscan history.

The young Dante wanted to play a role in politics. He joined the physicians' and apothecaries' guild in order to have a base of operations, although he did not practice medicine. But in those days, if you wanted to enter politics, you had to belong to a guild. Some historical records suggest Dante spoke or voted at various notable meetings of Florentine government. In 1300, shortly before his exile in 1302, he served as one of a small number of Priors responsible for civic affairs. Interestingly, the priors were often "sequestered" (to use a word from recent American politics) for their two month terms in the Palazzo Vecchio, so that they would be free from the influences of lobbying, vote-buying and other kinds of bribery.

Dante's tenure as a Prior unfolded as Guelphs continued to battle Ghibellines, as the Guelphs themselves split into Black and White factions, and as the political intrigues of Popes and Emperors, as well as a cast of kings, dukes, cardinals, and wealthy merchants were brought to bear on the city's politics. Dante went to Rome to try to negotiate with the Pope and his advisors, but failed in his diplomatic mission and ended up on a list of enemies charged with capital crimes. Threatened with a death sentence, he fled into exile, never to return to his beloved Florence.

Politics for Dante was not an abstraction; politics, like poetry, was a major portion of his life's concerns. He is a kind of amalgam of the roles of William Shakespeare, the great writer who defined the literary tradition in our language, and Thomas Paine, the bold political theorist who wrote beautifully about politics and actually took part in the great political battles of his day. In the *Divine Comedy*, Dante shows great enthusiasm for poet-Kings of the ancient world, especially King David, the Jewish king known for his leadership as well as his poetry.

Simultaneous with his work on the *Divine Comedy* in the early 1300s, Dante wrote a three volume political treatise, *De Monarchia*. The third volume made a powerful argument five centuries before Thomas Jefferson for the separation of Church and State. Devout as Dante was, he believed that the Pope should preside over spiritual affairs and the realm of the afterlife, while the Emperor should preside over temporal human affairs on earth. He expressed the view that both Pope and Emperor received their mandate equally from God, that both were human, fallible, and corruptible, and that many of the major problems in the bloody, fratricidal, constantly-at-war era in which he lived could be ascribed to religious officials seeking political power and political leaders betraying the real interests of their people.

Eternal punishments are designed to fit the crimes committed in life in Dante's *Inferno*. The punishments Dante imagines for the political factionalists and schemers—whether they are religious or civil—are particularly vivid: He condemns to the Inferno both the sometimes Guelph leader of Pisa, Ugolino, and his archenemy, the Ghibelline Archbishop Ruggieri. They dwell in Hell for all eternity, with Ugolino perpetually gnawing at the head of Ruggieri, while both are encased up to their necks in ice.

Dante uses the imagery of physical cannibalism as a metaphor for those who would cannibalize the common good of Florence or other city-states through partisanship, factionalism, and betrayal.

He returns to the horrific imagery of cannibalism when he arrives in the very base of Hell. There, he finds a monstrous Satan perpetually gnawing on the three worst people in history—Judas, who betrayed Jesus, and Brutus and Cassius who betrayed Julius Caesar, setting in motion the ultimate collapse of the Roman Empire. Proof of Dante's focus on politics being at least as strong as his focus on religion is that two-thirds of the "worst people in history" are political criminals—Brutus and Cassius—while only one enemy of Christianity, Judas, makes it into the clutches of Satan's mouth.

Even short of cannibalism, partisan zealots are pictured as suffering frightening fates. In Canto 6 of *Inferno*, Dante inquires about five leaders of both Guelphs and Ghibellines from the thirteenth century—people who had been in and out of power, people who had led battles, wars, purges, and murders of opponents. He is shocked to discover that every person he asks about has been condemned for all eternity to be punished in the Inferno, even those Guelph leaders whom he had been taught as a young man to honor and praise. (Canto 6 in each of the three parts of the *Divine Comedy* includes significant political debate and discussion, each time from the different perspective of the story as it unfolds in the *Inferno*, *Purgatorio*, and *Paradiso*).

Dante dispatches to the Inferno numerous political and religious leaders who promoted partisanship for their own selfish reasons and allowed Florence to be turned from a glorious city with relative unanimity of civic purpose in the days of his grandfather to a state of near-permanent civil war. Even though Dante fought on the side of the papacy at Campaldino, he condemns several Popes and numerous powerful religious figures to the Inferno for their hypocrisy and their promotion of conflict and factionalism for unholy goals.

On the other hand, Dante recognizes and praises a few among his own political opponents, whom he judged to be trying to do something virtuous for Florence. He promotes them at least to Purgatory (where there is hope of purging their sins) as a way of rewarding their bipartisanship in a difficult time. He constantly seeks to contrast Florence's bitter enemies from Pisa or Siena who did some good works or had a better approach to good government with the false patriots of Florence who were self-interested and hypocritical in their alleged love for their city.

Those who shied away from acting as zealots in favor of neutrality or resignation were also not exempt from Dante's particular kind of existential condemnation. Those who never chose sides, never took a stand, and shied away from making the right moral choice are unwanted in Heaven, ineligible for Purgatory, and not even claimed by Satan. They dwell in an antechamber of Hell where they will spend eternity with no one even knowing or remembering their names.

Pope Celestine V—the last Pope to choose to resign voluntarily prior to Pope Benedict XVI's decision to do so in 2013—abdicated in the late thirteenth century, allowing Pope Boniface VIII to take over. Boniface is skewered and satirized in ways that make it clear he was Dante's most hated enemy. This corrupt Pope ends up in the Inferno's nightmarish pit of the simonists (religious officials who sold out holy principles for money and power). The sin of simony can be analogized to today's political figures who sell out their principles—and their country—to lobbyists and other forces of big money politics. Boniface is clearly guilty of these crimes. But Dante makes the case that Pope Celestine, who was generally regarded as a saintly man, paved the way for Boniface as a result of his resignation. His "cowardice" makes him an accessory to Boniface's crimes, in Dante's view.

The gridlock that dominated Florentine politics is excoriated by Dante. He particularly condemns the way one administration passes a law only to have it overturned by the next. In words that sound torn from recent headlines about the efforts to overturn Obamacare in the courts after finally passing US healthcare reform legislation, Dante asserts that the society has to let new laws go into force for a good length of time, and have the public gain experience with them, before determining if they need to be changed or overturned. He criticizes lawmakers for the constant partisan shifts and personal power grabs. In a reference that sounds especially contemporary, Dante accuses the statesmen of his day of making laws in October that do not even last "until mid-November."

The overall political vision of the *Divine Comedy* holds few, if any, actual *solutions* for our problems today. Dante's idea of political utopia is a naive and nostalgic view of how well government worked in the glory days of the Roman Empire. He is basically on the lookout for a new Emperor who can be a modern Caesar. He thought he had found one in the young Henry VII, who became Holy Roman Emperor in 1312 and tried to bring peace to the warring factions of Guelphs and Ghibellines. But Henry died of malaria in 1313, having accomplished little other than earning a prominent place in Dante's political cosmology in the story of *Paradiso*.

While Dante is a deeply nuanced thinker about many things, his enduring affection for the Roman Empire is uninterrupted by troubling "details." Nowhere does he suggest he has any recognition that the slaves, the plebeians, the political opposition, the women, and those people living in lands conquered by Rome may not have shared his benign view of how well Caesar's Empire functioned.

We can learn much from the power of Dante's poetry, particularly in calling attention to just how abhorrent and dangerous partisanship and gridlock can be. Dante asks all of us, particularly those who would be leaders and lawmakers, to step off the road that leads to the dark forest and reexamine our lives, our beliefs, our morality, our civic-mindedness, our constant internecine political battling, and our level of devotion to unity and success for our people . . . before it is too late.

Beneath the Veil: Parallel Universes and *Inferno* Resonances

BY DAN BURSTEIN
Creator, author, and coeditor of the *Secrets* series

Beneath the fast-moving plot of Dan Brown's *Inferno*, there is a second, slower-moving plot unfolding. The second story—hidden in plain sight as it were—is the system of parallels, resonances, allusions, and interconnections between Dan Brown's s *Inferno* and Dante's original. This commentary will endeavor to paint a picture of what's going on below the surface of Brown's novel.

Arriving in chapter 58, readers of *Inferno* encounter this quotation from Dante: "O you possessed of sturdy intellect . . . observe the teachings hidden here . . . beneath the veil of verses so obscure . . .." Robert Langdon explains this quote to Sienna this way (although why Sienna, with her 208 IQ, needs explanation is not clear):

> "It's taken from one of the most famous stanzas of Dante's *Inferno*," Langdon said excitedly. "It's Dante urging his smartest readers to seek the wisdom hidden within his cryptic verse." Langdon often cited this exact line when teaching literary symbolism. Langdon tells his students that this line from Dante is the equivalent of "an author waving his arms wildly and shouting: "Hey readers! There is a symbolic double meaning here."

In case readers miss the import of this passage, Brown will go on to cite this same Dante quote—"O you possessed of sturdy intellect"—five more times in the next twenty-two pages, as Langdon and Sienna read the spiraling inscription left by Zobrist on Dante's death mask, trying to discern its meaning. When they finally decode Zobrist's message, they think they know where to go to find the next clue: to the "bloodred waters . . . of the lagoon that reflects no stars," which they interpret at first as meaning Venice. But later they will understand that the part about seeking the "treacherous doge of Venice who severed the heads from horses," while it mentions Venice, is actually pointing them to Istanbul, where Venetian doge Enrico Dandolo is buried.

So why does Dan Brown mention six different times a quote designed to remind readers that Dante created layers of symbolic and metaphorical meaning in the *Commedia* and may even have embedded some coded messages? Because Dan Brown is doing the same thing in his novel. It's as if Brown himself, not Dante (who is far more subtle), is the author who is waving his arms wildly and shouting out to readers that there's a symbolic double meaning here.

On the surface, Brown seems content to suffer silently (except for his laughter on the way to the bank) the slings and arrows of the many critics who think his writing is atrocious. Few other writers of action/adventure/suspense thrillers ever get reviewed at all. But since *DVC*, Brown has been routinely reviewed by the most prestigious cultural media. A not insignificant number of these reviews, however, are motivated by the critic's desire to participate in the competitive, intellectual sport of Brown-bashing, which usually includes an attempt by the reviewer to parody Brown's writing style in order to expose it as the moronic output of a "pop schlockmeister." (This epithet comes from Brown himself, who has a scene in *DVC* where Robert Langdon's editor, Jonas Faukman, feels compelled to remind our favorite symbologist that he is a "Harvard historian, for God's sake, not a pop schlockmeister looking for a quick buck.")

But Brown is playing a deeper game. He is developing a new genre of easy-reading, page-turning adventure novels that actually have Big Ideas in them (population trends, transhumanism, self-evolution, biotechnology ethics), as well as a wealth of cultural information on subjects (like Dante and Florentine architecture and history) that are rarely taught any more in the contemporary

American educational system. Given his own lifelong interest in puzzles, codes, cryptography, anagrams, and treasure hunts (his family designed his childhood Christmas mornings as treasure hunts involving puzzles and clues to locate the gifts), he has added a genuine measure of artisanship to his fiction. In all of Brown's recent books there are hidden levels of meaning. In *Inferno*, in particular, there is a hidden allusion to Dante and the *Commedia* at every turn.

In order to "get" these allusions and parallels, you have to be pretty familiar with Dante's work. Of course, understanding this hidden layer is not a prerequisite to understanding and enjoying Brown's novel. But the author is subtly encouraging his readers to read Dante and is subtly rewarding those who already know their *Commedia*. Below are a small sampling of the parallels between the fourteenth century *Inferno* of Dante and Dan Brown's twenty-first century version:

IN THE BEGINNING: LOST

Dante

Dante can't tell how he came to be in the dark wood of the opening scene of his *Inferno*. "How I entered there I cannot say."

Brown

Langdon awakens in what appears to be a hospital bed having apparently sustained serious injuries. At first he has no idea where he is. Eventually, when he sees the iconic buildings out the window he realizes he is in Florence. But he has no idea of how he came to be there.

MEMORY LOSS

Dante

Dante's memory is affected by the power of seeing the bright light of God in Paradiso, and he tells his readers he has become inarticulate about his experiences as a result. When it comes to trying to describe what happened to him in the Empyrean zone, his memory loss and heavenly transformation has reduced him to mere baby talk, he tells us, even though we know he is a great poet and wordsmith.

Brown

Langdon discovers early in the story that he has short-term amnesia. On Monday in Florence, he can't remember anything that happened to him since his last memory of being on the Harvard campus the prior Saturday.

BEING IN HELL TAKES SOME GETTING USED TO

Dante

Swoons (faints) several times as he begins to comprehend where he is and as he hears the tragic stories of the sinners in Hell, such as Francesca.

Brown

Langdon is highly disoriented in the opening chapters. He nearly passes out several times from the drugs he has been given. His "swoons" match Dante's.

TIMESPAN OF THE EXPERIENCE: THREE DAYS

Dante

Divine Comedy takes place over a three-day period that corresponds roughly to Holy Week, 1300.

Brown

One of the first things Sienna tells Langdon in the Florence hospital (which will later turn out not to be a hospital) is that it is Monday, March 18. The action of the story takes place over the next day and night in Florence, Venice, and Istanbul. Later we will learn there is a whole back story to Langdon's preamnesia activities in Florence on Sunday. By the third day, when Langdon is back in Florence for the epilogue, he will have spent about the same amount of elapsed time on this adventure as Dante believes he spent in the afterlife.

PERCEPTION OF TIME

Dante

Although Dante is only in the afterlife for three days, it seems to readers of the *Commedia* much longer. In the poem, Dante explains that time stops in Hell. He makes several references to frozen time.

Brown

Langdon's adventures seem like they would take much longer than the suggested elapsed time of about three days (including the preaction on Sunday that we learn about from watching the security tapes in the Palazzo Vecchio). Langdon loses his infamous Mickey Mouse watch at the beginning of the story (Sienna has taken it). When Langdon has his watch returned to him at the very end, it is a signal that the story is over and he can step back into the normalized river of time.

GREEN MY EYES AND BEAK-LIKE MY NOSE

Dante

The eyes of Beatrice are said in the *Commedia* to be like emeralds. Dante is depicted by several important artists who painted his portrait as having a beak-like aquiline nose.

Brown

Describes Zobrist as having green eyes and a beak-like nose.

PLATONIC BEAUTIES

Dante

For his tour of the afterlife, Dante has several guides, the most important of whom is his beautiful and much beloved Beatrice. Although he loved Beatrice in life, we are supposed to understand that their relationship was platonic.

Brown

Robert Langdon has several guides, the most important of whom is a beautiful woman (Sienna). Although Sienna tries to arouse Langdon to be interested in a relationship, he tells her he is too old for her. They have no sexual encounter in the story and we presume if they ever meet again their relationship will be platonic.

WHAT THE HELL?

Dante

Visits the most frightening and detailed vision of Hell ever described in literature. Also visits Purgatorio and Paradiso.

Brown

Langdon goes through Hell in Florence (as in prior books, Langdon frequently uses the expression, "What the hell?" when some plot point surprises him). An argument can be made that after suffering through hell in Florence, things get a little better in Venice and Istanbul, since he gains more information and starts to put the puzzle pieces together. So, perhaps Florence is the Inferno and Venice and Istanbul are Purgatorio. There does not seem to be any Paradiso, only an existential ending and epilogue.

FACTIONALISM, PARTISANSHIP, AND CIVIL WAR

Dante

Italy's excessive factional battles between Guelphs and Ghibellines (and, after the split between Black and White Guelphs, the even more ferocious battles between those formerly on the same side) dominate Florentine history and Italian politics for much of the thirteenth and fourteenth centuries. Ditto for the battles between popes and emperors. This history runs throughout the *Commedia*, with Dante highlighting themes of factionalism, betrayal, disloyalty, lies, frauds, etc.

Brown

Everyone in the story will change sides by the end. Zobrist, the arch-villain at the beginning, is cast by Brown as a hero by the end. Ferris, who seems very suspicious, will turn out to be OK, but Sienna, who is supposed to be Langdon's partner, will turn out to be Zobrist's disciple. Sinskey will have a major change of heart on the issue of population control by the end of the book.

WHAT'S REAL AND WHAT'S NOT

Dante

Makes no distinction between real historical characters and fictional ones from myth and legend. He meets both types in the afterlife.

Brown

His novels are a mixture of researched fact and utter fiction.

TRANSHUMANISM

Dante

Invented the term "transhumanize."

Brown

Makes the modern transhumanist movement a big part of the story of *Inferno*.

TAKING LIBERTIES WITH THE CLASSICS

Dante

Rewrites the story of Virgil's *Aeneid* and Homer's *Odyssey* for his own purposes and invents episodes and interpretations not evident in the classics.

Brown

Dan Brown rewrites Dante's *Inferno* for his own purposes, changing the details about the rings of Hell and the deadly sins to create puzzles and clues.

FLORENCE

Dante

Much of *Divine Comedy* draws on events that happened in Dante's life in Florence, although world history and many geographical locations figure in the poem. Dante tells a specific story in the *Commedia* about his own experiences in the Baptistery in Florence. He also mentions the Badia.

Brown

Florence occupies center stage for the first two-thirds of Dan Brown's *Inferno*, before the action shifts to Venice and Istanbul. Other locations mentioned in flashbacks include New York,

Chicago, London, and Manila. The Baptistery in Florence figures prominently in the plot, as does the Badia, where Zobrist jumps to his death in the prologue.

MEDUSA

Dante

Has an encounter in Canto IX of *Inferno* with Medusa. Virgil has to react quickly to cover Dante's eyes so that looking at Medusa does not turn him into stone.

Brown

Utilizes the actual sculptural upside down head of Medusa in the cistern in Istanbul as a plot point. When Langdon sees the signs pointing the way to the Medusa head, he senses that her ability to turn people into stone is a metaphor for the sterilizing of the human species that will occur if he doesn't find the virus before it is too late.

IDES OF MARCH

Dante

Both Brutus and Cassius, who conspired to assassinate Julius Caesar on the Ides of March, are in the worst and final part of Hell, eternally being cannibalized by Satan himself. Dante places such weight on the crime of the assassination of Caesar (and the downfall of the Roman Empire he believes it set in motion), that Brutus and Cassius make up two of the three worst sinners in history, with Judas, the betrayer of Jesus, as the third.

Brown

Brown gives contradictory timing information in two different places of *Inferno* about Zobrist's suicide. But one of the timelines suggests that Zobrist jumps from the Badia on or about the Ides of March.

PAST, PRESENT, AND PREDICTING THE FUTURE

Dante

Souls in the Inferno can see the long-term future and remember the distant past, but not present or immediate past. Several people Dante meets in the afterlife correctly predict his coming exile from Florence as well as other events. Dante cleverly sets *Divine Comedy* in 1300 against the backdrop of only the events that had happened by 1300. But he actually wrote the poem over the decade that followed his exile around 1302. So he knew what had already happened, but he uses the literary device of making the shades of 1300 look prescient.

Brown

Langdon knows a lot about the distant past. He seems to be able to remember verbatim his lectures given years ago on Dante and other subjects, but, because of his amnesia, he knows nothing about what happened to him in the recent past, particularly the last two days. He also understands very little about what is happening to him in the present, until he begins to put it all together in Venice. Brown's *Inferno*, like Dante's, is filled with predictions about the future—particularly Zobrist's forecasts for global catastrophe as a result of exploding population.

BODIES OF WATER

Dante

Multiple rivers crisscross the geography of Dante's *Inferno*. The rite of passage of getting across the river even to enter Hell is adapted from Greek mythology. One of the most frightening of Inferno's river systems is Phlegethon. This is a river of hot, boiling red blood. Sinners who themselves have spilled blood in violent acts are submerged in the river at various levels, corresponding to their degree of guilt and sin. Dante has much to say about rivers of the world, from his own home town Arno in Florence, to the problem of how the man from the Indus River (India) will achieve salvation if he has never even been exposed to the message of Christianity.

Brown

Langdon also confronts bodies of water. In his recurring nightmare, he sees a "bloodred river," with writhing bodies on its banks. Langdon and Sienna have to make their way through the watery grottoes of the Boboli Gardens to get to the Vasari Corridor. Like Dante crossing the river to enter the Inferno, Langdon and Siena are using the Vasari Corridor to cross the Arno. Part of Zobrist's inscription on Dante's death mask suggests they need to be looking for "the bloodred waters . . . of the lagoon that reflects no stars." That clue takes Langdon and company to Venice, where they must make their way into the city through the canal system by water limousine. Toward the end of the story, Langdon has to help Brüder find the plague bag in the cistern waters of Istanbul. For some reason we never see Langdon perform any of the swimming feats for which he has been famous in prior novels.

THE EVIL DITCHES

Dante

The eighth circle of Hell, where Dante places those who have committed fraud, covers a lot of Inferno real estate. There are so many different kinds of fraud that Dante has to devise a system he calls *Malebolge*—evil ditches—assigning a different type of fraud to each of ten ditches, with a different type of hellish punishment taking place in each ditch. *Bolgia* 2 is a place where insincere flatterers are punished by being steeped in human excrement, symbolizing the foulness of their false flattery. *Bolgia* 3 is the place where those who committed simony (religious officials buying and selling offices and power) are placed head first in holes in the rock with flames burning on the soles of their upside down feet.

Brown

Hiding from the Carabinieri and the manhunt the authorities are conducting for him, Langdon and Sienna take refuge behind a Porta-Potty near the art institute. "Langdon grabbed Sienna's arm and pulled her around behind the structure, forcing her into the narrow space between the toilet and the stone wall. The two of them barely fit, and the air smelled putrid and heavy." In other words, they have just landed in a space reminiscent of *Bolgia* 2 in the eighth circle of Hell. While hiding beside the Porta-Potty, Langdon will contemplate the excremental stench and think back to the bicyclist they just talked to, which in turn will remind him of *Bolgia* 3, where the simonists' legs, a bit like the bicyclist's, are flailing in the air as a result of their upside down treatment. This, in turn, is going to help him figure out what's wrong with the clues Zobrist has left him.

SCALING THE HEIGHTS

Dante

Escaping from the Inferno, Dante and Virgil confront the need to climb up Mt. Purgatory.

Brown

When the action in Brown's *Inferno* moves from Florence to Venice, it is metaphorically moving from Hell to Purgatory. In Venice, Langdon and Sienna have to scamper up out of the lower depths of St. Mark's church, helped out by an old Gypsy woman. It is a challenging climb, much as the ascent of Mt. Purgatory is challenging, but they make it.

THE CRIME OF NEUTRALITY

Dante

Dante is very critical of those who pretended to neutrality in the great political and moral battles of his day. Although the neutrals committed no specific crime, they are consigned to an area of Hell where no one will ever know their names or remember them. Their punishment for having been neutral in life is to become nonpersons for eternity.

Brown

Almost every one of our Dante experts wanted to weigh in on Dan Brown's epigraph and epilogue, which focuses on the problem of those who stay neutral in times of moral crisis. As I later discuss in the "Dolci" section of this book, Brown's epigraph that opens the novel is a version of a quote adapted from John F. Kennedy, who actually misquoted Dante. Nevertheless, the spirit of the point remains valid and is certainly Dantesque: when great moral issues face society, those who refuse to take a stand are committing a crime by their inaction. Zobrist and Sienna are very critical of those who stay neutral and won't see the problem of overpopulation for the crisis they believe it to be; presumably they speak for Brown himself.

IMMORTALITY

Dante

Dante deals with the desire for immortality and the possibility of obtaining it through writing books. He and his old mentor Brunetto Latini debate this in *Inferno*. In point of fact, Dante ends up becoming close to immortal through the *Divine Comedy*, which has lasted 700 years and is still going strong. In this respect, Dante has outlasted all his enemies and rivals. Many of Dante's characters—including Latini who was, at the time, Florence's most ambitious and best-known writer—are today remembered by history chiefly because of what Dante said about them in the *Commedia*.

Brown

Dan Brown discusses the work transhumanists are doing to extend human life. Many people in the real transhumanist movement see no fixed limit to human lifespan and believe the technology for "living forever" is advancing rapidly. Zobrist wants to be remembered as a modern Dante teaching humanity about its need for physical salvation and renewal. And he wants immortality. Indeed, he wants the world to remember him "as the glorious savior you know I am."

THE IMPORTANCE OF THE STARS

Dante

Ends each of the three books of the *Divine Comedy* with the word "stars."

Brown

Ends his novel with the word "stars."

Section 2
Bold New World

An Overview of Dan Brown's Arguments on Population Control, Technology, and Transhumanism

BY ARNE DE KEIJZER
Coauthor and coeditor of the *Secrets* series

Dan Brown consistently poses an existential question, and uses his books to seek the answer. The question is, "How do we become modern, science-minded people without losing our faith?" The answer in *Inferno* is different, in interesting ways, from what it has been before.

In Brown's earlier books, a reconciliation of his internal conflict between science and religion seemed more and more within reach. Transhumanism, which posits the idea of using technology to extend human physical, intellectual, and psychological capabilities beyond what is possible with just biology, would seem to represent a way toward that elusive balance. Yet Brown's ambivalence about transhumanism is expressed in his selection of Zobrist, a bioterrorist, as the seminal character in *Inferno*. This is an "end is nigh" book. The world is on the brink of collapse because of unrelenting population pressure. Any chance for human "enhancement" is subverted by a bioterrorist with a rogue virus in a sack in the belief that the post-human future justifies a sub-human act.

In Brown's 2009 book, *The Lost Symbol*, Katherine Solomon, Neoticist, and the lead female character (and, arguably, that novel's Beatrice) oversees a lab to produce evidence that "the realization that the mind's ability to affect the physical world . . . is the missing link between modern science and ancient mysticism." In *Inferno*, a transhumanist works in a lab to create the missing link between modern science and the Black Plague. In *The Lost Symbol*, the theme of "Ye are gods" ends with Robert Langdon and his companion contemplating the meaning of life. Is there a god? Is god an exterior force or is god interior to all of us? *Inferno* asks no such questions. Zealotry has replaced faith. The bad guy wins. Not only that, the bad guy has basically convinced everyone else that he was right. Even science must be distrusted because in this case it "would create a race of superhumans and perceived subhumans. . .the kind of situation that would be ripe for slavery or ethnic cleansing" (p. 295).

In this Section we analyze the "big issue" themes that underlie the plot of *Inferno*—the impending calamities associated with an overpopulated earth, the use and abuse of vector viruses, and the promise (or profound danger) of our continually-increasing ability to merge our personal biology with technology.

Malthusian Math

Dan Brown was just four years old in 1968 when Paul Ehrlich published *The Population Bomb*, a bestseller in which he warned that, "The battle to feed humanity is over. In the 1970s the world will undergo famines; hundreds of millions of people will starve to death." Because of explosive population growth, Ehrlich maintained (and does today) that the world is threatened by ecological disaster and major social upheavals. In stating this, Ehrlich expanded on and moved into a contemporary context views first articulated in the late 1700s by the cleric and scholar Thomas Malthus.

Ehrlich's *Population Bomb* dominated every discussion about the future of the planet for the next decade. We were perceived to be running out of everything, most especially oil, a perception reinforced by the oil shocks of the 1970s, gas lines, and the growing power of OPEC. We were thought to be running out of food and raw materials as well. Natural resources were finite and we were reaching the end of the earth's bounty. New technology had not yet shown another meaningful way forward. In this atmosphere, the arguments of Ehrlich and other neo-Malthusians made sense to many: If we can't expand the pie of global resources, let's limit the number of people trying to eat from it. Ehrlich was particularly controversial because of some of his proposals for solving the problem—especially a suggestion that the world consider government-imposed methods of sterilization to prevent further population growth. Forty-five years later, science has moved on, but, as our interview with Ehrlich makes clear, he continues to hold a pessimistic perspective. Dan Brown, despite his often stated belief in the power of science, technology, and human reason, emerges in *Inferno* as an Ehrlich acolyte, even borrowing from his four decade old suggestion about mass sterilization.

Malthus wasn't completely wrong. He was right in saying that in larger sense there is always going to be *some* limiting factor on population growth. The factors he knew about in his era were food, space, and disease so those are the ones he cited. Ehrlich modernized and amplified Malthus, adding birth control and other technology options as potential means of population control. His suggestion that these could be government-imposed gave *The Population Bomb* some of its controversy.

Technology wasn't much of a factor in the 1700s. Technology (including improved public health) has modified the timeline of overpopulation, but it hasn't negated the principle. Even transhumanists agree that there *is* some ultimate limiting factor. If it isn't food, it's waste. If it isn't waste, it's water. If it isn't water, it's space. No matter which card you play, at some point a limiting factor exists. Slowing the *rate* of growth extends the timeline; it doesn't change the outcome—unless and until, say the transhumanists, our technological future can intersect with our biological future.

Transhumanism is the ultimate *deus ex machina,* an argument that invokes an unknown, unexpected, and often previously nonexistent solution for an otherwise unsolvable problem. Transhumanists frequently offer "human ingenuity and creativity" or "advances in technology" or "technology extending human capabilities" to explain how population growth can be accommodated. After all, progress has already been made in agriculture, alternative energy, and the slowing of the growth rate. The interesting twist of *Inferno* is that Brown's invocation of technology by Zobrist as a "solution" to the problem is not a way to enable further population growth, which you would expect from a transhumanist, but a way to eliminate the problem and reduce population radically. The simplistic logic chain that Zobrist espouses goes like this: the Black Plague of the 1300s wiped out over a third of Europe's population in a few years. That "culling of the herd" led directly to the Renaissance, ergo, if we want to avoid the path we are on now to an awful new Inferno, and achieve a new Renaissance instead, we should forcibly cut world population by a third. It's a response that Malthus couldn't contemplate and Ehrlich could only dream of—action on population control simultaneously, globally, with laser-like efficiency, no pain, no side effects, and all accomplished by the will and ingenuity of one man deeply worried about the world situation.

Zobrist's actions function in the story not so much to render an actual solution as to raise a challenging and profound set of moral questions—*if* such a thing were possible, would it in any sense be the right thing to do? If it *is* the right thing to do, is any single individual morally correct in doing it without the knowledge or acquiescence of those on whom the solution is imposed?

A (Very Brief) History of Transhumanism

Transhumanism at its core is a simple idea—humans should not be limited by their biology. Through the use of technology, we can extend human capacities in mental, physical, psychological, and social realms.

Transhumanism as a term traces its origins to Dante's *Commedia*, discussed in Section 1 of this book. Precursors to modern transhumanist thinking emerged in the twentieth century, spurred by scientists studying concepts of radical life extension and the enhancement of humankind. Biologist Julian Huxley, prominent member of the British Eugenics Society and, ironically, the brother of *Brave New World* author Aldous Huxley, is believed to have been the first to use the word *transhumanism* in its modern sense.

Transhumanism coalesced into a movement in the 1960s through the teachings of F.M. Esfandiary, who began the convention of transhumanists adopting names that reflect their first and middle initial and the year in which they will turn 100 years old. So, Esfandiary became FM-2030, although in point of fact, he died in 2000 at age seventy. FM-2030 makes an important cameo appearance in *Inferno*. In 1983 Natasha Vita-More, whom we interviewed for this book, authored the "Transhumanist Manifesto." In 1998, the British philosophers Nick Bostrom and David Pearce founded the World Transhumanist Association, an international organization that promotes transhumanism as a subject of scientific inquiry and public policy. The organization recently changed its name to Humanity+, which is also referenced by Brown in *Inferno*.

As with almost any human intellectual movement, the transhumanist whole is made of varying strands and strains, from advocates for cryogenics to those who foresee science fiction-inspired cyborgs.

The aspect of transhumanism with which we tend to be most familiar, and the path that Dan Brown takes in creating his plot, emphasizes the use of futurist technologies to bring humankind into a post-biological limitations world, using such tools as genetic engineering, bionics, virtual reality, artificial intelligence (AI), or some combination of them. People such as Ray Kurzweil and David Orban, who is interviewed in this book, believe that by mid-century humans and technology will become one, often referred to as The Singularity. This will be a watershed moment, when exponentially smarter machines transform our world in powerful ways, positively impacting our society's intelligence, capabilities, resources, health, and even radical life extension.

Such advances should (and can) help solve the most urgent challenges facing humankind, transhumanists say, from ushering in an era of broader individual choice about what to do—or not do—with biological enhancement technologies.

The people most interested in transhumanism and the power of new technology to solve global problems such as climate change, environmental degradation and resource scarcity, are not generally troubled by population trends. They believe that we can stay ahead of the population curve through resilience and innovation, a point

Jamais Cascio makes in his interview. This establishes the key moral and ethical conflict that animates Brown's *Inferno*—a division in the transhumanist path, with one road leading to a hopeful future based on belief in the capacity for continued sustainable population growth while the other path leads to immediate, unilateral action by an individual to "fix" what he is convinced is unsustainable growth. As Vita-More points out, the transhumanist movement draws some "crazies," a few of whom may believe that Zobrist-like action must be taken to ensure the post-human future. But this is far from being a mainstream transhumanist belief.

Though the transhumanist movement is largely secular, its critics sometimes observe that its missionary zeal carries religious undertones. There is an undertone of "We know what is best, and we are morally *obligated* to help the human race transcend its biological limits." This attitude, say the critics, is the most dangerous aspect of transhumanism. Francis Fukuyama, the political scientist and social commentator best known for his book *The End of History*, worries that, "If we don't develop a humility of evolution soon, we may unwittingly invite the transhumanists to deface humanity with their genetic bulldozers and psychotropic shopping malls." Several of our experts address this controversy, arguing that the biotechnology revolution will liberate human beings to achieve their full potential by enabling us to make choices and flourish.

Most transhumanists know that it is not the number of people on the planet that is our challenge, it is a combination of the complexity of our systems and the new challenges to the species. To overcome these problems we need new technology. The Fukuyamas of the world, meanwhile, want to restrain that technology because they think they know what the human essence is and they don't want to see it eroded. Meanwhile, the transhumanists think the human essence can be many things, and we shouldn't sit around trying to preserve the basically religious era view of human essence when we face so many challenges.

One could speculate that Dan Brown himself might be a secret follower of the transhumanist movement, suggested, among other things, by referring to himself in code on the cover as DG-2064.

Perhaps he admires the movement in the way he has expressed admiration for the Freemasons, the transcendentalists of *The Lost Symbol*. There is commonality: Belief in the power of science to transform our understanding of the world and use it for the common good; an interest in alternative ways of looking at the world; and, a way of looking at the most fundamental aspects, literally, of our being.

But if Dan Brown is a transhumanist, he has at best twisted it. At the end of the book all three of the main characters, Langdon, Sienna, and Sinskey continue to believe in radical means of controlling the world's population growth. Dr. Sinskey lets it be known that even if WHO is successful at reengineering the virus they "might not even *want* to counteract it" and suggests the need for a "viable alternate plan" that is more "selective." In a word, eugenics. Sienna agrees to attend the emergency WHO meeting not because she wants to stop population control but to continue to do it "transhumanist style" through random genetic engineering.

How Good Is the Science?

Dan Brown has clearly done his homework in the area of viral vectors and genetic engineering (one leading virologist we contacted declined to be interviewed because of a nondisclosure agreement with Brown). He makes a convincing and clever case whose scientific underpinnings are for the most part at least minimally plausible, although not probable. But where does his science stop and his fiction begin? The answers are not designed to quibble with Dan Brown. His job as a novelist, after all, is to take information, some accurate, some wrong but interesting, from different fields and weld together a plot in a way that has you believing it is true or could be true. Dan Brown's commercial success at it is a tribute to his craft, even if the science in his books doesn't always hew to reality.

Viruses show symptoms and get transmitted when they are aerosolized—dispersed as tiny particles that float easily from carrier to the next victim. Hacking and sneezing are symptoms of a cold; sneeze, and you spread the virus. But the human-to-human virus Zobrist has created is designed to go right for our DNA and make changes in our genetic software, while remaining asymptomatic. So how does the virus spread? Here is how Brown describes the process:

> The contents of the Solublon bag had apparently bubbled up to the surface and aerosolized viral particles into the air. *It wouldn't take many, Sinskey knew. Especially in such an enclosed area.* A virus—unlike a bacteria or chemical pathogen—could spread through a population with astounding speed and penetration.
> (*Inferno*, p. 433)

And how would the virus work once it is in our DNA? Brown cites examples:

> The Ebola virus impaired the blood's ability to coagulate, resulting in unstoppable hemorrhaging. The hantavirus triggered the lungs to fail. A whole host of viruses known as oncoviruses caused cancer. And the HIV virus attacked the immune system, causing the disease AIDS.
> (*Inferno*, p. 434)

On the fundamental nature of viruses and their ability to alter genes, Dan Brown is right say the experts. Some types of viruses actually physically insert their genes into the host's genome. Viruses of this type have in fact recently been replicated in a laboratory by the two virologists Brown mentions by name in the book—Ron Fouchier of the Erasmus Medical Center in Holland and Yoshiro Kawaoka at the Department of Veterinary Medicine at the University of Wisconsin.

The two, working independently, managed to create a highly pathogenic mutant H5N1 virus (better known as bird flu). As Brown says, it can be transmitted mammal-to-mammal, through aerosolized droplets. Announcements about their work did indeed ignite the "firestorm of controversy" Dr. Sinskey predicts in the novel. Among the issues are whether scientists should be free to do this kind of work and share the information in the name of the public good, as our expert Gregory Stock favors. Or, in the interests of public safety, should some sort of government control be established so such information doesn't fall into the hands of a Zobrist? This is a course of action favored by another interviewee, Lauria Garrett. Meanwhile, the US National Science Advisory Board for Biosecurity (NSABB) has called for a moratorium on this research until the risk of its publication can be weighed against the benefits.

Fouchier himself seems undaunted by the controversy, saying publicly that worries about the virus getting out of hand are misplaced: "Bioterrorists can't make this virus. It's too complex. And rogue nations that do have the capacity to do this don't need our information." Meanwhile, as Laurie Garrett tells us with concern, Fouchier continues his work.

The consensus among the experts we talked to is that Fouchier is probably right, but the example of Zobrist should be a teachable moment. Sometime down the road, such a virus could fall into the wrong hands.

On the science, and as reflected in our interviews, it seems highly improbable that now or any time in the near-term future anyone could come up with a vector virus that effectively and randomly sterilizes a third of the population with one week of exposure, while not having noticeable side effects. There are easier ways to do destroy parts of the human race. Bioterrorists could come up with some bio-plague that would kill large numbers of people, or cause ebola-like suffering, but being specific enough to sterilize and to find a way to do it randomly, without other effects, seems highly unlikely.

Zobrist never said with any specificity *what* gene was targeted. There is no single "fertility gene" that one could disrupt or co-opt. Reproduction is a complicated process. The idea that you could disrupt on a mass global scale the highly robust process of human reproduction, which has been evolved over hundreds of thousands of years to favor everything that enhances survival of the species, is low probability for even the most brilliant scientific team, let alone a single individual. That this virus would work in such a way that some of the people became infertile and some did not is piling improbability upon improbability. Moreover, the "Zobrist virus" would have to be continuously released or population growth would resume, just as it does after plagues and other species-threatening events.

Most of our experts also thought that the notion of "one brilliant guy, light years ahead of everyone else" is not supported by any reality. Every generation has its bright lights and they lead the way, but biotechnology today is a huge and highly collective pursuit. The thinking is done collectively, as is the verification. Researchers publish. Information becomes public. Does someone eventually put stuff together in a new and different way, for which they justifiably get a Nobel Prize? Of course. But usually, it's not a case of them being that far ahead of everyone. This is not to say that there isn't a growing "do-it-yourself" alternative biotechnology movement that increasingly resembles the early days of Silicon Valley entrepreneurs working on computer technology in garages. There is such a movement and it will pose many new questions as it grows. But something as unprecedented as a vector virus that could affect human reproduction worldwide, both male and female (two highly differentiated reproductive systems), all from a single Solublon bag being dispersed in a cistern in Turkey is simply not in the cards in the decade ahead. Which, come to think of it, is really not that far down the road.

As for the social dimension, Dan Brown depicts the virus as randomly affecting one-third of the entire population, male and female, making them infertile. As a result, Brown implies, the population growth rate drops by one-third. But this is fundamentally flawed logic, says David Shugarts in his essay in Section 3. "It would only be approximately true if the affected people married each other. If the one-third of the affected males and one-third of the affected females were to marry exclusively unaffected partners, that would result in *two-thirds* of couples being infertile, since it takes two to tango."

The scientists we talked to also pointed out that there would be many ways around this kind of mass infertility. At the moment, there's the whole set of technologies around artificial insemination and *in-vitro* fertilization. Can there be any doubt that within a few years it will be cloning, and perhaps growth from embryonic stem cells? Simply blocking fertility would barely blunt population growth and might in fact accelerate it. Faced with mass infertility, the most likely response would be more technology solutions, resulting in a sort of transhumanist vs. transhumanist duel. With a technology override, and unrestrained by their natural fertility *or* age, people would find it far easier to have children—women wouldn't worry about menopause, because it wouldn't matter. Just go down to the egg store, have them transfer your good genes into an ovum, and away you go.

Asked what the future holds, Brown's character Elizabeth Sinskey, the director-general of WHO, says it well: "I'm afraid it's only going to get murkier. We're on the verge of new technologies that we can't yet even imagine."

Perhaps we can't, but the experts in this section are willing to try. They show us how far we have come and speculate on where we are going. The ability to escape our long evolutionary history of biological determination is here. We are already self-evolving and we will undoubtedly continue to do so. Whether we, as a society, can find ways to maximize the benefits of our new technologies and self-evolution powers and limit the dangers and downsides, remains to be seen. Brown's *Inferno*, for whatever its shortcomings, stirs the pot of a conversation we need to have.

Demografiction

BY JOEL E. COHEN

Abby Rockefeller Mauzé Professor of Populations at
The Rockefeller University and Professor of Populations
at the Earth Institute of Columbia University

If Bertrand Zobrist had consulted a competent demographer, he would not have pursued his purported "solution" to problems of rapid human population growth.

To recall, Zobrist randomly sterilized one-third of the world's people (with no by-your-leave). If this fascist intervention had no effect on the birth rates or death rates of the other two-thirds, what would be the demographic consequences?

Earth had about 7.1 billion people in 2013, so the sterilization would leave about 4.7 billion people unaffected. Since the unaffected people would be a random sample from the population, their numbers would grow at the same rate as the whole population in the absence of sterilization. The rate of growth per year of the world's population is 1.1 percent (United States Census Bureau estimate for 2013) or 1.2 percent (Population Reference Bureau's 2012 World Population Datasheet). Nobody knows the global population growth rate exactly because many countries have no recent demographic data.

If the unsterilized people continued to increase in numbers at 1.2 percent per year (I will return to this implausible assumption in a moment), then these 4.7 billion would grow back to 7.1 billion people by the year 2047. The growth rate of 1.1 percent per year brings the population produced by the unsterilized 4.7 billion to 7.1 billion people by the year 2050, only three years later.

Zobrist's "solution" is no solution at all, only a temporary delay, if it results in no change in the birth rates or death rates of the unsterilized.

Now let's go back to my "implausible assumption" of a fixed annual percentage of increase per year. (Whether it's 1.1 percent or 1.2 percent doesn't matter.) This assumption is the definition of exponential population growth: a constant annual percentage of increase. (Think of the size of the population as the value of a bank account that grows at a fixed interest rate.) Zobrist assumes exponential growth when he lectures Dr. Elizabeth Sinskey:

> "The time bomb is no longer ticking. It has already gone off, and without drastic measures, exponential mathematics will become your new God ... and 'He' is a vengeful God. He will bring to you Dante's vision of hell right outside on Park Avenue ... huddled masses wallowing in their own excrement. A global culling orchestrated by Nature herself."

In fact, contrary to the assumption of Thomas Robert Malthus in 1798 and many neo-Malthusians since then, human numbers globally have hardly ever grown exponentially. For most of human history up to the early 1960s, despite major fluctuations like the Black Death, the annual percentage of increase of the global population was itself increasing. Demographers say that global population growth was super-exponential. (Think of a bank account in which the interest rate rises in proportion to the balance accumulating in the account. If you find such a bank account, I want to know about it.)

Super-exponential population growth ended dramatically in the early 1960s, though no one knew it at the time, when many people in developing countries began having fewer children. The Census Bureau estimates that the all-time high growth rate of global human population, just over 2.22 percent per year, was reached in 1963. The annual rate of increase then fell by more than half, to 1.09 percent per year in 2013, just fifty years. The growth rate of the human population has been anything but constant. It has been falling dramatically for the last half-century.

"It is difficult to predict, especially the future," goes a standard joke among demographers. The Census Bureau projects that the world's population will be growing by 0.47 percent per year by 2049. This rate of increase is less than half the current growth rate. In the low variant projection of the United Nations Population Division published in 2012, global population growth ends altogether by the middle of the twenty-first century and a slow decline begins, with no help whatsoever from Bertrand Zobrist.

The recent and projected slowing of global population growth is good news. But it is far from the whole story. About one-sixth of humankind, mainly in the least developed countries, still suffers exceptionally high population growth rates. Authoritarian interventions like those of Zobrist are no more appropriate for these unfortunate regions than for the world as a whole. The multifaceted strategies that respect individual human dignity and improve human well-being while lowering population growth rates include education for all boys and girls; improvements in the status of women through legal rights, credit, and employment opportunities; raising the age of marriage; reproductive healthcare and family planning; reductions in the death rates of children (so that parents feel less need to bear many children as old-age insurance); economic development; and modernization in all its variety and imperfection.

In this work of what the Dutch demographer Anton Kuijsten called "demografiction," Zobrist's central and fundamental error is his assumption that human numbers are the major or sole threat to the future well-being of humans and life on Earth. On the contrary, for example, from 1900 to 2008, carbon emissions from fossil fuels increased sixteen-fold globally. Over this same interval, global human population increased roughly 4-fold (3.8-fold or 4.3-fold, depending on the estimate of global population in 1900). Thus carbon emissions per person roughly quadrupled. More recently, between 1990 and 2008, carbon emissions from fossil fuels increased by about 50 percent while global population size grew about 27 percent. The increases in emissions per person are at least as much of a threat to the stability of the atmosphere and Earth's climate as the increases in the number of people.

While today's rich countries were the main emitters of carbon dioxide in the past, now the responsibility for carbon dioxide emissions is shared between rich and poor countries. Beyond sheer numbers of people, how people choose to live and make their livings, and what they value in their own lives and in the lives of their descendants, determine their own, and their descendants', well-being.

Zobrist, smiling confidently, tells Dr. Sinskey: "Any environmental biologist or statistician will tell you that humankind's best chance of long-term survival occurs with a global population of around four billion." It sounds pretty authoritative, doesn't it? Not so fast. I reviewed estimates by reputable scientists and scholars of Earth's human carrying capacity in my 1995 book, *How Many People Can the Earth Support?* Twentieth century estimates of the human population ceiling ranged from fewer than one billion to more than 1000 billion. Another study by Jeroen C. J. M. van Den Bergh and Piet Rietveld in 2004 found a similar wide range of estimates of Earth's human carrying capacity.

These estimates of human carrying capacity range so widely because they rest on widely divergent assumptions. No single number for global population can possibly tell you where humankind's best chance of long-term survival occurs. Human carrying capacity depends in part on how people, alive now and yet to be born, answer a host of questions that range far beyond demography.

What political institutions will resolve conflicting interests, allocate power, and establish law? Will people settle their political differences by contaminating large regions of Earth with radioactive fallout or by negotiating peacefully? What technologies will people use? Will people grow their food and fiber by mining aquifers, eroding top soils, exhausting the forests, and depleting the oceans, or by protecting the fresh waters, lands, woods, and seas that nurture us and other species? What average level of material well-being and what distribution, with how much inequality, will people desire or accept? What economic arrangements will regulate production, distribution, exchange, and consumption? What demographic institutions and policies will influence families, child-bearing and child-rearing, care of the elderly, migration, and urban life? What physical, chemical, and biological environments will people prefer or find acceptable? Parks or parking lots? Jaguars with four wheels or jaguars with four legs? Will people want a world that is livable and beautiful for five years or five thousand years or five million years? What level of variability and risk will people accept (environmental, economic, and political)? What values, tastes, and fashions will govern human behavior? Will we return to the Easter Islanders' taste for colossal *mo'ai* or Aztec human sacrifice? Will we continue to permit people who are poor or unemployed to go hungry? Will people continue to poison themselves with tobacco, excessive alcohol, and addictive drugs? Answers to all of these questions influence how many people Earth can support.

In addition to these largely unpredictable human choices, we understand very incompletely the constraints that the natural world imposes. How much we invest in understanding the natural world will also influence Earth's human carrying capacity, because our knowledge will influence how we use and accommodate ourselves to Earth.

Had Zobrist really wanted to make the world a better, more secure home for humans and other species, he might have attended to the quality of the process of bringing about change as well as to his goal. Those billions of people Zobrist sterilized, and the billions more in the families they belonged to, had no voice in the change imposed on them. Neither did the many tens of millions who died in the twentieth century at the hands of Hitler, Stalin, and Mao. "Father Knows Best," a popular network radio and television show from 1954 to 1960, is dated as comedy and obsolete as a strategy of governance. Consulting with people who are affected by potential change improves human well-being by granting people the dignity of having a voice in the processes of decision and change. Who knows? It could improve the outcome of change as well.

"You Simply Have to Be Insane to Think that You Can Just Continue to Grow Forever on a Finite Planet"

AN INTERVIEW WITH PAUL EHRLICH
Bing Professor of Population Studies, Stanford University, president of Stanford's Center for Conservation Biology, and author of *The Population Bomb*.

Paul R. Ehrlich has been warning us about the near-at-hand calamities associated with too many people on the planet for the last four decades. Despite some controversial calls and what many of us see as countervailing trends—vast improvements in the ability to feed people, lower population growth rates in many countries, more education, and unprecedented technological progress—he stands by his general thesis. If anything, he suggests here, the threat posed to civilization as we know it from an exploding population has only gotten worse.

Public concern that rapid population growth was a direct threat to human survival and the environment were not new when he published The Population Bomb *in 1968 (*Time *had a cover story on it in the January 11, 1960 issue, for example). But the book's relentless "we are on the precipice" tone, its bold scenarios for the disasters to come, and the suggestion that governments in some parts of the world at least consider imposing mandatory sterilization, galvanized the public. Hugely controversial,* The Population Bomb *made him instantly famous—even notorious in the eyes of his many critics, among whom Dan Brown is clearly not one.*

Ehrlich has continued to be an activist on behalf of the cause. He recently helped form the Millennium Alliance for Humanity & The Biosphere (MAHB), for example, whose goal is to get hundreds of non-governmental organizations to work together more often and coordinate their efforts. He also works on behalf of legislation covering such areas of interest as endangered species and the preservation of genetic resources. By training he is an entomologist and contiues to do research in the structure, dynamics, and genetics of natural butterfly populations.

In this interview Erlich tells us why technology optimists have been continually wrong, why we would be better off having fewer rich people in the world, and why climate disruption is much more serious than Obamacare or the debt crisis, among other topics. Asked if he thought it unfair that he was being considered by some as the role model for Dan Brown's Zobrist character, Erlich—who once suggested governments might consider putting sterilizing agents into the water supply—offers an unhesitating answer: "No."

Your book, *The Population Bomb*, published in 1968, made you instantly famous for the dire warnings that exploding population growth against finite resources would lead to disaster, even starvation. Now, two generations later, have your views changed? Are you a bit more optimistic?

Basically, the situation has only gotten worse since then. Population size has doubled, the number of starving people has increased, and there are now probably 800 to 900 million undernourished people and roughly another two billion—combined, almost half the population—who are micronutrient malnourished. So, neither I nor my colleagues have seen any significant progress.

Yet some of the alarming trends you wrote about, such as mass starvation and increasing death rates, haven't come about. The Green Revolution in agriculture and the technological advances in medicine and other areas related to well-being have raised living standards around the world. It seems we are resilient and keeping ahead of the curve.

Actually, that's mostly hogwash. We have lost roughly 200-300 million people to starvation and starvation-related disease since *The Population Bomb* was written, which is almost the equivalent of the population of the United States. And while there has been substantial diminishing of birthrates, the United Nations just raised their median estimate for 2050 to 9.6 billion people. That may or may not come to pass. But the problems we wrote about are close to precisely the same.

Sure, the green revolution in the poor countries did spread with a rate that the agricultural people did not expect. But it was clearly short term. Basically, as its founder Norman Borlaug said, the revolution bought us a few decades to kill the population monster, yet we have done little about that.

To bring the pending disaster home think of it this way: To take care of the people we have today over the long run, and without improving their condition, we would likely need at least another half a planet. To raise everybody to the standards of the United States or Britain, you would need four or five more planets. We're not going to get them.

The technological optimists have been continually wrong, not continually right. We were going to have nuclear power that was going to provide us with energy too cheap to meter. We were going to farm whales in atolls, get leaf protein from leaves, and raise bacteria on sewage in order to feed people and get everybody wellnourished. The optimists just haven't delivered.

The early results of climate disruption, the spreading of toxic chemicals from pole to pole, the problems with nuclear weapons, and the threats of huge epidemics are all tied to population size. You simply have to be insane to think that you can continue to grow forever on a finite planet.

Dan Brown, clearly as concerned about the population explosion as you are, created an antihero named Zobrist who saves the world from itself by releasing a virus that will "cull the herd." Since you have suggested that sterilants would be a way to reduce population growth it is tempting to suggest that Zobrist is a fictionalized version of you. Is that an unfair characterization?

No, it's not really unfair. It is clearly the business of society, and that may mean government, to do something about the size of the population. The issue, then, is what do you do? I absolutely do not believe, for example, that every woman has the right to have as many children as she wants, or every man, any more than anybody has the right to steal as much stuff as they want.

When we talk about putting sterilants in the water supply, obviously people wouldn't like that. But wouldn't it be wonderful if people had to take an antidote in order to *have* a baby. That would get rid of the entire abortion controversy, the entire issue of whether or not people were given contraceptives at certain ages, and so on. Every child would be a wanted child. It would be a wonderful world.

As for Dan Brown's "Zobrist virus," if it affected a random third of the population and that this was something that could be reversed, it would be much superior to the sorts of things we're doing now, like starving people to death and having some people overreproduce and having many people overconsume. But, of course, being able to create such a virus that would be completely safe is pure fiction.

If population growth is slowing in the developed countries and gaining in poorer countries, don't strict population control measures have an inherent bias against the poor, the nonwhites, and the nonhighly developed countries?

There certainly could be. One has to be very alert to prevent that. But I believe that if you could sterilize the rich people at a higher frequency than the poor people, you'd be even better off because of course it's the rich people who are attacking our life support systems, consuming too much and despoiling the environment.

That is why I said that if the virus Dan Brown proposes really was random, or slightly more likely to make a rich person sterile than a poor person, I'd be more in favor of the plan. Because, of course, the most overpopulated nation is the one that you and I are living in right now. The US has the third-largest number of people, and when you factor in how much each one of us, on average, consumes, we're still way more threatening to human life-support systems than China and India.

Speaking of China, in your second book, *The Population Explosion*, you wrote approvingly of China's one-child policy, which most of us would characterize as coercive. Don't such measures violate our sense of human rights?

I would much prefer noncoercive measures of population control. On the other hand, human beings have a right to have grandchildren. They have a right for their grandchildren to live in decent environments. They have a right to be well-fed and well-educated. But such human rights are countered by the idea that everybody has the right to have as many kids as they want. There were unquestionably difficulties with the Chinese situation, but population growth slowed. The Chinese themselves say they're in much better shape today because of that program.

People can invent any kind of rights that they want, but they've got to do some analysis. For example, where does the right for everybody to have as many kids as they want fit in? Is that the same as the right for everybody to steal as many cars as they want? What if every man or woman has as many children as they want, and they all want ten kids, should that be a "right"? What are the consequences?

I have very little patience for this inventing rights crap. It's been around for a long time, it's never analyzed, it's simply stated. It's what we used to call proof by vigorous assertion.

One of the biggest changes in recent years has been our ever-increasing ability to modify our own DNA as well as to create mammal-to-mammal viruses. A Zobrist figure could soon create a vector virus in their garage from off-the-shelf bio-engineered material and let it loose on the world. What do you think, is there any moral or ethical basis for people taking evolution—including population control—in their own hands?

No, I think that there's not. This is something that has to be done socially, done collectively. We're a social animal. We've got to have a reasonable discussion of this but, discouragingly, we don't seem to have a reasonable discourse in the United States on this important topic. How we deal with the world's resources and the environment are critical but in the last Presidential election no one even asked the candidates: 'what do you think about climate disruption?'

People don't understand that climate disruption is so much more serious than the Obamacare plan or the debt crisis. You can't negotiate with nature. Even a relatively minor increase of a few degrees during the growing season can shrink the grain harvest in major food-producing regions. And, growing populations dump ever more greenhouse gases into the atmosphere, likely making it ever more difficult to produce the additional feed needed.

As for ethics, I would ask, is it ethical for the fossil fuel industry to pay a whole bunch of liars and cooperate with a whole mob of morons to confuse people about the climate disruption? Seriously, why was there no discussion?

Is there anything that could make you optimistic? Is there an innovative solution you know of or can imagine that would avoid the kinds of disasters you believe are at hand?

That is exactly what I am working on. We have an organization called the Millennium Alliance for Humanity & The Biosphere whose goal is to get hundreds and hundreds of NGOs to work together more and coordinate their efforts. We cannot solve this piecemeal and we have to face the fact that our governance system is broken, that our international system is broken, and that therefore we have to get together at the grass roots level and change the way we do the whole thing. It's probably pie in the sky but there are examples in history, big and small scale. Think of the big changes in race relations and women's rights. It shows that by tackling big issues together you can sometimes solve them.

In the end, I'm hopeful, but not terribly optimistic. As was the case decades ago, were you to ask me what I think the chances of us avoiding a collapse in civilization are I'll say they are pretty slim. Some of my colleagues think they are much, much slimmer than I do. But you don't even hear any discussion of it. Maybe Dan Brown's *Inferno* will help start that.

— Interviewed by Arne de Keijzer

The End of the World Isn't as Likely as Humans Fighting Back

AN INTERVIEW WITH JAMAIS CASCIO
Distinguished Fellow, Institute for the Future, and Senior Fellow, Institute for Ethics and Emerging Technologies

One might say that Jamais Cascio is the anti-Dan Brown: he believes in the future of possibilities, not a future of doom. Yes, he worries about the big challenges to twenty-first century human civilization and warns that the earth might not even make it to ten billion people unless Western diets and post-industrial consumption patterns change. But where he parts company with the gloom and doom of the neo-Malthusians, including Dan Brown, is his faith in our ability to meet those challenges by reinventing climate management systems, known as geoengineering. As he explains here, "Such a world would be more than simply sustainable; it would be regenerative and diverse, relying on the capacity not only to absorb shocks but evolve them. In a word, it would be resilient."

Jamais Cascio has worked in the field of scenario development for over a decade, and in 2010 was named a Distinguished Fellow at the Institute for the Future. He is also a Senior Fellow at the Institute for Ethics and Emerging Technologies. His work appears in a wide range of publications and Cascio has also been featured in multiple television programs. In 2007, his original work on calculating the carbon

*footprint of cheeseburgers—yes, cheeseburgers—
went viral. Cascio is also author of* Hacking
the Earth: Understanding the Concept of
Geoengineering.

Unrelated, but still topical to Inferno, *he has
designed several science fiction game settings, including "Transhuman Space: Broken Dreams" (speculating on the future of the developing world) and
"Transhuman Space: Toxic Memes" (examining
future popular culture and political movements).*

*In this interview, Cascio explains why we don't
need drastic action on the population front, why the
"Zobrist solution" from the Dan Brown novel will
only lead to even greater population growth, and the
three scenarios he believes can steer us sustainably to
the future.*

Dan Brown clearly seems to have joined the Paul Ehrlich club
of neo-Malthusians who predict imminent, world-scale calamities if we don't dramatically reign in population growth. Radical
intervention, they say, might be desirable, even necessary.

Population growth is a valid concern, to be sure, and there's
no doubt that the kinds of environmental problems we are seeing now—and that will be on the rise over the coming years—are
exacerbated by population growth. However, this does not trans-
late into a need to do something drastic and immediate. That's
applying short-term, reactive thinking to a complex problem, just
the kind of thinking that Zobrist would undoubtedly hate!

Here is why: Earth's population growth is actually slowing,
and the United Nations is now predicting a peak population well
below their own projections from earlier years. It turns out that
human societies do a very good job at limiting their own populations as they become economically more secure and, most importantly, as their women become more educated. That is why you're
seeing a *decline* in population throughout the developed world

(even the United States would soon be seeing a shrinking population if it wasn't for immigration). Economic growth and education also put societies on a pathway to being able to adopt more sustainable and efficient technologies. It's an all-around win.

Still, we seem to be continually reminded that we are on a fast track to global collapse by not meeting quickly enough the challenges of climate change, environmental degradation, water shortages, running out of livable space, and so on. Yes, the rate of population growth has slowed but it will still reach nine or ten billion by mid-century. Isn't there ultimately a limit to earth's carrying capacity?

While the risk of global collapse is rising, so is our ability to grapple with it (and neither is growing exponentially). When we look ahead at the challenges of the years to come, we have to remember that we'll be facing the problems of the future with the tools, ideas, and minds of the future, too.

That will be the case with population. There is an ultimate limit to earth's carrying capacity, but it will be greater than what we can see today.

Is a Zobrist-like, one-person biological "solution" becoming more plausible as genetic technology advances?

In the abstract, a single person unleashing a global genetic intervention (at least a simple one) could be possible sometime in the next few decades. But what would-be Zobrists will have to keep in mind is that the ability to detect and counter such attacks will be advancing as well, and the number of specialists seeking to defend the human population will vastly outnumber the number of renegade genetic engineers. On top of that, we are building a better global protocol for dealing with pandemics—identifying them, isolating them, and preventing their spread. Anyone considering something like this would have to deal with the fact that we're building precisely the kind of infrastructure to detect and counter such an intervention.

Of course, this all assumes that such an intervention would even work as planned. The kind of thing that Zobrist has in mind would require a far more advanced understanding of genetics than we have today. It may not even be possible at all.

You have discussed the fact that short of an extinction-level catastrophe such as earth being hit by an asteroid, the future will be applied "unevenly," with diverse populations confronting different problems, with different outcomes. Does that argue for or against a Zobrist-style selective solution?

Any kind of one-size-fits-all solution is going to have enormous unwanted consequences. A Zobrist-style sterilization infection applied evenly around the world may temporarily cut birth rates in some nations to a more sustainable level, but other places with already declining populations, such as Japan or Italy, would see their populations collapse. Conversely, applying this intervention just in high-population regions would quickly be seen as a return to imperialism at best (where someone from a more "advanced," powerful position decides what's best for the weaker parts of the world), genocidal racism at worst.

Imagine what would happen if something like this succeeded. Western nations, the United States in particular, would be accused of being behind such an attack (no matter if Zobrist proclaimed his personal responsibility on every channel and web page). There is a very real chance that panicked, angry nations would want to start a war. At the very least, you would see trade embargoes and political unrest, all ultimately *slowing* the development of new, world-changing technologies.

And here is the kicker: Zobrist's intervention would be counterproductive in the long run. In each country affected there would be campaigns to learn who was infected and who was immune and for "the fertile" to do their patriotic duty and have lots of babies. We already have an example: when birth numbers fell below replacement levels in the 1970s, Singapore encouraged parents to have more babies, especially those with more education and higher incomes.

It's altogether likely that not only would the population recover within a couple of decades, we would actually see a *faster* rise in population than ever before. And it would all be Zobrist's fault.

What you seem to be saying is that in spite of all the daunting challenges facing the world we should remain optimistic. You have said, "Apocaphilia is trite at best and counterproductive at worst." So cheer us up. You have proposed three scenarios for a sustainable future. Would you explain them?

None of these scenarios for the future is meant to be utopian. They all have significant drawbacks, depending upon your and society's points of view. And, the working goal of my project leading to these scenarios is to envision what a successfully sustainable world could look like, and working from there to think through how we get there.

The first scenario is the "we get our act together" future, where governments enact policies (and businesses embrace them) that rapidly bring down greenhouse gas emissions. Temperature spikes are prevented by active intervention in the climate (something called "geoengineering"), and the carbon already in the oceans and air is pulled out through a variety of complex chemical processes. This is a top-down, almost military scenario, one in which we become sustainable because the alternative is chaos.

The second scenario is the "we clean up afterwards" future, where we are hit by some of the big global catastrophes, manmade or natural, and have to deal with the aftermath. Here, most of the big institutions we have depended upon for decades (or centuries) are either broken or no longer trustworthy, and there is a massive political and economic shakeup. Targeted use of high-technology items parallels widespread adoption of back-to-nature communities. Imagine the Amish with 3D printers, ultra-efficient solar panels, and ubiquitous environmental sensor grids and you start to get the picture. This is a bottom-up scenario, but one that most people would find unfamiliar at best.

The last scenario is the "we get weird, and that's good" future, where advances in technology—envisioned by some transhumanists and other futurists—allow a revolution not just in how we live, but in our relationship with the planet. Super AI plots out ideal strategies for sustainability, diamond-based nanomachines literally suck the carbon out of the atmosphere and oceans to make more of themselves, robots do most of the work, and a happy, healthy population enjoys art, education, and probably lots of sex and drugs. This may sound highly unlikely, but it's actually much more plausible than you might expect—and very few people over twenty would even begin to know how to handle such a world.

Speaking of transhumanism, futurist concepts such as artificial intelligence, Singularity, bioengineering, life extension, and Cyborgs all fit under the transhumanist or post-humanist banner. Is one technology any better suited to the future than another? When will we know that we have arrived at the inflection point toward that future, and what should we look for as signposts along the way? What, if anything, do you worry about as people experiment with these directions and trends such as do-it-yourself biology and transhumanist technology movements proliferate?

Technologies that are likely to be valuable and useful over the course of the next few decades will tend to have a few things in common:

> • They will be more *open* than restrictive—able to connect to a wide array of other systems, flexible in their use, ideally able to be understood and altered or fixed by end-users.
> • They will give us a better *understanding of the world*, whether through sensors or analysis or connections. They'll make the world more transparent, and make the likely consequences of our actions more visible. They'll help us understand the consequences of their use.

- They will help *reduce our environmental impacts*, whether by reducing the amount of energy we use, limiting our resource needs, or allowing us to see our impacts in order to make smarter choices.

In this sense, things like artificial intelligence or biotechnology aren't good or bad for the future in the abstract, but entirely in how they are deployed. And, it is probable that many of the uses of these emerging systems will be aimed at short-term returns, not long-term value. Unfortunately, privileging the short-term over the long-term is exactly what brought us into the mess we're in now.

You have suggested there is an analogy between modern times and the incredible advances in human brain power, skills, and cooperation that followed the retreating Ice Age, allowing for the development of writing, cities, agriculture, advanced symbolic thought, and so on. What are some of these forward-leaping, positive trends that may similarly create new ways to improve our thought processes and abilities to cooperate presently? Advances that may enable us to successfully tackle some of the big problems? And isn't this the X factor that Dan Brown leaves out of his story—the uniquely human capability to rise to the challenges of major problems and find new solutions?

There is a fascinating pathway of development for many of our present and emerging technologies: increasing both our understanding of the world and our ability to understand the consequences of our actions. Something as simple as a real-time mileage readout on newer cars (especially hybrids) changes driving behavior. You can see, moment by moment, how your driving habits affect your fuel economy. People who start driving hybrids often see better mileage a month or two later than when they first bought the car, not because the car is getting better over that time, but because *they* are getting better.

This is the technological pathway that will help us deal with the big challenges we will face in this century. One of the important rules for futurists and strategic foresight specialists who focus on the environment is never to rule out human ingenuity. Not that we'll develop a techno-fix for every problem, but that we'll gain a better understanding of how we got into this mess, and develop innovative responses that allow us to change the rules of the game.

The risk isn't that we won't be able to figure out how to deal with the global problems we face; the risk is that there will be those who want to take shortcuts that make problems worse in the long run, or that result in the suffering of millions (or billions) or people.

You have proposed that we "reinvent climate management" to assure a sustainable future, presumably through technologies such as geoengineering. That seems a tall order in the current political climate.

When I talk about reinventing climate management, I am not just talking about technological options like geoengineering—in many ways, the use of geoengineering actually makes many of the political and economic problems associated with global warming *worse*, not better. I'm actually thinking more about the need to develop the kinds of institutions for communication, education, and diplomacy that will allow for greater cooperation around environmental issues. And, if you think that a technological response would be difficult in the current political climate, this is orders of magnitude harder.

My concern about geoengineering technologies is that they would be used to suppress some of the symptoms of global warming, but mostly without directly addressing the causes. They would do things like hold heat down by pumping particles of stuff like sulfur dioxide into the stratosphere, blocking a little bit of incoming sunlight. This alone wouldn't solve the global warming problem, because without cutting carbon emissions, we will still be poisoning the oceans and would have to put more and more stuff into the atmosphere to block more and more sunlight. It's a tourniquet, not a cure.

Ideally, we'll be able to get more political cooperation as a younger generation comes into power and as environmental solutions that offer widespread economic and social benefits become more prevalent. In this sort of future, climate management will be reinvented precisely because it is how we will improve our lives, not just because we are trying to head off disaster.

How do you think people and governments would react if there were a visible impending crisis approaching? Would governments suddenly swing into cooperative action? Or would the atmosphere of polarization and partisanship only get worse?

How governments around the world would react to an impending crisis, especially one that could wipe out much of human civilization, would largely depend upon how much time we perceive ourselves as having to confront it, how certain we were of the level of the threat, and what kind of effort was required to meet the challenge. In the past, we have managed to come together for other large-scale problems, and not just in terms of fighting against a common enemy in a war. The Montreal Protocols banning CFCs, for example, are a terrific example of how the global community can work out solutions for global problems.

In that case, the problem wasn't immediate, we had some years before it really threatened the planet as a whole, the scientific evidence was strong (especially once the hole in the ozone layer started to show up), and the needed response was, in the global economy, quite manageable.

The closer the threat is to happening, the more likely we are to respond with desperation; the more costly the response would be to those in political and economic power, the more likely we are to respond with dismissal. What it often comes down to is how visible the threat is—is it something tangible, understandable (and scary) to the everyday citizen? Is it something that has obvious bad effects worth sacrificing for? Is the solution something that makes sense to people?

The situation gets much more complicated when the threat comes from the actions of one or a few global actors (countries, leaders, supervillains). The temptation to assign blame and push all of the responsibility for the solution onto those who caused it is awfully strong. And while this makes sense in the abstract—you really should clean up the messes you make—many of the true global threats (like climate disruption or the collapse of fisheries) can't be solved by any one country, no matter how powerful.

The question then becomes, can we get over our need to point fingers and dismiss solutions that adversely affect us in time to avoid global catastrophes?

What kinds of constraints, if any, would you put on creating technology-driven evolution? What are the ethics of becoming our own gods?

Stewart Brand, editor of the eco-minded *Whole Earth* catalogs from the late 1960s and 70s, once wrote, with regards to humanity's growing power and effect on the world, "we are as gods, and we may as well get good at it." As I've noted in talks where his comment has come up, he never actually specified *which* gods he was thinking about. At this point, I am inclined to think he meant Loki (the Norse god of mischief and movie supervillain).

We tend to think of gods as having two key characteristics: *omnipotence*, the ability to do just about anything, and *omniscience*, the ability to know just about anything. The thing is, to the degree that we're getting closer to being able to become "our own gods," it's really only about the first characteristic. We're able to affect each other, our planet, our futures in ways that would truly astound someone from a few generations ago, and be impossible to comprehend for someone from a few centuries ago. Yet we still lack the kind of deep understanding of the complexity of the world that we need to be able make wise use of this power.

The constraints I would like to see are those that demand that we improve our understanding of the consequences of our actions.

The tools for doing so vary, and none of them are perfect: simulations (which are getting better and better); controlled experiments ideally in ways that are cut off from any possibility of harming others; transparency of all of the data from our research and experiments (so that others can learn from what worked and what didn't); and the use of scenarios and futurism to try to imagine unexpected outcomes by, in the words of Hermann Kahn, "thinking the unthinkable."

There's an old saying, "it's easier to get forgiveness than permission." The more powerful we get, the less wise that path becomes.

—Interviewed by Arne de Keijzer

I Am Not Zobrist

AN INTERVIEW WITH LAURIE GARRETT
Senior Fellow for Global Health, Council on Foreign
Relations and author of *The Coming Plague*

Laurie Garrett has been on the trail of outbreaks and epidemics worldwide since the 1990s, winning a Pulitzer Prize for her reporting on the Ebola virus in what was then Zaire along the way. Her book, The Coming Plague: Newly Emerging Diseases in a World Out of Balance, *published in 1994, was a best seller and continues to be a benchmark in the field. She joined the think tank staff of the Council of Foreign Relations in 2004, where she is responsible for covering the intersection between global heath and public policy.*

Garrett's link to Inferno *is obvious: Zobrist, Dan Brown's fictional zealot, harangues Dr. Sinskey, his fictional chief of the real life World Health Organization in a darkened conference room at the real life Council on Foreign Relations on New York's Upper East Side. It is there that Zobrist warns Sinskey in an apocalyptic speech that if WHO remains unwilling to take action against the "hell just below our feet," he will offer the world his own solution.*

Garrett, who is deeply engaged in researching viruses and plagues and ways governments might be able to cope effectively with them, felt compelled to write a commentary for CNN in which she made sure no one confused Brown's fictional CFR with the real one. Alluding to the scene where Zobrist basically takes fictional WHO chief Sinskey hostage, Garrett said: "I am the only trained biologist working in

the New York headquarters of the Council on For-
eign Relations, where I am senior fellow for global
health. I've never kidnapped WHO Director-Gen-
eral Dr. Margaret Chan, but I have been known to
corner her for some whispered one-on-ones."

Garrett's work is not theoretical. Nor is she
dealing with something that exists only in the imag-
ination of thriller writers. This is scary, real-world,
real-time stuff. A SARS-like virus, dubbed "Middle
East respiratory syndrome" (MERS), broke out in
Saudi Arabia in 2012, has killed forty-five people
as of mid-2013, and has now also been detected in
Europe. The slow spread rate (at least to date) may
make the fictional Zobrist's expected success rate
even less plausible, but it does demonstrate his point
that WHO has little direct control over the research
and no power to impose solutions (it does stimulate
research and advances in epidemiology and assists
governments with their health policies).

When we asked Laurie Garret what she thought
of Inferno, she was blunt: "Silly but thought pro-
voking." What follows is the thought-provoking
part, made all the more so because, as she tells us, Ron
Fouchier, the real-life virologist mentioned by Dan
Brown in his novel, has moved to patent the genomic
sequence of the MERS virus and place restrictions
on who can have access to it. To date, it seems that
neither WHO nor the governments eager to develop
diagnostic tests have had access. Welcome to the scary
world of viruses and plagues and the battle between
the public good and the power of one.

Readers meet Bertrand Zobrist, the brilliant Swiss billionaire, transhumanist, and bioterrorist on your home turf: the
Council on Foreign Relations. "The rings of hell await," he tells
the head of the World Health Organization there, but could be

forestalled by the thinning of the population herd. Let's start with some fact checking. Have you seen any mad scientists roaming around the halls lately?

You are kidding, right (laughing)? Actually, we are here to do the opposite: helping to save lives by understanding viruses and plagues and the policy measures governments might take to control them.

The World Health Organization (WHO) *is* real, of course, and headed by Dr. Margaret Chan. You have worked with her. Do you think she is pleased to have Dr. Elizabeth Sinskey as her doppelganger, and at the way her organization is portrayed?

On the record, there is no reaction, but she knows about the book, of course. What I can tell you is that the book's criticism of WHO as an organization that doesn't take population growth seriously is pretty ridiculous. WHO and its allies in the UN system have done a tremendous amount for family planning and are big supporters of condom use to block transmission of sexually transmissible viruses and bacteria.

If you are going to be angry about the lack of promotion of family planning in the world, you should start with why so many countries, including the US, oppose, as a matter of political principle, funding family planning.

The novel's Dr. Sinskey travels around the world with her own security detail to deal with threats like the Zobrists of this world, and by any means necessary. Just like Dr. Chan?

Spoiler alert! She doesn't have a private C-130 transport and the ECDC (European Center for Disease Prevention and Control) doesn't have a whole bunch of military-trained cadres in flak jackets that can, with impunity, and no international visa requirements, pop in, with all their armaments, from one country to another. Moreover, WHO is in such deep financial straits that its epidemic response division is basically broke.

More seriously, Dan Brown mentions the work of Ron Fouchier and Yoshihiro Kawaoka, who independently of one another created a highly pathogenic virus in their labs. How well does Dan Brown represent that research?

He does. Fouchier and Kawaoka were able to make deliberate genetic changes in the H5N1 bird flu virus in order to see in the lab what it would take to turn it into a mammal-to-mammal transmitter, as opposed to a bird-to-bird and occasionally bird-to-mammal one.

The work was wildly controversial and continues to be. There are many, many people in government and in various scientific societies that think that what they did was terribly irresponsible. Yes, they were subjected to tremendous scrutiny and both teams executed their work in very high security laboratories with maximal protective things. Kawaoka even disabled his experimental viruses so that they couldn't easily cause any serious disease in human beings. These guys may have been responsible, but the next guy might not be.

The story is not over. Since *Inferno* was published, Fouchier has been mired in an overlapping controversy involving the MERS virus that is now circulating in Saudi Arabia. It is frighteningly similar to the deadly SARS virus. In an even more unsettling development, Fouchier has moved to patent the genomic sequence of the MERS virus and is placing restrictions on who can have access to it.

The whole question of dual-use research is of great concern and something that I've put a significant amount of time into. We at the CFR are about to release a whole package of information about it from a policy perspective.

So Dan Brown isn't just making this stuff up.

Synthetic biology is real. The ability to construct microbes is real. Two years ago, Craig Venter, the biotechnologist, announced that he had successfully made a 100 percent previously non-existent species, an actual bacterial life form. This really got everybody's attention.

We have gone from the hypothetical to the all-too-real far faster than anybody thought we would. Craig Venter operates in the private sector, so his work was all outside of most of the regulatory systems that exist inside the United States government, much less the non-existent international regulatory apparatus.

It is becoming increasingly clear that viral genetic material can become a permanent part of the human genome. More and more of the human genome and of other higher-order animals turns out to have been originally a bacterial genome or a viral genome that ended up being inserted.

So to the degree this process has occurred, Brown is not wildly out of line. But there is nobody preparing anything of this kind that I'm aware of.

Can viruses be designed to attack one-third of the world's population randomly? Without people knowing they have it?

I think that this is a really crucial error in Dan Brown's book: he doesn't offer any way that this virus would be transmitted from one person to another. How is this getting around the world? There is a reason microbes have to cause symptoms. The symptoms are essential to transmission.

True, he tells us how, generically, airborne transmission of viruses occurs, which is accurate. And, yes, his WHO gang figures out that the epidemiology supports the notion that airborne transmission is happening, based on numbers of people having casual contacts.

But, that method of transmission doesn't refer specifically to the virus that has been unleashed by Zobrist. Moreover, Brown also asserts at the end of the book that the virus causes no symptoms and nobody would know who got it, who didn't, and therefore who was sterilized. So if people never get the sniffles or coughs, how are they transmitting the virus? The notion that you would have a massive scale of infection that results in the transformation of their genome without anybody knowing they were infected is not credible.

Should we be optimistic, then, that an individual bioterrorist isn't going to get a hold of this stuff in the next five or ten years and be able to wreak havoc?

Guardedly.

First, I think any would–be terrorist that has the sophistication to execute a genomically–based horror has a lot easier things that they can do to cause massive havoc than to a create a vector that carries genetic signaling into the human genome and alters it. I think nature shows us that it is capable, and natural evolution is capable, of providing us with more than enough horror. We don't need, really, to conjure nightmarish visions created in some man–made laboratory.

Second, the danger as I see it will not come from a single mad scientist. The greatest threat is from the astronomical proliferation of high-security research laboratories around the world, increasing the probability of an accidental release of viral material. Even in US top–security, bio–safety level four and bio–safety level three facilities, more than 100 researchers have become infected in the last ten years with agents they were studying. The idea that someone could accidentally get infected and then take it out into the community was borne out in 2005 in Beijing, when a research team accidentally released SARS in the lab. People infected with SARS went out into the community and infected others in Beijing.

That's the worry. We can't regulate nature. Something may be percolating that we have not anticipated and will be shocked by, as H7N9 showed us this year. But we can control our own research and, if we care enough, mitigate the dangers by doing more to regulate it.

— *Interviewed by Arne de Keijzer*

Transhumanism and the Promise of the Future

AN INTERVIEW WITH NATASHA VITA-MORE
Chairman, Board of Directors of Humanity+ and author of the "Transhumanist Manifesto"

As Dr. Elizabeth Sinskey informs Robert Langdon, transhumanism "transcend[s] the weaknesses inherent in our human bodies...[and uses] all the power at our disposal to improve us as a species."

That promise lies in a combination of artificial intelligence, genetic engineering, and human-computer integration to significantly enhance both our problem-solving and biological selves. The biological aspect includes the radical extension of human health and lifespan, eradication of disease, elimination of unnecessary suffering, and augmentation of intellectual, physical, and emotional capacity.

Natasha Vita-More is particularly interested in this latter aspect of the movement. Characterized by The New York Times *as "the first female philosopher of transhumanism," Vita-More authored the seminal "Transhumanist Manifesto" in 1983 and is currently Chair of the Board of Directors of Humanity+, a transhumanist organization that counts nearly 6,000 members.*

Asked for her opinions on the way transhumanism is portrayed in Inferno, *she makes it clear that the Zobrist approach is diametrically opposed to the goals of transhumanism. Although there may be some "extremists" attracted to the movement, she says, and wonders if Dan Brown might have met one of them, she assures us that transhumanism does not promote coercion in any form. Instead, it embraces individual choice and self-directed evolution. Vita-More also talks about the origins of the transhumanist movement, its relation to religion, the desire of some to change their names (her first name was originally Nancie), why she believes the gap between the wealthy and the poor will continue to narrow, and the promises of autonomy and diversity she believes transhumanism will bring. Readers wishing to delve more deeply into the movement might be interested in her new book,* The Transhumanist Reader: Classical and Contemporary Essays on the Science, Technology, and Philosophy of the Human Future, *co-edited with Max More.*

Zobrist, the man who believes in transhumanism so deeply that he has an H+ tattooed on his shoulder, turns out to be a bioterrorist. Readers might be forgiven if they end up with the impression that transhumanism, with its lofty goals, will instead bring us a harsh future. Was Dan Brown unfair to transhumanism?

It is evident that Brown has misinterpreted the scope of transhumanism and its cultural currency. Historically, we have witnessed the misuse of transhumanist ideals and attitudes in many literary contexts. The character Zobrist seems to be psychologically confused and may not even understand the ethical nature of transhumanism. Here we have a character that claims to be manipulating genes for the common good but is so out of touch that his behavior is more sociopathic than moral. He seems to be more of a conspiracy theorist than a rationalist. Anyone can borrow a term, or symbol, and use it for effect.

Transhumanism as a philosophical construct promotes inquiry into human existence as it relates to the future uses of technology to intervene with the limits of biology. As such, it advocates the proactive, ethical use of technology. This approach is contrary to the coercive actions of Zobrist in his attempt to manipulate society. Perhaps Zobrist's sequestering himself within his field and not being more of a cyberneticist or whole-systems theorist agitated his mind, resulting in his being psychologically distraught. While he may have a scholarly understanding of ethics and social values, he falls short in understanding long-range planning and systems thinking.

I also want to make it clear that transhumanists are not focused primarily on overpopulation. It is concerned with human enhancement on all fronts, from prolongevity to the environment. Like the vast majority of demographers, many transhumanists and futurists see that the population in some countries is declining and there is evidence that this could become a long-term trend globally.

Dan Brown writes that "H-plus is the symbol of the transhumanist movement." Is he correct, technically speaking?

While I realize some may think it is only a matter of typography, "H-plus" is not the codified symbol for the transhumanist movement. There are several ways to shorten the name of "transhumanism," and the most commonly used one is H+; i.e., the symbol for plus, not the word. To further clarify: Humanity+ is the name of the organization that put on the H+ Summit at Harvard to which Dan Brown refers, but because the symbol "+" cannot be used in domain names, our organizational website is "Humanityplus.org," no dash. Finally, a circled "h+" (not capitalized) is the logo for our online magazine.

Can you give our readers a brief overview of the roots of transhumanism and how it evolved from your perspective?

Humankind has always sought to understand existence and the process of evolution. We apply emerging technologies and scientific insights as tools to help form scenarios for resolving issues that have daunted humanity for eons, such as disease and death. Such technological innovations, coupled with the deeply exploratory nature of the human brain and its problem-solving capabilities, have triggered a passion among many people to seek still further and to dig more deeply.

So what are transhumanists seeking? For me, it is to resolve the age-old issue of disease and death. If humanity could intervene positively to overcome our biological limitations, imagine what life would be like! I don't mean this rhetorically—life would not be a state where each day we are aging and ultimately dying.

Reaching back to its roots, Dante used the verb *transumanare* or *transumanar*, which can be translated as "go outside the human condition and perception." T.S. Eliot used the word "transhuman- ized" in his play, *The Cocktail Party*. Ideas about humanity and evo- lution were also prominent in Julian Huxley's writings. Notably, Fereidoun M. Esfandiary, who changed his name to FM-2030, outlined the transhuman future in the late 1970s. In 1983, I authored the "Transhuman Manifesto," emphasizing radical life extension. However, the well-known philosophy of transhuman- *ism* was authored by Max More in 1989. The cultural movement had its roots in the Extropy Institute in the 1990s. The world- wide *society* of transhumanism emerged from the Extropy Institute and later the World Transhumanist Association, now known as Humanity+.

I should note that there is a difference between "transhuman- ism" and "the transhuman." Transhumanism is focused largely on a technology-directed evolution to enhance intellectual, physical, and psychological capacities. The transhuman pertains to a person who emphasizes self-directed human enhancement. Obviously, these two concepts are complementary—even integrative—and the tools devel- oped by the former will facilitate our ability to practice the latter.

Speaking of FM-2030, why do you think he was referenced directly in Brown's *Inferno*?

I do not know why he played off FM-2030 and the character FS-2080 (Sienna Brooks), other than to refer to a prominent indi- vidual. Maybe at some point Brown attended FM-2030's classes at UCLA or the New School in New York City and got some ideas and skewed them a bit for effect. Or maybe he attended an event FM and I hosted in Los Angeles. The Extropy email list was the first transhumanist list on the net, dating back to 1991, and it still is active. On the list have been some icons—Marvin Minsky, Eric Drexler, and others, so maybe Brown had been clandestinely on that list. Interestingly enough, I recall on a few instances an extremist that would come to an event, so it could be that Brown observed someone going off on a tangent about overpopulation. [Although Dan Brown was living in Hollywood in 1991/1992, there is no evidence he attended any of these events—*ed*.] Actually, this could have occurred anywhere. Many people come and go because they are attracted to the vanguard.

Transhumanism seems to mean a lot of things to a lot of different people and to speak in many voices, now and in the past. What is the common bond among people with such a broad range of interests? Is it a grounding in science fiction?

Science fiction has marvelous stories and a large audience, but human enhancement, radical life extension, cryogenics, and the Singularity are not about science fiction. They are concerned with human futures and, in the case of the Singularity, being aware of what could occur if supercomputing intelligence outperforms human intelligence. Transhumanism is fairly pragmatic, given the time frame we live in. Unique to transhumanists is a fun-loving *joie de vivre* plus a strong awareness that ethics are essential in all stages of how the future could play out.

Given *Inferno's* plot, it does not seem illogical for some to draw the conclusion that transhumanists may approve of using either overt or covert means for global genetic manipulation, or other technological means, to control the population.

Controlling people through an undisclosed, unilateral manner is coercive. Since transhumanism embraces individual choice, it is ethically, socially and politically inappropriate to coerce people, especially through something as dangerous as global genetic manipulation. This type of behavior is aggressive to a point of anti-social. A more logical way of looking at this is to educate people to be responsible about their lives. If people have enough knowledge to be responsible about their health, finances, families, etc., then they would be able to determine how many children it is wise to have. Given the state of things today, a person living on welfare would be irresponsible to keep having children.

Is there a religious, or at least a spiritual dimension to transhumanism?

Both sets of beliefs seek enlightenment, but religion is a system of faith and worship. Transhumanism is a system of critical thinking. Some transhumanists try to combine these two systems and rationalize religion, but the bottom line is that there is no "worship" within philosophical inquiry.

Nevertheless, critics of transhumanism believe it has a dark soul. Here are some of their arguments. While cognitive enhancement holds out the promise that people can become more productive, more intelligent, wealthier, and healthier, isn't it also true that it threatens to widen the gap between those who can afford to adopt the technology of transhumanism and those who can't? In other words, the post-human future may widen the gap between rich and poor, between the developed and developing world, between parents who can afford to "enhance" their children and those who can't.

One could say the same thing about television, computers, or the smart phone. Making this type of assumption simply does not make sense, because people have become freer, healthier, and more prosperous for the last century through broadening democratic processes and economic growth fostered in large part by capitalism. Let's look back over the eons: rulers had kingdoms; landlords had serfs; we can find evidence of wealthy having slaves throughout cultures. The gap between the wealthy and the poor has narrowed to a point where today even the poor have a television, a computer, or a smart phone. In most countries, anyone can go on the Internet at any time. Knowledge is power, and information is the most abundant resource we have today. We need, and are moving toward, a society where people become more and more aware and informed about their own lives and their environment, and encourage others to do so as well.

Critics say transhumanism is basically eugenics hiding under the promise of self-improvement. In the end, bio and genetic engineering, Singularity, the control over the length of a lifetime, and so on, will be coercive. We will lose our autonomy.

Eugenics has a terrible connotation because of the horrors committed in the past. Contrary to this tragic practice, transhumanism ardently supports the concept of morphological freedom, meaning that people have a right to enhance their bodies and the right not to be coerced to enhance their bodies. Coercive practices are anti-transhumanist. Human rights and transhuman rights are paramount.

People should have autonomy. With our right to choose what we want to become, some people may select to retire, grow old, and enjoy life. They may want to remain biological humans. Some may go back to school, develop new skills, and enjoy living longer. They may want to become transhuman. Either way, it is an individual's choice. The transhumanist perspective encourages self-responsibility, which, coupled with diversity, offers more freedom of choice and fewer universal dictates on what is the common assumption that all people on the planet ought to be characterized by a certain set of values. This notion simply does not work in a world that has numerous cultures and belief systems. The issue here is that we are changing and incorporating more technology in and around our lives. Everyone's life has been improved by technology, and our responsibility is to use technology as a tool that helps improve our lives, not threaten us.

The ethics of playing god with our own evolution, let alone society's, seems questionable at best. A transhuman or post-human future tells people: If you don't get with the program you get left behind.

If playing god means being aware of our physiological health and psychological state of mind, then this is a moral responsibility and an ethical thing to do. But confusing the notion of a religious God with the act of self-responsibility is an oxymoron because the term God in that context signifies the creator of the universe and ruler of people, not a personal choice for creating wellbeing and happiness.

The fear that any of us could fall behind and not keep up with the future, or with others, can be overwhelming. Imagine being on a sinking boat and there are only a few life rafts. Who gets on them? This is a twentieth century notion. In the twenty-first century, our ability to connect through the Internet, our openness on social interfaces such as Facebook, and our ability to communicate with people throughout the world easily, changes the dynamics of the sinking ship scenario. In other words, there are not just a few life rafts to fit a limited number of people.

You came to embrace transhumanism as part of the human quest to ward off death and do everything in our power to keep living. Is the aim of technology-driven humanism to give us the tools to achieve immortality?

Technology is a tool. A tool is made because there is a need that is not being met. One distinct need that is not being met for most people is how to stay alive as healthfully and as long as possible. The term immortality is actually a misnomer, because no one can absolutely guarantee to live forever (outside narratives of religious salvation or reincarnation). Instead, I use the phrase radical life extension, because the aim is to extend life beyond the biological maximum age with no definitive timeframe and with the option that a person can take a retreat from life, drop out for a while, and then reconnect.

I am also driven by a need to explore and a need for peace. The tension between these two objectives is apparent in the narratives of my work. Looking back over artistic works, performance art, videos, bioart narratives, and my future body prototype design, I have been connecting the dots (from atoms to pixels) between the human need to explore and the innate desire for love.

What do you think would be the ideal conditions under which society will be able to embrace transhumanism?

A confident society composed of people who have a sense of self-worth.

What kind of social, political, scientific, cultural, biological, and technological changes will we need?

The transhuman condition would be the result of an advanced inquiry into human potential, greater emphasis on diversity, a letting go of what has been drilled into the minds of people that there are universal norms that humans are required to live by. When we first went into space, there was a great joy of adventure and hope for the future. That is what we need today. We need a social paradigmatic shift where people would let go of their angst about each other and enjoy the amazing innovations we have at our fingertips. Just think about the fascinating results of the Internet, Facebook, TED, Humanity+, H+Lab and Transhumanist Knowledge and Media Center (both my projects), GF2045 Congress, Quantified Self, Institute for Ethics and Emerging Technologies, and so many more inspiring projects.

In the end, do you think Dan Brown helped the cause of transhumanism, or damaged it? Did he make it sound like a conspiracy in the way he made the Illuminati the dark side of *Angels & Demons*? Or did he endorse transhumanism as a way to the future, with the "good" side of his character Sienna?

There is something to be said about good outwitting evil, so Sienna is a marvelous character. But I think transhumanism would make a thrilling and dramatic story if presented as it really is, overcoming human limitations, namely death (not overpopulation), and the unique characters that have represented it over the past thirty years. Transhumanism is a love story between humans and life. At any moment, it could be gone.

— *Interviewed by Arne de Keijzer*

"Whether You Think the Future Makes Sense or It Doesn't, It is Here. Get Used to It."

AN INTERVIEW WITH DAVID ORBAN
Futurist, CEO of Dotsub, and former chairman of Humanity+

David Orban is not mentioned by name in Inferno, *but his presence is palpable. He was behind the true-life notices posted all over the Harvard campus announcing an H+ Summit thought by Robert Langdon at the time to be "some kind of chemistry conference" (Chapter 67). Orban was one of the organizers of that summit and served as its chairman. His stated goal was to "cut across the limits of deep specialization of people concerned with the impact of technology on the human condition" and bring them together under the umbrella of transhumanism.*

Orban himself is deeply immersed in the search for that moment when computers will be linked directly to human intelligence, both as an entrepreneur—he is CEO of Dotsub—and teacher on the faculty of and an advisor to the Singularity University, an interdisciplinary university whose mission is to "educate, inspire, and empower leaders to apply exponential technologies to address humanity's grand challenges."

Our interview was wide-ranging, but several larger themes stood out. One is Orban's view that human enhancement technologies are not a zero-sum game. Another is the need to protect the rights of all individuals to make their own choices, including those who want to participate in enhancement technologies and those who don't. Orban also reminded us that biological evolution is an ongoing river—its flow doesn't stop with us. The accumulation of knowledge and the continual work to apply it to our biology will not stop. Change will continue whether we wish it to or not. The challenge is to create the technologies— and the ethics—that will help us move to the next stage. As for those who charge transhumanists with wanting to liberate the human race from its biological contract, Orban pleads guilty, and happily so, noting that there is nothing sacred in biology.

Dan Brown uses the Humanity+ Summit held at Harvard in 2010 as a plot point that in effect associates the philosophy of the bioterrorist Bertrand Zobrist with the concepts of transhumanism. You were the organizer of that conference, and bioengineering was one of the many subjects on the agenda. Was Zobrist there?

I looked up the list of registered attendees and I can confirm that there was nobody called Zobrist at the conference, nor Dan Brown for that matter. At least not under their own names . . . .

More seriously, you were chairman of Humanity+ at the time. What were the goals of the Summit and what were its accomplishments?

Humanity+ is an international nonprofit membership organization that, under the banner of transhumanism, advocates the ethical use of technology to expand human capacities. At the beginning of 2010, Alex Lightman (the Executive Director of Humanity+) and I thought that the time was right to have a conference that would synthesize what are otherwise often distinct domains of expertise: technology, business, social change, media, human-computer integration, and so on. We wanted to motivate mind-shifting ideas and bring them to a wider audience.

The event was very successful. With more than fifty speakers and about 500 attendees over two days, live streamed to thousands of additional viewers worldwide, we achieved our goal of bringing our themes to a wide audience. I am especially proud of how many of our speakers went on with their research, radically novel at the time, and won prizes as well as academic and financial support. Ed Boyden, for example, gave a talk on "Controlling Brain Circuits with Light," and in 2013 he won the Grete Lundbeck European Brain Research Prize. Stephen Wolfram spoke for the first time about the ontological consequences of his worldview and the principle of computational equivalence that he formulated.

Is Dan Brown fair to transhumanism? He seems to write positively about aspects of the movement, but then there is the anti-hero, Zobrist, who believes in transhumanist principles so deeply that he has an H+ tattooed on his shoulder and turns out to be a genetic terrorist. Readers might be forgiven if they end up with the impression that transhumanism will bring us a harsh future.

It is a given that a thriller, in book form or as a movie, will be more successful representing a dangerous situation and a menacing future, rather than Utopia. A partial representation in support of his plot line and of the narrative tension can be appropriate. So I am not bothered about the question of "fairness."

Real-world transhumanism is a very rich and complex philosophy, encompassing disparate views, some of which are actually quite mainstream, while others that are seemingly radical now are bound to be absorbed by the global consciousness. Still others are going to stay radical for a long time or forever. What they have in common is the belief that the acceleration of technological applications can have a beneficial impact on the daily lives of billions of people.

As technology evolves, increasing energy availability, food productivity, manufacturing capability, and the speed and depth of information and knowledge available to all, it is up to us to decide how we want to apply it, and to find new ways to organize it, in order to live our lives and progress towards our individual and collective goals.

One of the major themes of that 2010 H+ Summit was the increasing democratization of science and the emerging promise of the citizen scientist. Dan Brown makes the case that this could be an extremely dangerous proposition. Do you share that concern?

For the past 500 years, every change that took away power from an elite and made it more widely or universally available has been met with agitated, sometimes hysterical, and even repeatedly violent reactions. Do you dare to read the Bible in your own language rather than hear it passed from the pulpit in the Latin version as it was for centuries? Blasphemous heretic! Do you think that women should vote, and that their brain is capable of absorbing the information needed, or that they should work outside of the home? You'll destroy society! And so on . . .

There is no question that giving the power of scientific inquiry—both theoretical and experimental—to everybody is as risky and as exhilarating as these and many other changes. It will bring the possibility of mistakes and dangers that have to be contained, or at least minimized.

Of course, we have to develop guidelines on how to responsibly handle the power of these rapidly evolving technologies. Only an open, rich, and articulated public debate can make progress toward the right balance in the use of these tools.

A great example of this is the Asilomar Conference of 1975, where the nascent field of molecular biology saw its practitioners agree on guidelines on how to responsibly handle the power of this new technology. Those guidelines remain in effect to this day. MIT's yearly IGEM (International Genetically Engineered Machines) competition is among the best current attempts to broaden and popularize the understanding of what synthetic biology can do, and how to use it for the good of humanity.

Individuals do not need official seals of approval to use their head. There is nothing better than allowing them to think, learn, and prepare.

Dan Brown is certainly on point when he notes that we have huge, multiple crises to overcome, among them economic uncertainty, climate change, social and political upheavals, and rapid population growth. Still, those in favor of human enhancement technologies seem a generally optimistic lot, believing in our collective resilience.

There is no guarantee that we will find a solution to all of our challenges forever. We can only try, and in my opinion only technology and its advances can allow us to progress in this search for solutions. Human civilization has gotten where it is now, for the good and the bad, through the progressive acquisition of knowledge. Yes, we have multiple, huge crisis situations to overcome. My bet is that further knowledge and the spreading of the tools to acquire and apply that knowledge will get us through these crises.

Relinquishing technology, abandoning the illuministic program of understanding the world through reason, is a choice we are free to make. But that will guarantee that our civilization doesn't survive. There are indeed those who appear to want that, and who see a positive in this apocalyptic outcome. Fortunately, at least for the moment, they have not been able to impose their will. Education, learning, research, and applications of our understanding to the problems we face continue. With the right policies and with a little bit of luck, things can actually go well.

Critics of transhumanism believe it has a dark side. Cognitive enhancement may hold out the promise that social productivity increases dramatically and that people become wealthier, healthier, and generally freer, but that is for a small elite. It could also widen the gap between rich and poor, the educated and not, and the developed and underdeveloped world. Another line of argument has been put forward by Francis Fukuyama, the Stanford political scientist and social commentator, who basically accuses transhumanism of wanting "nothing less than to liberate the human race from its biological constraints." Shouldn't we be worried about that? Aren't the ethics of our increasing ability to play god with our own evolution highly dubious on legal, humanistic, and religious grounds?

One of the great challenges of the future, which is already showing up today, is going to be the way society will need to structure itself to respect the right of those who do not want to participate in the enhancements that are available. In the past, we have been horribly unable to realize the inhumanity of our actions, or we chose to ignore them. Nevertheless, with some "enhancement" of knowledge we came to an understanding of how those who choose not to participate should be handled. Society must find ways to correctly balance the right of the individual and that of the group, and the solutions will not be universal, but have to be wisely understood in each context.

Human history very clearly shows that our trajectory is not a zero-sum game. We don't gain only if others lose. When we learn something and apply that knowledge, everybody wins; we all progress. The positive applications of technology are not in balance with the negative ones; the first vastly outweighs the second.

As for Fukuyama's accusation, guilty as charged. There is nothing sacred in biology, which itself is happy to exterminate millions of species in its natural evolutionary process as it discovers new ways of doing things. One of the most radical changes occurred two billion years ago, when the anaerobic bacteria that dominated the planet for a billion years were almost totally wiped out by oxygen breathing ones, and relegated to forgotten niches under the ocean close to volcanic vents. Is there dignity in a child dying of diarrhea at age four? Is it the honorable thing to suffer from cancer for years, rather than opposing cancer, finding its causes, and if possible curing it? Nature is not sacred, illness is not to be respected, dying is not good.

What would be the ideal conditions under which society will be able to embrace transhumanism? What kind of social, political, scientific, cultural, biological, and technological changes will we need? And how will we know if we have reached the transhumanist epoch?

There is no there, there. You can't go to Google Maps and search for the path toward the country of Transhumanism, unless you misspell it Transylvania.

An open, strong society that recognizes its challenges and opportunities, that provides individuals with increasing degrees of freedom, and where the future is proactively designed rather than blindly stumbled upon, is one that will be richer, not only in material goods, but also in the broad spectrum of opportunities and choices that it gives to its members.

Another benefit is that the more robust a society, the more it can afford to be tolerant—tolerant toward different ways of life, different goals, desires, behaviors. We have to be careful, however, not to fall into a trap of false symmetries. Tolerance is desirable, tolerance of intolerance is not. You can't earn my respect by imposing restrictions on freedoms and then, hiding within the rules of an open society, designing closed cultures of restriction.

Bioengineering and genetic manipulation have gone mainstream, and the tools for using them are better and better known and easier and easier to put our hands on. Do you fear a future Zobrist? Are there any second thoughts about the road forward, or at least cautions? Is there a role for the government, or should it stay out of the way and let science and the free market proceed unrestricted?

Being cautious and avoiding risk at all cost is the accepted principle today, the precautionary principle. The opposing view, the proactionary principle, takes into account the opportunity cost of inaction. What good would we *not* do if we are paralyzed by our risk analysis?

Yes, smart solutions require constant vigilance. No given approach is valid forever. Just because market forces appear to find optimal ways to allocate certain resources, it doesn't mean that only market forces can do so, or that they always will. The interactions of individuals, corporations, and society require a constant reevaluation of what the best tools are in different situations. Antitrust, regulatory bodies, international treaties, public debates, professional associations, open standards, certifications . . . are only a few of the tools that are at our disposal and that we have to use, refine, and apply as appropriate.

Dan Brown has said that his books are an expression of his search to balance religion and science. We have talked about the science. Does transhumanism also offer a belief system?

The transhumanist philosophy doesn't require a naturalistic world view, but it has little to say about metaphysical components of those who need religion to make sense of the world. Our incomplete understanding of the universe is not a sign of anything more than our ignorance. Our desire to learn more and overcome that ignorance is a fundamental part of the philosophy.

So what is going to happen? How will humanity change? How will humans adapt to a world that is shaped by their technological creations?

Humanity+, which represents the world's transhumanist associations, is dedicated to proactively exploring the space of possible answers to these and other questions without Pollyanna-ishly naïve optimism, but rather with a rational, non-zero-sum analysis, unclouded by dogmatic prescriptions.

So what is the future going to bring us? It is going to bring us a lot of change. And whether you agree with the direction of this change, whether you think this makes sense or it doesn't make sense, it is here. Get used to it.

— *Interviewed by Arne de Keijzer*

Nothing Is Going to Be the Same

AN INTERVIEW WITH GREGORY STOCK
Biophysicist, biotech entrepreneur, and founding director of the Program on Medicine, Technology and Society at UCLA's School of Medicine

It would be surprising if Gregory Stock's many thought-provocations on the biotech revolution had not influenced Dan Brown in his research for Inferno. *Among other things, Dr. Stock contemplated as far back as 1987 in his* Book of Questions *a virus remarkably similar in its impact on population growth to the one Dan Brown has used in his plot: a birth control virus. Stock, who used the idea of a virus like this to raise challenging questions to get society ready for the issues coming our way in the twenty-first century, tells us that he enjoyed discovering that Dan Brown had transferred his hypothetical ethical question into a significant element of* Inferno's *plot.*

In this interview, Stock explains his idea about the virus further. He also offers a series of remarkable observations on recent evolutionary advances in human biology, the need for individual trial and error in laboratory experiments, the ethical issues raised by our increasing ability to be gods of our own evolution, and his concept of a global superorganism in which humans are as intimately interconnected with the tools of technology as the cells in our own bodies.

Dr. Stock is a leading authority on the broad impacts of genomic and other advanced technologies in the life sciences. His books include Redesigning Humans: Our Inevitable Genetic Future;

Engineering the Human Germline; Metaman: The Merging of Humans and Machine into a Global Superorganism; *and the bestselling* Book of Questions. *He is also currently Chief Scientific Officer of Ecoeos, a personal genomics company, and serves on the boards of Signum Biosciences and Napo Pharmaceuticals.*

Gregory Stock was the founder and director of the influential Program on Medicine, Technology and Society at UCLA's School of Medicine. The program, begun in 1997, was designed to explore critical technologies poised to have an impact on humanity's future and the reshaping of medical science. Interestingly, Fereidoun M. Esfandiary, the founder of transhumanism known by his code name FM-2030 (and referenced by Dan Brown in Inferno*), also taught at UCLA, offering related courses in the 1980s. What would Robert Langdon make of that?*

What do you think of the "Zobrist scenario," the ability of a billionaire biochemist to create a mammal-to-mammal virus that will change someone's DNA?

To alter an existing virus to modify someone's genetics is easy and already being done routinely in animal research and various human trials. To do so broadly to everyone, and in the nuanced way that Zobrist does, is an entirely different story. The idea that one person could design and execute a present-day version of the Black Plague, much less a novel birth control virus such as that described in the book, is unrealistic. Early attempts would fail and have many secondary consequences. Enormous learning from trial-and-error would be needed, as well as many conceptual breakthroughs. This is not about some abstract clearly defined puzzle, it's about ourselves as organisms and how we work. It's about biological complexities and redundancies and interwoven connections, and we are at an early stage in our understandings in these realms. Designing a virus such as Brown describes would require a long process of effort and insights, of developing *ad hoc* solutions to a sequence of challenging problems. It would build on failures. It would not be the product of some brilliant insight or two by a mad genius. But for a work of fiction, the concept is a good one, and the novel is a page-turner.

Creating a highly contagious virus that did not show any symptoms either in the person transmitting it or in the person contracting it might be theoretically possible, but seems highly unlikely. It is incidental to the plot development in any event.

Didn't you once express your own idea for a birth-control virus that would control population growth?

Yes, in *The Book of Questions*, my best selling collection of provocative dilemmas, first published in 1987 and just revised and rereleased. The book touches on quite a few issues related to the biotech revolution. The particular question you're thinking of went something like this: "Someone worried about population growth releases a virus that renders every woman sterile in any month she doesn't take a cheap fertility pill. The person turns himself in, claiming he's saved the world by making it take a conscious effort to conceive a child. What should be his punishment? Would you release such a virus? How much do you think it would reduce pop-ulation growth?"

I enjoyed seeing Dan Brown run with this issue so effectively. I never tire of these sorts of questions. They catalyze stimulating conversation.

Stepping back and thinking about the big picture, there is a general impression that significant evolutionary advances in human biology will occur in the not-so-distant future. What do you think?

Meaningful changes in human biology will require quite a few generations, I suspect. But two massive evolutionary break-throughs are underway right now. They are absolutely unprecedented, not just in human history but also in the history of life.

The first is the silicon revolution. Nonliving material is being infused with a level of complexity that rivals life itself. In essence, we are awakening the inanimate world—animating the inanimate. Nothing will ever be the same.

The second is the biotech revolution, a child of the silicon revolution. Life has begun to achieve an awareness of its intimate workings at such a level of sophistication and nuance that it is beginning to alter, adjust, and control its own processes. We have as yet taken only a few baby steps, and unsteady, sometimes clumsy ones at that, but they are of enormous significance. Life is seizing control of its own evolutionary future, and again, nothing will ever be the same.

Consider the possibilities being unleashed. Life is animating the world, gaining control over its own processes, and melding biology and technology. Humans are transforming themselves through prostheses, implants, pharmaceuticals, vaccines, and a blur of technology that we are surrounded by, immersed in, and intimately tied to; for example, our cell phones, computers, Internet connections, and such.

Will these lead to our being able to reshape our own biology? Of course. And why would we not do that? When have we ever in our history not used technologies that large numbers of us see as beneficial in one way or another? We struggle to understand and cure cancer and other diseases, spending huge amounts of money trying to develop relatively uncontroversial therapies.

Success in these efforts will demand intimate understanding of cells and living processes. But with such understandings will come the power to achieve far more controversial possibilities: altering reproduction, enhancing immune response, even controlling aging or extending life span. We cannot know in advance which such possibilities will be realized first or which will prove intractable. But without a doubt, once such technology becomes available—and probably well before it is either safe or reliable—it will be broadly employed.

Is it damn the torpedoes and full speed ahead then? If we can do this, will we do it? Won't we worry about potentially disastrous consequences?

Yes, we will do these things if they are possible, and yes, we will fret endlessly about the potential consequences. Both lines of reasoning are all too human. But looking more deeply at this issue, I think that too many people look at the world and ask themselves something like the following: "If I were God and could control and shape it, how would I redesign the world? Which technologies would I allow? Which would I restrict?" To me, this is a silly game. It is a conceit. The world is what it is. There are powerful dynamics at work in it. And we control much less about the future than we think. Why not try to understand the forces at play and where they are carrying us, and how we might align that process with our values?

When I reflect about the possibilities of the future, I don't think that we are headed towards some perfect realm. There will be many wonderful things, but there will be problems as well, many even more significant than those of today. But we cannot go back, and I suspect that from the vantage point of someone a century or more from now, the present time will seem quite magical.

Magical? Do you mean that people a few generations from now will look back and actually romanticize this moment? That is a startling notion.

Dan Brown's book refers to the Black Death, when a third of the population died in the middle of the fourteenth century. But any real understanding of that hell has largely faded from view, and its aftermath is somewhat romanticized in the book, just as it tends to be in the general culture. Yes, there were dire consequences from the Black Death, but society survived. The plague didn't derail civilization, it signaled the birth of the Renaissance, a time we see as uniquely creative, almost magical.

When people look back at this moment they won't think of it as the time when we destroyed the planet. They will overlook our many difficulties, just as we do when we look back at early eras like Greece or Rome. Human endeavor is not fragile and teetering on a precipice as sketched by Brown. The human enterprise is far more robust than most people believe or admit. And some of that may be because it is so disorienting to imagine what the world might become with even a century of technological advance at the current pace.

Our emerging capacity to modify biology and animate technology will be the cornerstone of future society and of the lives of future humans, whoever or whatever they become. Would it be surprising if future humans looked back at this transitional moment with a sense of wonder? This is when it all began. Future humans may well say: "What a moment to have been alive, to have watched these amazing developments and to have been their architects."

Which brings us back to the question of "we." Should control of our biological future reside solely in the hands of individual scientists, with its risk of negative consequences, intended or not? Or does the "we" mean government-created, cautious protocols to try to prevent the obvious risks and dangers?

Progress today is emergent. There is no script. Control does not reside in the hands of a few scientists because no one is in control. We each play our parts, but it is hard to say, even in hindsight, which parts were the most critical. The dynamic for change is powerful and the future largely obscure to us. But if it comes to what to worry about, I think that government abuse should be much higher on the list than individuals who freely do research or make genetic choices about themselves and their families. Most people are actually pretty responsible about such choices, because they want to better their lives, and they know that if they make a bad mistake, they and their families will be the ones to suffer the consequences. Who wants to serve as a cautionary tale for others? Unvetted technology applied broadly is what generally causes the biggest problems. This is our real danger, and it is generally the province of governments, particularly ones convinced of the rectitude of their own designs and showing less caution, since it is usually not the decision-makers themselves who suffer from mistakes.

With cloning, extended longevity, and so on, we need to be careful about potential problems. But the real danger is broad implementation from on high, rather than engaging in diverse trial and error at an individual level. In fact, we need the small mistakes, because they purchase collective wisdom for making better choices.

Let's go back to the symbiotic relationship between human culture and technology. What will come from the joining of these two?

Extraordinary possibilities and lots of problems. A global superorganism is being born. Let me elaborate. Life on earth exists at only a few levels of organizational complexity, and breakthroughs to a new level have happened only a few times in the history of life. For billions of years after life first arose there were only bacterial cells, essentially little bags of biochemistry. Then eukaryotic cells evolved. These advanced cells are a million times larger, have separate internal compartments and structures—a nucleus that houses the cell's DNA, mitochondria that produces energy, and so on—many with bacterial origins. Thus, the transition to this next organizational level was the result of symbiotic associations of organisms at the previous level. Such symbiosis repeated itself over a half-billion years ago, when complex multi-cellular life arose from complementary, cooperative, interacting associations among these complex single cells and ultimately produced all of today's large life forms. And now a new transition is occurring, toward a global superorganism in which humans are as intimately interconnected as the cells in our own bodies. We are glued together by complex technologies: computer, telecommunications, and transportation systems to name a few.

Moreover, this new layer of quasi-biological organization manifests the same biological systems as other more familiar life forms. We see metabolic processes, where nutrients such as chemicals, oil, and energy are distributed through the system, processes for eliminating wastes, cognitive functions arising from layers of interwoven interpersonal and computational activities facilitated and multiplied by the Internet and other hi-tech neural-network-like connections. A sort of global mind has already come into being from this rapidly intensifying activity.

Our individual understanding of this global entity and its timescales is necessarily modest. But we're now living within a throbbing global whir of activity that is a very lifelike integration of technology and biology into a powerful new organizational level of being. Technology and biology are not in opposition, they are aligned and growing ever more mutually linked and interdependent.

Just think, you can travel between London and Tokyo and remain under a roof the entire way. People in cities do not even begin to grow enough food to sustain themselves; they depend on a vast network of farms, trucks, railroads, highways, storage depots, food processing and distribution systems, and all the technological, financial, and cultural systems that support and integrate these activities. This global human-centered superorganism is not some abstract future construct. It is here and now.

These are the kinds of concepts and possibilities being discussed by the transhumanists that Brown refers to. These are the possibilities that Zobrist was afraid would never be reached.

Brown's novel suggests that humanity is racing towards a cliff, perhaps while trying to strap a hang glider onto its back. For many, the idea of such an imminent reckoning is almost comforting, not only because such a looming catastrophe can be used to justify anything one believes will make a difference—for example, Zobrist's release of an infertility virus—but because it allows us to avoid seriously thinking about where the world might really be headed, those unsettling and unfamiliar possibilities ahead of us on many, many fronts.

So, while I agree that we may face disasters of one sort or another, I think it very unlikely that they'll approach the scale needed to threaten the overall entity—this super organism that is the manifestation of human endeavor and the vessel housing civilization. I disagree with Dan Brown's underlying thesis that the world is fragile and nearing catastrophe, that just a little more population growth would put us over the edge. That vision is great for the dramatic tension he needs in the novel, but it greatly underestimates the robustness of the evolutionary transition now underway. Life is penetrating to a new level of organizational complexity, and it is hardly surprising that this birth, like any other, is messy and chaotic.

Critics of controlling our own evolution believe that, while it sounds beneficial, the results will only be beneficial to some. Greater divisions in society will arise, like a wider gulf between the enhanced and unenhanced, between the rich, who can afford to alter the DNA of their children to make them smarter, and the poor, who will be left sitting in the back of the class, or between those in developed and developing countries. What are your thoughts on this?

I think this reflects a fundamental misunderstanding of the nature of technology. An instructive example of how technology actually infuses into society can be found with computers. Twenty years ago, the richest person in the world could not have purchased a computer that could hold a candle to what anyone in the middle class can get today. The same is true of phones or medical technology. If you were massively wealthy and could, for example, construct your own Internet, it would be useless because its value comes from the participation of others. The same holds for genetics. Knowing your own personal genome—at a cost of tens of millions of dollars less than a decade ago—would have been of little value to you. Only as the cost of obtaining genetic information began to get low enough to look at the genetics of lots of people and correlate it with detailed information about health status did personalized genetics and healthcare become possible.

The real gulf is not between the rich and the poor. It is between one generation and the next. A child born today will have access to technologies that today's adults will never see. And the same is true of whole societies. Exploding middle classes in India and China have ready access to cell phones that were unavailable a generation ago to the wealthiest individuals in the wealthiest nations on Earth.

You don't seem to worry much about the ethics of all of this. Perhaps you think these changes will inevitably happen and the ethics will take care of themselves.

I would recharacterize that: Most ethical discussions in this realm involve crude abstractions of reality and operate at a symbolic level far removed from the complexity of the real possibilities now emerging. It is almost like arguing about how many angels can dance on the head of a pin.

The most meaningful ethical concerns I see are those that relate to specific, concrete situations we actively grapple with all the time. Key issues in medicine like whether people give informed consent, understanding the choices and risks they face, are put at added risk for purely experimental purposes. Is it ethical, for example, to force people whose only hope of life is some experimental drug into a clinical study where they have a fifty-fifty chance of getting a placebo?

Interestingly, if you look closely at the moral arguments people have made about new technologies like *in-vitro* fertilization (IVF), stem cells, genetic engineering, or cloning, you'll find virtually the same arguments being repeated for each new technology. The unfamiliar is threatening until it becomes more familiar. *In-vitro* fertilization was staunchly opposed by those like Jeremy Rifkin and Leon Kass, who later came to accept it and then repeated almost identical arguments to oppose cloning.

As for safety, we are better off making little mistakes that help us understand the true risks we face, rather than worrying in advance about every potential danger we can imagine. We need real information about both risks and rewards before we can decide how best to balance them or seriously discuss what's right and what will serve us.

Agonizing about imagined moral and ethical choices involving ill-defined future technologies is hardly the way to shape technology policy. Our ignorance is too deep. I try instead to understand the realities of new technology and communicate their challenging implications. As for controls, I think people should be given information and allowed to make their own choices until real problems arise that must be collectively handled.

If I had access to a longevity pill, what would be the chances that I'd use it?

If people could take a pill to triple their vital lifespans, so that they'd be functioning at the level of activity and intellect of a fifty-year-old until they were, say, 150, most people would take the pill. Sure, they might be opposed to life extension at a philosophical level, but as long as there are more appealing possibilities than debility and decrepitude, few seem willing to go gently into the night to make way for others. We try so hard to cure cancer and heart disease and avoid age-related illnesses. So, if I could actually offer you that pill, I suspect you'd ultimately take it. And I think that once enhancement technologies exist, people will almost certainly use them. Banning them would merely drive them underground and reserve them for the wealthy, who are best positioned to circumvent such restrictions.

If you were asked to design an optimal path for a massive program for the development of technology such as human genetic engineering, what would it look like?

Not so different from what is occurring today. We'd be putting a lot of money into understanding our genome, into dropping the cost of genetic sequencing, and into unraveling the biology of various diseases. We'd be putting a lot of effort into IVF, embryo handling and storage—which are major focal points of infertility research today—and we'd be learning how to manipulate genetic vectors, another focus of current research.

One thing that would be different, though, is that I'd simplify and reduce today's regulatory constraints on clinical research, making it much easier for well-informed individuals to knowingly use new, inherently risky therapeutics. Our present regulatory regime inhibits the translation of biotech breakthroughs into useful therapeutics, without bringing us much additional safety. We need a regulatory environment that better balances considerations of risks and rewards. Inaction carries a price.

If enhancement technologies become potent, which I think may well happen within the next couple of generations, a radiation of new developments will occur. Biology will become more like technology, and our biology may gradually transform in ways that reflect our beliefs and values. And if that happens, things will become very strange in the coming centuries.

Strange, but life-altering in a profoundly affirmative sense, I presume.

I hope so, but you never know for sure. It's such a privilege to be able to observe this extraordinary transition in the evolution of life and the changes underway today. I take pride in being in the midst of it too, because we, as individuals, as a society, as a civilization, are the architects of this amazing transition. The reason, of course, that this is so challenging for everyone is that we're more than observers and architects; we're also the objects of this. This is about our futures and those of our families and friends. It should be quite a ride. We definitely live in interesting times.

— *Interviewed by Arne de Keijzer*

Section 3
Dan Brown Decoded

Dan Brown, the Infernal Novelist

BY DAVID A. SHUGARTS
Investigative reporter, author of *Secrets of the Widow's Son*, and contributing editor to the *Secrets* series

David A. Shugarts has contributed some of the most interesting and memorable commentaries to our Secrets *series of books about the fiction of Dan Brown, beginning with our bestselling* Secrets of the Code *in 2004.*

Trained as an investigative reporter, Shugarts has been the first to crack a number of Dan Brown's codes and puzzles over the last decade. He found the famous message left by Brown on the cover flaps of The Da Vinci Code—*bolded letters that spelled out, "Is there no help for the widow's son?"—and deduced from there that Dan Brown's next book would be set in Washington, DC, and feature the Freemasons and their role in American History.*

In 2005, Shugarts published Secrets of the Widow's Son, *a book that sought to analyze and predict what would be in Dan Brown's next book before Brown had even published it. As it turned out, it took Dan Brown four more years to publish his next book,* The Lost Symbol. *But when TLS finally arrived in 2009, it turned out to be set in Washington, DC, against the backdrop of the Freemasons, just as Shugarts had predicted. Moreover, Shugarts had made over 100 specific content predictions that were proven correct. These ranged from things like Albrecht Durer's Melancolia II playing a role in the plot to the moon rocks in the stained glass windows of the National Cathedral showing up in the story. One European blogger wondered: During those long years that Dan Brown was working on* TLS, *maybe he had developed a bad case of writer's block—and turned to Shugarts'* Secrets of the Widow's Son *for ideas!*

For our 2006 paperback edition of Secrets of the Code, *Shugarts wrote a 20,000 word mini-biography of Dan Brown that remains the most insightful commentary into the personal and intellectual life experiences shaping Brown as an author and thinker.*

In the following essay, Shugarts probes Dan Brown's Inferno *for codes, plot flaws, and mistakes of various kinds, and also looks at the riches of Florence that Dan Brown chose not to include in his latest novel. David A. Shugarts, your captain for this excursion, may be the world's leading expert on the mind of Dan Brown. Enjoy the voyage.*

Each upcoming Dan Brown novel sends me into a heightened mode of anticipation, and that's a big part of the fun. It's a truly pleasurable experience to pre-wander through history, art, and literature, guessing what secret lore will be revealed in a new Robert Langdon novel. And when the book arrives, there is always a strong plot to compel me to turn the pages—and often a series of plot flaws to stoke the engines of my interest and further research.

So it is with *Inferno*, Dan Brown's fourth novel in the Robert Langdon series and the latest since 2009's *The Lost Symbol* (*TLS*). That novel followed *The Da Vinci Code* (*DVC*) in 2003 and *Angels & Demons* (*A&D*) in 2000.

However, one of the most striking things about *Inferno* is that we have seen a pronounced drop in the plethora of codes, ciphers, and puzzles that we had come to expect, both contained in a Dan Brown novel itself and in the pre-publicity. The puzzle quest has been a major attraction for me and a number of other readers, some of whom are much more energized by these quests than by the content of the books themselves.

Harking back to the summer of 2009, Dan Brown's publishers spared no effort in pre-publicity for *TLS*, with several months' worth of intense challenges, played out on Facebook and Twitter and Dan Brown's websites. There were well over 100 clues, riddles, puzzles, rebuses, and arcane symbols. Eager fans raced to identify and solve them. The eventual contest in the countdown to the release of the book led to the award of thirty-three signed copies of *TLS*.

For *Inferno*, the pre-publicity effort was not in the same league. It involved only a few dozen clues disseminated through social media, a smartphone app, and the award of only seven signed copies. It seems quite evident that the publishers made a pencil calculation and concluded that they could not justify a *TLS*-level effort.

And the book itself has very few puzzles and only one "code," the reshuffled advice *cerca trova* ("seek and find") that is found on a flag on a Giorgio Vasari mural. Perhaps more importantly, *Inferno* has none of the participatory nature of previous novels. Whether it was the urge to rotate a copy of *A&D* to read the ambigrams, or to ponder the pyramid's symbols in *TLS*, Dan Brown had always engaged the reader in the chase. In *Inferno*, readers are basically stuck watching Robert Langdon stumble along the trail. No reader could ever have guessed that *cerca trova* would somehow lead to Dante's death mask. And once the riddle written on the Dante mask is revealed, it is entirely up to Langdon to solve it.

Early in the book, Brown chose two symbols to depict graphically (the "biohazard" symbol and the tragedy/comedy masks). It looked as though there might be a lot of symbols for readers to view, perhaps of significance to the plot. But then the spigot was turned off and, for the rest of the 463-odd pages, there were no further symbols. I thought for sure he would remark about the crest of the Medici family, which can be seen practically everywhere in Florence. It has a number of "balls" and it sparks no end of puns among tourists and travel writers. (The balls are actually thought to be pills, since the Medicis were said to have started in the medicine business.)

A hallmark of Dan Brown's previous novels was the presence, either actual or implied, of nefarious groups of conspirators. Whether it be shadowy factions of the Catholic Church, the Illuminati, or the traditional chart toppers of conspiracy groups, the Freemasons, Dan Brown took on the heavyweights. In *Inferno*, the two "conspiracy" groups are the World Health Organization and the Consortium, his anonymized name for a company that, among other services, specializes in providing alibis for people who want to cheat on spouses. Sorry, this just isn't in the same league as the Illuminati!

But you do have to give Dan Brown credit for his choice of a villain and his mission to spread a "plague." Global overpopulation does pose a mega-problem, a higher order of magnitude than, say, blowing up the Vatican with an antimatter bomb, as in *Angels &Demons*. *Inferno* turns out to be more topical and a more issues-oriented book than most of his prior works.

Treasures of Florence

As I anticipated the release of *Inferno*, I delved into many aspects of Dante's beloved Florence, its history, art, architecture, and culture, attempting to guess at things that Dan Brown would simply have to include. When the release date came, I had the pleasure of seeing some of the items on my list emerge in the novel. But a lot of items I was most interested in seeing how he would treat were either overlooked or left on the cutting room floor. Here is a smattering of hits and misses:

Florence boasts a number of foods that are special (it is renowned for gelato), but there is one dish that I was sure Dan Brown would mention: *lampredotto*. And sure enough, he did. He put it on the very first page of the narrative! What I didn't anticipate was that he would hold his tongue and not explain what *lampredotto* is. Usually served in a sandwich, it is a form of tripe, in this case the fourth stomach of the cow. It is a Florentine peasant's dish handed down from centuries ago but still popular today. You can still buy it fresh on the streets of old Florence but . . . why would you want to?

When you learn about the Vasari Corridor, the not-so-secret passageway snaking its way from the Palazzo Pitti across the Ponte Vecchio all the way to the Palazzo Vecchio, you can easily see something Dan Brown would just have to incorporate in *Inferno*. He did, of course, making it a central part of the extended chase sequence. In order to work it in, he had Langdon and Sienna begin at the Porta Romana, jump the wall into the Boboli Gardens, and scurry to the Palazzo Vecchio. The sculpture and architecture that are mentioned in this sequence are great, of course, but it ignores the vast Uffizi Gallery, a treasurehouse of art that easily equals or exceeds many other grand museums of the world.

In fact, it has been said that the core of the old city has the highest density of art in the world. Because of this, there is even an unusual psychiatric affliction called "Florence syndrome" (sometimes called "Stendahl syndrome" after the nineteenth century author who was the first to remark on it). Also known as hyperkulturemia, it is defined as a "psychosomatic disorder that causes rapid heartbeat, dizziness, fainting, confusion, and even hallucinations when an individual is exposed to art, usually when the art is particularly beautiful or a large amount of art is in a single place." It was identified by an Italian psychiatrist in 1979 after he had seen more than 100 patients from among visitors to Florence. I thought this would be tailor-made for the tweedy Professor Langdon to expound upon. Dan Brown could have used Florence Syndrome as an alternative explanation for Langdon's fuzzy-headed amnesia. But alas, he never brought it up.

Dante, perhaps the most famous of Florentines, was banished from the city for the latter part of his life, and died in Ravenna. The people of Ravenna honored him with a tomb and faithfully kept his bones, even to the point of hiding them when it was feared they would be stolen.

Why might they be stolen? Well, Florence had realized that Dante was passing into literary immortality (and indeed, at one point was proposed for sainthood), and the Florentines wished they could bring him back (or at least his bones). In fact, Florence in 1519, led by Michelangelo, got Pope Leo X to order that Dante's remains be returned. Ravenna invited the Pope's representatives to open the tomb, which was found to be empty. (Dante's bones had been hidden in a church wall and were not rediscovered until 1865). In the belief that they would eventually get Dante's remains, Florence in 1829 had built a tomb for him within the Basilica of Santa Croce, but it remains empty.

After all of the tombs and crypts that we've seen in Dan Brown's other novels, it seemed to me it would be irresistible for Brown to bring Langdon around to Dante's tomb, only to reveal that it does not contain Dante's remains. Well, Brown didn't rise to the bait. This information doesn't appear in *Inferno*.

There is another striking case of bones that are not quite in the right place: the bones of Galileo. Although Galileo was born in Pisa and much associated with that city, he also was a professor at Florence's Accademia delle Arti del Disegno and spent the last years of his life in Arcetri, not far from Florence.

For obscure reasons, although most of Galileo's bones are buried beneath his ornate tomb in the Basilica of Santa Croce in Florence, three of his fingers, a vertebra, and a tooth were separated from the rest of his remains. These relics had various provenances but all ended up at the former Science Museum in Florence, now know as the Galileo Museum. Galileo's middle finger received its own customized glass display.

Given that Dan Brown has written about the putative ancient conflict between science and religion personified in Galileo's famous dispute with the Catholic Church, I was expecting Galileo might figure in the plot of *Inferno*. At the very least, I thought the gesture of his erect middle finger would be impossible for Dan Brown to ignore. Nonetheless, he did.

In fact, I really expected to hear a lot more about the other famous figures in Florence's history. Dan Brown rushes right past the works of Leonardo da Vinci, Michelangelo, and dozens of other Renaissance artists from Florence. He likewise gives short shrift to Machiavelli.

While I considered hints that the Black Plague might figure in *Inferno*, I frankly did not anticipate the use of the "plague doctor," a mask tradition that comes from Venice. I was betting on a group of cloaked figures known as the *Incappucciata*. They originally were a group founded by porters in Florence in 1244, one of the oldest charitable institutions in the world, known as the Arciconfraternita della Misericordia di Firenze (Brothers of Mercy of Florence). They initially were known for charitable works such as providing dowries for indigent girls, helping people in need, and burying paupers. When the outbreaks of plague came, they were the ones who carried the sick to hospitals and the dead to graveyards. All the way into the twentieth century, they were known for walking the streets of Florence in black robes, hoods, and masks. They seemed perfect for a role in *Inferno*, but Dan Brown didn't pick them.

Florence was essentially ground zero for the Renaissance. It was also a center of neoplatonism plus studies of arcane threads of history, such as hermeticism, magic and the occult, and the Kabbalah. Under Lorenzo de Medici, Florence patronized the highly influential translations of Plato by Marsilio Ficino and nurtured Giovanni Pico della Mirandola. These all represent the kinds of historic threads that Dan Brown traced in other novels, but failed to even mention in *Inferno*.

If Dan Brown warp-drives past the majesty and richness of Florence's history, he hits hyperdrive when he gets to Venice and Istanbul. I would have at least expected some mention of Marco Polo, one of the most famous of Venetians, not to mention Aldus Manutius, the printer who gave the world its first portable copies of the classics.

The long history of Istanbul, formerly Constantinople, formerly Byzantium, is a progression. It started out as Greek and then became a capital of the Roman Empire, which by then was Christian. Eventually, the European world came to be divided between a Catholic Church under the pope in Rome, and a rival Eastern Orthodox Church under the patriarch in Constantinople. Venice at times stood between them and independent of them, and at times Venice even defended Constantinople and enjoyed a tax-free status in its port. So, the looting of the city by the forces of the Fourth Crusade in 1204, co-led by the Venetian doge Enrico Dandalus, was a case of Christian against Christian, and a former ally made into an enemy. This is not explained in *Inferno*, although the very same treacherous doge is at the heart of the Venice/Istanbul part of the plot.

There is a tragic connection among all three cities: Florence, Venice, and Istanbul at various times were all afflicted by devastating plagues. But to tell the complete story, one would have to start at least at the Plague of Justinian in 541 AD. This crippled Constantinople and laid waste to many parts of the Middle East, felling an estimated twenty-five million people. It kept returning in subsequent generations up until around 750 AD. In Venice, there was a terrible plague in 1347 killing an estimated 40 percent of residents, but there were also outbreaks in 1575 and in 1630, the last killing about a third of the population. In Florence, the most devastating outbreak came in 1347. But one study found outbreaks in 1430, 1437, 1449, 1478, and 1527, the last killing about 20 to 25 percent of the population. But this is way too complicated a story for Dan Brown, we would have to agree, so he grossly abbreviated this history. One very important thing to note, in my view, is that Dante lived and died before any of the major outbreaks of plague.

Brownisms

Occasionally, Dan Brown pulls a little literary stunt where he asserts some zany notion and attributes it in a manner similar to Fox News ("some people say . . ."). My all-time favorite comes in

Angels & Demons when Brown tells us that obelisks are "referred to by symbologists as 'Lofty Pyramids.'" There's only one symbologist who says that, and he's fictional.

There's a priceless example of this in *Inferno* on page 314 when Brown claims that the facade of St. Mark's in Venice, having so many doorways, is "sometimes accused of offering 'an embarrassing surfeit of ingress.'" Who talks like that?

Another Brownism awaits on page 317. The passage relates how Langdon once went to an event at New Hampshire's historic Runnymede Farm, home of a fabled Kentucky Derby winner, and saw a performance of a troupe called Behind the Mask, mounted on stunning Friesian horses and wearing dazzling Venetian costumes. Langdon researches the breed and we have this assertion as a result: "the powerful bodies of the early Friesian horses had inspired the robust aesthetic of the Horses of St. Mark's."

Well, there simply is no basis for saying that Friesian horses have any connection with the Horses of St. Mark's. However, there *is* a connection between Dan Brown and the Friesian troupe. It turns out that Runnymede Farm is not five miles from Brown's house, and in New England, neighbors help neighbors. The historic farm fell on rough times in recent years, and Dan and Blythe Brown have been lending support.

Pagan Origins

One of Dan Brown's favorite themes is to expose the underlying pagan aspects of symbols and sacred sites. In *DVC* and *A&D* especially, he is careful to point out where the great Christian cathedrals have been built atop the ruins of temples dedicated to Roman or Greek gods. He takes pains to explain that symbols like the pentagram or the six-pointed star have origins that pre-date any Christian usage.

In *Inferno*, Brown misses several important opportunities of this kind. Indeed, his hero Robert Langdon seems almost totally to forget all of that pagan lore and its interconnections with the Christian church.

A glaring example is his quotation from Dante's *Paradiso*:

> But Florence, in her final peace, was fated
> to offer up—unto that mutilated
> stone guardian upon her bridge—a victim.

The context for this quotation was to mention the murder of Buondelmonte de' Buondelmonti that took place in 1215 at the Ponte Vecchio and served as the legendary starting point of a century or more of conflict between the Guelph and Ghibelline factions of Florence.

But Dan Brown left a huge unanswered question here: What was the "mutilated stone guardian upon her bridge"?

The answer: a statue of Mars, the Roman god. What this says about Florence is very revealing, and the very kind of thing Robert Langdon, in his past adventures, would have stopped to explicate.

According to legends, the Romans founded the city of Florence in the first century BC. The Romans dedicated a grand temple to Mars as the protector of the city, with an equestrian statue. Some say this temple was at or near the site of today's Baptistery, others that it was near the Piazza della Repubblica. Early on, when Christianity came to Florence, a cathedral was founded and paganism was swept aside. The Florentines moved the statue of Mars to a pedestal along the Arno as a result. When the Goths took Florence, they in turn tossed the statue into the river. In the rebuilding of the city by Charlemagne late in the eighth century AD, it was recovered and, although damaged, was placed on a pillar near the north end of what is now the Ponte Vecchio. The statue was "mutilated," but to the Florentines it represented a layer of divine protection. Even though Florence had taken first St. Reperata, as well as St. Zenobius and then the venerable St. John the Baptist, as patron and protector, the common people were not ready to abandon respect for Mars. The statue was still there during Dante's lifetime, and he referred to it in the *Divine Comedy*. It eventually was washed back into the Arno in a flood in 1333.

Another example of forgotten pagans comes when Langdon reflects on the Harris Tweed logo, an "iconic orb adorned with thirteen buttonlike jewels and topped by a Maltese cross. *Leave it to the Scots to invoke the Christian warriors on a piece of twill*," Langdon thinks to himself in his inimitable Italic style.

What Langdon fails to mention is that the symbol in question is a stylized depiction of the Sovereign's Orb, one of the United Kingdom's crown jewels. It stems from the acquisition of the UK's earliest trademark in 1909 by the Harris Tweed Authority. It's true that this royal orb signifies the British monarch's role as Defender of the Faith, but the full Christian story dates back to a symbol called the *globus cruciger*, symbolizing Christ's dominion over the world.

As Langdon should know, the *globus cruciger* is descended from a pagan symbol, the *globus terrarum* ("world of the lands"). This was a simple sphere that was held (or sometimes trod underfoot) by Roman gods, such as Jupiter or Salus. It symbolized a god's dominion over the earth.

Where Are the Editors?

Inferno, like other Dan Brown books, contains some passages where Dan Brown has made simple writing errors that should have been caught by careful editors. Every writer makes these mistakes, but top writers should get the services of top editors.

Late in the book, Langdon wakes up aboard the *Mendacium*. He knows it's some kind of a boat because of the "portal window." It should be "porthole."

Another minor transgression: Langdon passes the fountain of Neptune and notices the "three-pronged trident." (Unless you believe your reader is a dolt, you don't need to say "three-pronged." The word "trident" comes from the Latin *tri dentes*, or "three teeth.")

When Langdon is explaining the concept of using gesso to prepare a surface for painting, he tells Sienna the surface has "teeth." Says Langdon, "In the art world, this rough texture is called teeth, and painters prefer to paint on a surface that has teeth because the paint sticks to it better." WANTED: Editor experienced in the fine arts. Artists say a surface has "tooth," not "teeth." It may seem ungrammatical, but that's the way artists say it. Getting this wrong makes a fictional professor of art history look like a boob.

At times Dan Brown can get downright silly. At one point, Langdon agrees with something Sienna has said, so he nods. The only problem is, she's in front of him on the Trike and cannot see that. Likewise, on the C-130 flight from Venice to Istanbul (essentially due east), Langdon comes up to the cockpit door to bask in the warm sunlight. This isn't possible, since it's late afternoon and the sun is low and behind the airplane.

Sometimes Brown leaves a clear contradiction in different passages *on the same page*. On page 138, he introduces a graph that he says was published by the World Health Organization listing "key environmental issues deemed by the WHO to have the greatest impact on global health." To pound home the point, he spells out a bunch of items, ending with "and global sea levels." Then, in an unusual novelistic touch, he presents the graph itself. The only flaw is, "global sea levels" is not on the graph.

Much more glaring is page 318, where Dan Brown tells us the legend of the Horses of St. Mark's. First, he relates that "the horses arrived in Venice in 1254, and were installed in front of the facade of St. Mark's Cathedral." Three paragraphs later, however, he quotes a website that says the "decorative collars were added in 1204 by the Venetians to conceal where the heads had been severed to facilitate their transportation by ship from Constantinople to Venice."

It's not just that this calls attention to a nagging unanswered historical question (what happened to make the trip last fifty years?), but it makes the Venetians appear to be uncannily prescient, to have added the collars five decades before the horses arrived at their destination. A tiny amount of editing would have avoided this problem.

Dan Brown says that Napoleon put the horses on top of the Arc de Triomphe in Paris. He misses a nuance of triumphal arches that he ought to know well from his research walking around Paris. The *famous* Arc de Triomphe is actually the Arc de Triomphe de l'Étoile. The horses were *not* placed on this arch. Rather, they were on the much smaller Arc de Triomphe du Carrousel, which ironically stands within a stone's throw of the Pyramid at the Louvre, "hidden in plain sight" near one of Langdon's favorite spots.

Time and Date Settings

Inferno is the first Dan Brown novel where you can determine exactly what date the main action is supposed to have taken place: Monday, March 18, 2013. In all the other novels, you can only vaguely deduce the approximate year, approximate time of the month, etc. But Brown spells out that it's Monday, March 18, when Langdon wakes up in the hospital and then it only takes a bit of deduction to figure out the year. First of all, the last year in which March 18 fell on a Monday was 2002, and then in 2013, and not again until 2019.

But the clincher is, we have been told that Sienna is thirty-two years old, and then we are told that she is known by her code name, FS-2080, which, in the transhumanist identity system, denotes the year of her 100th birthday. Thus, she was born in 1980, sometime later than March 18; she will turn thirty-three sometime in 2013.

This sets up Brown for a minor plot flaw. When Langdon calls his friend and editor Jonas Faukman in New York, it's about 10:28 a.m. in Florence and about 4:28 a.m. in New York, based on the text of *Inferno*. Faukman thinks to himself: *They don't teach time zones at Harvard?*

Well, it's not exactly the time zone that's wrong. It turns out that the US switches to Daylight Savings Time on the second Sunday in March, thus March 10 in 2013. However, Italy did not switch to "Summer time" until March 31. Therefore, on March 18, if Langdon calls at 10:28 Florence time, it's 5:28 New York time.

Seeing Things

Inferno contains some striking examples of how Dan Brown can look at something and not really see it accurately. A fine case is a remark about Langdon seeing a statue at the Porta Romana, "depicting a woman departing the city gates carrying an enormous bundle on her head."

Clearly, our famous art historian has not done his homework. Yes, there is a statue of a woman. But the "enormous bundle" is actually a second, roughly stylized human figure, prone, with an upturned face, so that it gazes behind the supporting figure.

The sculpture is called *DietroFront*, or "Turnabout," by Michelangelo Pistoletto, a modern artist. It also has been called "About-Face." It consists of two figures, one of which strides forward, while the other gazes behind. In an interview, Pistoletto said it represents a dual look forward into the future and backward into the past. He is pleased that it is situated at the gate of Florence, looking toward modernity, while remembering the Renaissance of the city's earlier days. It was originally unveiled at nearby Fort Belvedere but moved to its current location in 1984. (By the way, Pistoletto recently made headlines by decorating another of Dan Brown's favorite art objects, the Louvre Pyramid in Paris, putting a complex infinity-like symbol on its front face.)

Dan Brown really blows it when it comes to describing the iconic gondolas of Venice. He has the water taxi driver, Maurizio, tell us that there is only one piece of metal on the boat, at the bow, called the *ferro di prua*. This completely misses the ornate piece of metal found at the stern called the *risso*. Brown further tells us a gondola is "nearly forty feet long," when the specification for a gondola is 10.75 meters, or about thirty-five feet. Brown correctly notes that the gondola's hull is built asymmetrically, resulting in a noticeable list. But he says this list is to the *left*. As anyone who really looks at Venetian gondolas can see, the list in fact is to the *right*.

Travel Arrangements

In previous novels, Dan Brown has often been confused about directions and routes of travel. In *The Da Vinci Code* and *Angels & Demons* in particular, he typically and amusingly sent Langdon east toward a landmark that was actually west, or the wrong way down a one-way street.

In *Inferno*, there is less of this kind of thing, but Brown does seem to see Florence as lying east and west of the Arno, when most people would call this north and south. Indeed, the Oltrarno district is defined in virtually all guidebooks as the "south" bank of the Arno. Some *Inferno* characters drive around Florence seeming to be unaware of the restricted sectors where it takes a special permit to operate a motor vehicle. This includes the basic zones around all the tourist attractions north and south of the river.

Where Dan Brown gets completely implausible, however, is in the realm of air travel.

He tells readers that the NetJets representative cheerfully promises to have a Cessna Citation Excel routed to Florence from "Monaco" in less than an hour (this kind of speedy repositioning is itself extremely implausible). But the glaring flaw here is that Monaco does not have an airport, so no one in professional aviation circles would say that they have a jet "positioned in Monaco." (There is an airport nearby in Nice, France, however.)

The next part of the plan is where things really get loony. The NetJets rep schedules the plane into Lucca Airport, about fifty miles west of Florence. This is implausible on two counts. First, the Lucca runway is too short for a Citation Excel. Second, it makes no sense because Florence's own airport is only about five miles from the city (just off the same highway you would use to get to Lucca).

When Brown needs to transport Sienna Brooks from Venice to Istanbul, he conjures up another private jet, a Cessna Citation Mustang that flies out of the airport on Lido Island. This doesn't make a lot of sense, since the runway at Lido is not paved—it's grass. At the destination, Brown has the plane land at Hezarfen Airfield. Again, that runway is too short for the jet.

When the WHO agents learn Sienna is in transit to Istanbul, one yells, "Then call the European Air Transport Command! Have them turn the jet around!" This is nonsense because the EATC doesn't have any control over civilian flights, and none of the countries on the route of flight are even participants in the EATC.

In Venice, Langdon and his companions hire a water taxi to go from the train station down the Grand Canal to St. Mark's. The driver, Maurizio, promises it's the fastest boat in all of Venice. We are given the impression that the boat roars down the canal at top speed. Well, it's just not possible. That's because the speed limit on the Grand Canal is seven knots (eight mph) and Maurizio would be risking his license—and therefore his livelihood—if caught. And he almost definitely would be caught, because in 2007 Venice installed a sophisticated camera and computer system that monitors all the boat traffic on the canal. Its name is Argos, which Professor Langdon would recognize as an alternative name for a 100-eyed giant of Greek mythology. One reason for strict low-speed rules on the canal is that the historic buildings suffer greatly from erosion by wave action, such as constant wakes.

There are a couple of cases where Dan Brown gets travel parameters very right, and he deserves credit. When he sends Langdon, Sienna, and Ferris off to Venice in the train known as the Silver Arrow (*Frecciargento*), going 174 miles an hour and making the trip in about two hours, he's absolutely right, and he's calling attention to Italy's marvelous high-speed rail system. When the WHO team has to hustle to get from Florence out to the Lucca airport in less than fifty minutes, a trip of almost fifty miles, it sounds pretty unlikely at first. But that's before you learn that the A11 Autostrada has a speed limit of eighty-one mph. It's part of an excellent network of motorways in Italy.

Techno Babble

Ever since my teenage days when I read Sir Arthur Conan Doyle's tales of Sherlock Holmes, I have come to expect a high standard among mystery-thriller writers. If Doyle told us that a victim of cyanide poisoning had a residual smell of bitter almonds on his lips, that turned out to be absolutely true (even though most people don't know what bitter almonds smell like, as opposed to sweet almonds).

Dan Brown has a far different standard of accuracy on matters like this. A central plot tension device of *The Da Vinci Code* was the fragile cryptex, which contained a message written on a piece of papyrus suspended inside a vial of vinegar. According to Dan Brown, the papyrus would dissolve instantly if it made contact with the vinegar. Well, that just isn't true, and anyone can obtain some papyrus (believe it or not, it's available) and test the notion at the kitchen table. (A piece of papyrus after some hours will eventually separate into the strips that it's made from, but it doesn't dissolve. We performed this experiment in 2004 and documented it as part of our research for *Secrets of the Code*.)

In *Inferno*, Dan Brown tells us that the plaster death mask of Dante has been inscribed with a message, which was then covered with a coat of gesso. He smells the mask and concludes that it's acrylic gesso because it smells like "wet dog." He calls this good news because it's "water soluble." He wets a towel and in a few minutes rubs off the gesso to reveal the message.

Well, we imitated Langdon's purported process by casting a molded piece of plaster of Paris, waiting for it to dry, then painting it with a single coat of acrylic gesso.

First of all, acrylic gesso doesn't have any appreciable smell after it is dry. (We did find some online references to artists' brushes acquiring a foul smell after being used in acrylic gesso, however.)

When we scrubbed the dried gesso with a wet towel, it didn't seem to be exactly "water soluble." It softened a bit when dampened, but this only allowed a little bit of the gesso to slough off under heavy scrubbing. It was evident that it would take hours to get all the gesso off, if it was even possible at all. Myth busted!

There are other cases of technical nonsense in *Inferno*. The ornately carved object that slides out of the "biotube" has a function. "It's a Faraday pointer," says Robert Langdon. He muses that he was given one once, and then describes the technology: "When the device was agitated, a metal ball inside sailed back and forth across a series of paddles and powered a tiny generator."

Langdon's explanation of how it works is ludicrous. But self-powered shake-lights do exist. This kind of device actually involves a small rare-earth magnet that slides back and forth within a coil, creating the Faraday effect, which is used to charge an ultracapacitor. The capacitor then discharges through a light-emitting diode (LED) lamp. In fact, although a pointer based on this technology is going to be nearly impossible to find, a flashlight like this is widely available, priced at under $10.

On page 410, Brüder is at the cistern and whips out his trusty Tovatec penlight. Dan Brown twice refers to its piercing "halogen beam." However, actual Tovatec lights have LED lamps, not halogens.

Early in *Inferno*, we are given an accurate explanation of a "suspended particle device" glass used to turn partitions from transparent to opaque aboard the *Mendacium*. In my view, it's funny that Dan Brown felt he needed to explain this, since forms of what is now commonly called "smart glass" or "switchable glass" have been around at least since 1982's *Blade Runner* in fiction, and have been used in real life in many buildings throughout the world for at least a dozen years.

The entire notion of hiding the "biotube" in a special pocket in Langdon's jacket is badly flawed. It's not even clear what the goal of this would be, since Langdon was sneaked into Florence without a passport and so he did not pass through Customs. Therefore, he doesn't need to make it a matter of spycraft, since he isn't going through a metal detector or a pat-down. He could have simply put the biotube into the pocket of his trousers.

But, assuming he needs to hide it, a newly sewn pocket at the nape of the jacket is preposterous. It will not hide a rigid six-inch tube. Most jackets lie tight against the wearer's back, and the object would appear as a prominent, very odd, bulge.

What is really amazing is what else Langdon appears to carry around with him, somewhere in his jacket or pants. When the time comes for him to examine the Dante death mask, he whips out a pair of surgical gloves. And a few minutes later when he needs to steal the mask, he miraculously produces a large Ziploc bag!

The Finer Things

It seems likely that wealth and access to well-heeled people has introduced Dan Brown to some very exclusive products. The niftiest one, in my view, is the single-malt Scotch that the provost turns to (after being on the wagon for fourteen years). It is a bottle of Highland Park, fifty-year-old vintage.

Highland Park is an Orkney Island distillery dating to 1798. It bottles whiskies aged twelve to forty years, typically, but in 2010 it released a special fifty-year-old scotch, in elegant designer bottles sheathed in silver lattice. There is still a small supply available through the company's web site at a mere £10, 000 a bottle (about $15,000 at the current exchange rate).

The bottle is 0.7 liters, or about 23.67 ounces (US). If the provost pours a "standard" drink of 1.5 ounces, then his dose of whisky is worth about $950!

Malthusian Math

If you examine the entire premise of Zobrist's infertility virus, you can look at it on a very basic level, or it can be very complex. On the complex level, the details of population growth or decline are an intricate ballet of factors, and it takes experts to make wise comments on that level. Except to say that much, it's really far beyond my ken, and I defer to any genuine experts.

But there are certain very simple aspects of Zobrist's plan that amount to plot flaws, in my view.

For instance, as Dan Brown depicts the effects of the virus, it is said that it will affect a random one-third of the entire population, male or female, making them infertile; as a result, Brown implies, the population growth rate drops by one-third.

But this is fundamentally flawed logic. It would only be approximately true if the affected people married each other. If the one-third of affected males and one-third of affected females were to marry exclusively unaffected partners, that would result in *two-thirds* of couples being infertile, since it takes two to tango.

Second, as Dan Brown describes the continuing effect on future generations, it "would be similar to that of a recessive gene . . . which gets passed along to all offspring, and yet exerts its influence in only a small percentage of them."

Wait a minute—isn't this a glaring contradiction? If the virus continues to thrive, it would affect a random one-third of future generations. If it behaves like a recessive gene, it would affect a smaller portion. (When a gene is recessive, its trait is inherited only by individuals who get one gene, or *allele*, each from their mother and father.) Which is it? How does it go from being so virulent that it affects one-third of all people alive today, but then suddenly becomes recessive?

It's also important to note that a large part of the world's population has stabilized its growth. Brown says the world is daily adding "the equivalent of the entire country of Germany." This is an odd choice, since Germany, like most of Europe, has a current population growth rate of 0.0 percent. The most populous country, China, has achieved a dramatic decrease in growth rate since it began a "one child policy" in the late 1970s; its population is now only growing at 0.47 percent.

Time Slips

There is a pretty glaring loss of about an hour, early in the book. Langdon gets a time check at 6:00 a.m. on Sienna's cell phone when he calls the "consulate" from her apartment. The phone call brings a promise that someone will be there within twenty minutes, and actually, both Vayentha and the SRS team show up promptly. So it is probably about 6:30 or 6:45 a.m. when Sienna and Langdon zoom off on the Trike moped. We next pick up Sienna and Langdon as they are driving along the Viale Niccolo Machiavelli and Langdon muses that he had "just seen" the silver-haired woman. Logically, they can have traveled only about two or three miles, in a hurry. It should be about 7 a.m. But they pass a chapel clock that is chiming 8 a.m.

There are some clear contradictions within the plot as to timing of certain events. A hinge point is the suicide of Bertrand Zobrist. On page 26, we are told this happened "several days ago." But on page 180, it's a different story: "six days ago, Bertrand Zobrist threw himself off the top of the Badia tower."

And then there is a sharp discrepancy over the date when Langdon was brought into the hunt by Sinskey. Today, in the novel, is Monday, and the last thing Langdon can remember was walking toward a Saturday night lecture at Harvard (page 15). However, we can discount Langdon's version because he has a drug-induced form of amnesia. But we have two other citations, and they conflict. On page 267, it says, "Sinskey had first met Robert Langdon four nights before." On page 292, it says, "Almost two days ago, when Sinskey recruited Langdon . . ."

Logically, based on the action that is described retrospectively at various points in the text, Langdon was shanghaied on Saturday night, flown to Florence and set loose there on Sunday evening. So his recollection actually isn't faulty, the page 267 reference is.

Another issue related to time (tenuously) is the Doomsday Clock. On page 213 of *Inferno*, Dan Brown gives this dialog between Sienna and Langdon:

"Zobrist illustrated his point with a 'Doomsday Clock,' which showed that if the entire span of human life on earth were compressed into a single hour . . . We are now in its final seconds."

"I've actually seen that clock online," Langdon said.

Well, Langdon is wrong. There is a well-established Doomsday Clock; it's online at thebulletin.org and it has been around for many decades, but it has never had anything to do with overpopulation. The clock was actually set up in 1947 by atomic scientists and referred to the threat of global nuclear war. In 2007, some scientists added concerns about climate change. The clock started at 11:53 pm, got as close as 11:58 in 1953, and is now at 11:55.

Mysteries to Ponder

Usually, a good mystery writer takes a moment near the end of a book to wrap up all the loose ends. But Dan Brown leaves a really tantalizing loose end in *Inferno*. On page 86, we learn that Sienna's computer is registered to "someone with the initials S.C." As we progress through the book, we do learn that her name is Felicity Sienna Brooks. But we never learn what S.C. signifies. Is this something Dan Brown intended to leave unanswered, or it is just sloppy writing?

We don't ever learn the relevance of the solemn date inscribed on Zobrist's plaque: "In This Place, On This Date, The World Was Changed Forever," even though there are six different references in the story to the exact same plaque. We can deduce that the date in question is March 19, 2013, but what does the date signify? Why would Brown, who usually picks dates with attention to their numerological or symbolic connotations, choose this specific date?

We do learn about the transhumanist naming convention, where you follow the example of the founder, Fereidoun M. Esfandiary. You take your first and middle initial and add the date on which you would turn 100 years old. Thus, the founder renamed himself FM-2030.

On page 321 of *Inferno*, Sinskey gives two further examples of transhumanist name conversions: DG-2064 and BA-2105.

The first of these is surely the new transhumanist name for Daniel Gerhard Brown, the author himself, born in 1964. There is another instance of "DG-2064" to be found in faint lettering on the dust jacket of *Inferno* as well.

Is this just a playful author teasing the reader, or has Dan Brown gone over to transhumanism?

Further, has Dan Brown come completely under the sway of those who espouse an extreme solution for population control, as does his character Bertrand Zobrist? Shortly after the book's release, Brown in an interview referred to Zobrist as the "hero" of *Inferno*. Ordinarily, *Robert Langdon* would be considered the hero. Is this a Freudian slip by Brown?

And we are left wondering about a boy or girl now eight years of age: who is BA-2105?

"I Need Another Clue"

BY CHERYL HELM
Dan Brown codes and puzzles expert

People could be forgiven for speculating at one point that Cheryl Helm was actually Dan Brown, cleverly hiding in plain sight. There was the mysterious email address and the uncanny knack for being ahead of everyone else in deciphering the tantalizingly clever codes and puzzles posted on Inferno's *website. There was the shared dedication to amateur musical performance and, obviously, to intricate puzzles. And a "he" posing as a "she" is actually something Dan Brown has done before, using the name Danielle Brown for his first book,* 187 Men to Avoid. *(Presumably the list did not include Robert Langdon.)*

When our colleague David Shugarts introduced us to Cheryl's uncanny work we knew we had to tap into her experience as a puzzle master and so arranged to meet her. We can report that there is a real Cheryl Helm and that she is not the "he" who wrote Inferno. *She is, however, a talented singer and arranger of early music and composer of early-music-inspired choral works, a doting grandmother, and, yes, a master at uncovering Dan Brown's hidden messages with a true love of doing so. One could almost say obsessively so. She was part of the "posse" of clue hunters prior to the publication of* The Da Vinci Code *(for which she won several prizes),* The Lost Symbol *(more prizes), and now* Inferno.

One of the pleasures of decoding Dan Brown is not just in solving his puzzles, but the opportunity it gives for entering the doors of his wonderful library, rich with cultural history, all relevant to the plot. If you thought the Roman numeral VII was just a Roman numeral VII, then you don't know Dan Brown, or Cheryl Helm. Here is her journey of discovery down the "rabbit hole" that was Dan Brown's pre- and post-publication mystery tour for Inferno.

Little did I know when 2013 began that Robert Langdon would soon trample on my tranquility in his Somerset loafers. Then all hell broke loose. On February 20, NBC's *Today* show revealed the cover of Dan Brown's novel *Inferno* and my addiction to unsolved puzzles and love of plunging down rabbit holes kicked in.

I expected a trail of puzzles, codes, and hints, as had been done for his earlier books. I was not disappointed. Having played along on *The Da Vinci Code, Angels and Demons,* and *The Lost Symbol* quests—I still have my Cryptex, a signed Illustrated *DVC*, and my autographed *TLS* first edition prizes—I know if an image appears on a Dan Brown cover, it means something to *someone*. It might be a message to family, friends, or even foes, and it may or may not relate directly to the text within, but it's there asking to be solved.

Brown, who grew up with the fun of creating and solving puzzles as a regular feature in his family's home life, seems to enjoy teasing and challenging us while we await the actual publication, and many of us enjoy taking the bait. The forces he and his team deploy for publicity purposes turn some of us into late-night cryptologists and internet search zombies. For *Inferno*, we saw travel photos, cryptic statements, Facebook posts, Tweets, video clips, multiple book covers, and an intriguing reconfiguration of his official website, *DanBrown.com*. And while some of the pre-release hints eventually turned out to be decoys—Dan Brown has said publicly that he purposely created misleading clues to the contents of *Inferno* to throw the cottage industry of his followers off the scent—they were still worth the effort. As with many journeys, getting there really can be half the fun.

The majority of pre-publication hints and clues were posted on Facebook and Twitter. Some have since been incorporated into the Dan Brown website. But originally they appeared as random nuggets eagerly anticipated by we self-appointed sleuths. One group of clues, posted as "Monday Masterpieces" on Facebook and Twitter, was clearly intended to inspire us to delve more deeply into Dante's epic poem, the *Divine Comedy*. These included illustrations (sixteen so far) taken from four specific manuscript editions of Dante's work: four images from Sandro Botticelli's 1481 edition (Florence), three from Alessandro Vellutello's 1544 edition (Venice), five from one known as "Yates Thompson 36," located in the British Library with *Inferno* illustrations by Priamo della Quercia (Siena, mid-fifteenth century), and four from Gustave Dore's 1861 edition (Paris).

Two other manuscript editions also appeared in the photo clues. One is by Francesco di ser Nardo da Barberino (Florence, 1347) and is one of the oldest surviving editions of the *Divine Comedy*. It ends with a brief notation on Dante's death and burial, ironically not in his native Florence but in Ravenna, where he had lived out his life in exile. The other manuscript edition found in the clues is by Lodovico Dolce (Venice, 1555), and has the distinction of being the first known version to include the word "Divina" ("Divine") in the title. Identifying these particular manuscripts was a high point in my own route to *Inferno*.

Other clues guiding us toward the central themes of Florence and Dante included a photo of Florence's Laurentian Library dome (home of a copy of Johann Neumeister's first print of the *Divine Comedy* but on loan to the Palazzo Vecchio's museum, where Langdon encounters it), the oculus of the Boboli Gardens grotto (where Robert Langdon and Sienna Brooks hide from the WHO SWAT team), a snippet of a music score that turns out to be a motif of Liszt's *Dante Symphony* (the work being played in Istanbul's ancient Basilica cistern, where Zobrist's plague is unleashed), and the *Head of John the Baptist* sculpture by Igor Mitoraj (hinting at the Florence Baptistery).

Another tip, the city of Toledo's coat of arms, led me to Eleanora di Toledo (1522-1562), the royal consort of Cosimo I de'Medici, Duke of Florence and the first Grand Duke of Tuscany. Their patronage and wealth were prime factors in the Italian Renaissance. Eleanora's funeral dress happens to be displayed in the costume gallery of the Palazzo Pitti, another landmark in Langdon's escape route.

The "Seven Deadly Sins" videos

A recurring design feature of *DanBrown.com's* home page is a set of independently scrolling layers that visually reference his previous novels. In the underlay, for example, are the images of da Vinci's *Last Supper* (*The Da Vinci Code*), Brumidi's *The Apotheosis of Washington* (*The Lost Symbol*), and Bernini's *Fontana dei Quattro Fiumi* (*Angels & Demons*). Taken together, the overlay graphics include what I believe to be seventeen alchemical symbols.

It was not a surprise, therefore, to find that the layering technique also showed up in the "Seven Deadly Sins" videos posted on Facebook in the week before *Inferno's* release. These videos also provided a treasure trove of puzzles to unravel.

The first video, Envy, opens with an eye symbol and Caravaggio's *Young Sick Bacchus*. The Caravaggio dissolves into Andrea del Sarto's *The Holy Family with the Young St. John the Baptist*, and the del Sarto melts into Francesco Melzi's *Vertumnus and Pomona*. Watching the sixteen-second video, one's attention is drawn primarily to these Renaissance paintings, but at the time marks at 1 second, 4 seconds, and again at 9 seconds, I noticed a faint image underlying the main image. That image is of *Invidia* (Envy), by Pieter Bruegel the Elder, a 1557 engraving from the *Seven Deadly Sins* series (most likely as published by Hieronymus Cock in 1558). Pausing the video at these intervals reveals three different parts of the *Invidia* tableau depicted.

Each of the seven videos features its own set of three Renaissance paintings, though on the Lust video we are treated to a glimpse of a fourth: Titian's *Venus and Adonis*, in which Adonis is spying from the upper right on another painting, Bronzino's *Venus, Cupid, Folly, and Time*. While I have glimpsed five of the ghostly images of Bruegel's engravings underlying these seven videos, the other two elude me—if they are there at all.

In addition to videos and photos, another group of clues came from the novel's pre- and post-release US covers as well as the covers of international editions. Early in the trail of clues, seven small closeups taken from the pre-release US cover were posted. The first to appear was Roman numeral VII with a quote from Dante's poem that included the line "*I will be first and thou shalt second be.*" The next was the Italian word *sei* (six) presented as a piece of graffiti on a wall section from the cover's image of Florence, the third a closeup of the letter *W* making it appear as Roman numeral V, and so on until "The Final Clue," which was *I*, the first initial of the book's title.

That Roman numeral VII turned into what I came to call "The Mystery of the Disagreeing Covers." The puzzle begins with the passages early in the novel where Langdon begins his quest to recover his lost memory and save the world (*Inferno*, chapter 15):

> As Langdon had seen many times in this painting [Botticelli's *Mappa del'Inferno*], the tenth ditch of the *Malebolge* was packed with sinners half buried upside down, their legs sticking out of the earth, But strangely, in this version, one pair of legs bore the letter *R*...

> Langdon followed her outstretched finger to another of the ten ditches in the Malebolge, where the letter *E* was scrawled on a false prophet whose head had been put on backward...

Other letters now appeared to him... He saw a *C*
on a seducer being whipped by demons... another *R* on a thief perpetually bitten by snakes... an
A on a corrupt politician submerged in a lake of
boiling tar...

He returned his gaze to the uppermost ditch
of the *Malebolge* and began reading the letters
downward, through each of the ten ditches, from
top to bottom.

C...A...T...R...O...V...A...C...E...R

The puzzle is simple, but also clever in that the solution is
hidden in plain sight. Yet for me there is a problem—actually two
problems: the math and the sequence.

The problem starts with the slightly different versions of
the cover between the "teaser" that appeared online and the one
wrapped around the actual physical book. Both offer the same
dominating image: a medallion featuring a portrait of Dante similar to the more familiar one by Botticelli. Superimposed over the
portrait are a hub and nine concentric rings inscribed with Roman
numerals I through IX in succession, from the perimeter inward
to the hub. Preceding each numeral is a short vertical bar which
can be followed as an axis through the center to the opposite side
of the ring and a single letter. (Roman numeral I points to "C", II
points to "A", and so on.) The numerals and letters swirl into one of
Brown's favorite concepts, the Fibonacci spiral. Taking these letters
in the order corresponding to their companion numbers they read:
CATROACCR.

But what was Dan Brown trying to tell us with the word
CATROACCR? At the time, aware only of the US pre-release
cover, I started the hunt for a solution. The word did not yield to
anagrams in English, Latin, or Italian related to Brown's implied
themes. I tried the decoding methods I used in prior quests, but

still had no breakthrough. I manipulated the rings and the image hoping to winkle out a clue to unlock the puzzle. I wrote that sequence of letters dozens of times until it was etched in my mind. It seemed impossible until finally, on March 19, one of the "Monday Masterpieces" led to a solution. It was a Botticelli illustration of Dante's *Inferno*, Canto XV, where Dante encounters his late mentor, Brunetto Latini, who was as deep into Florentine politics as his pupil Dante. With that hint, a quick internet search yielded the "aha!" moment puzzlers love.

One of Latini's writings was titled *Il Tesoretto* and that pattern of letters suddenly clicked into place. CATROACCR, by way of a devilishly simple cryptogram, became TESORETTO. It also revealed a direct link to a video clue: Dan Brown emerging from a hidden entrance to one of the Palazzo Vecchio's secret passages. That passage connects the small *Studiolo* built for Francesco I de' Medici (1547-1587), to the chamber known as the *Tesoretto*, both designed by artist and architect Giorgio Vasari. (The phrase "*Ve... sorry...*" in the book's opening pages, which hints at an apology, turns out to be referring to Vasari instead—another bit of playful misdirection.)

Another puzzle solved. Well, not exactly.

Down yet another level

Soon after I thought I had successfully decoded the pre-publication US cover, the Italian cover came to my attention. Its medallion was different. It had the same nine circles, but its outermost ring had *two* letters instead of one (and additionally revealed that the penultimate letter wasn't "C" as it appeared on the earlier low-resolution image on the website of the US version, but was actually an "E"). This changed CATROACCR into a *ten*-letter string: CATROVACER. Tantalizingly and, as we shall see, significantly, when the US edition was released on May 15, 2013, its cover medallion had changed to match the Italian one. That single added letter would prove to be central to a major clue in the novel.

In chapter 20, Langdon has an epiphany behind a Porta-Potty, a sly reference to another kind of hell. He realizes Zobrist had rearranged the ten *Malebolge* ("evil ditches") of Dante's eighth circle of hell as represented in Botticelli's *Mappa dell'Inferno*. In addition to reordering the ditches, Zobrist also inserted letters, one per ditch. As Langdon presents the solution in chapter 23—"If these levels were a deck of ten cards, the deck was not so much shuffled as simply cut once"—the top three ditches had been moved to the bottom but otherwise still in order. All that was needed was to move the bottom three back to the top to put them in proper order and unscramble CATROVACER. Put that way, it works.

But after Langdon points out the difference between Botticelli's *Mappa* and Zobrist's altered one, Sienna's statement in chapter 23 seems to indicate this solution is off by one: "Okay, I see that. The first ditch is now the seventh." This harks back to the Roman numeral VII clue with the caption "*I will be first...*" exactly mirroring Sienna's words but with the personal pronoun "I" now turned into the Roman numeral, thereby moving it into the first position. But if the first ditch were now the seventh, the order would be ATROVACERC, not CATROVACER.

For this to work, the first ditch would need to become the eighth. The book's card-deck-cutting solution calls for ten letters, but the pre-release cover only had nine. You could say that had the book been published with the teaser cover the encoded puzzle would have been one card short of a deck. My hunch is that the first cover was a typo, but when it turned out to be uniquely solvable within Brown's themes, there was no reason to rework it before the actual release. So is it a further puzzle, or a snafu? I'd call it a lucky stumble.

Now that *Inferno* has been published, other cover secrets can be found, many of them less tangled. In addition to the medallion puzzle, there are faintly visible codes. Two are transhumanist references; *H+* (a magazine of the transhumanist movement) and "DG 2064" (possibly Dan Brown's transhumanist codename) are on the back. A Dante canto and verse reference, "VI 74 75," is on the spine; the mnemonic SALIGIA that refers to the seven deadly sins is encoded in bold letters on the flap notes; and "1265," the presumed year of Dante's birth, is on the outer edge of the back flap. The latest secret I have found may be a mirrored pair of small Dante profiles on the back cover incorporated into the torn-edge graphic near the spine.

While we puzzle hunters have deciphered many of Dan Brown's clues, there are still other unsolved puzzles, codes, and website "Easter eggs." Brown has hinted that some are inside jokes for his own and his editors' entertainment. Facebook and Twitter clues also remain that have not yet been tied to the book, and *Dan-Brown.com* will undoubtedly continue to evolve and incorporate more puzzles.

Meanwhile, and perhaps in response to all this code-cracking, Dan Brown has announced that the cover still has more secrets to reveal. Thus far I've found six. Or maybe it's seven.

I need another clue.

Section 4
The Dante Baedeker

Firenze: A Dante Travel Journey

BY DAN BURSTEIN
Creator, author, and coeditor of the *Secrets* series

When I was twelve years old, my parents made their first trip to Europe. Among the souvenirs they brought home was a poster from Florence. They had been there during celebrations commemorating 700 years since the birth of Dante Alighieri, and the poster they brought back depicted an image of the Poet reputed to have been painted by Dante's friend, the artist Giotto. That poster, that pensive and patient portrait of Dante, has been a constant source of inspiration throughout my life. Today, forty-eight years later, it still has a prominent place in my home.

I have been to Florence a number of times in the intervening years. But together with my wife, Julie and our son David, I made a special trip there in the spring of 2013 specifically to look at what remains of the city that Dante knew and loved, and to learn about some of the mysteries and intrigues in Florentine history to properly frame our research into Dan Brown's *Inferno*.

Among the high points of our spring in Florence was a visit to the Bargello Museum, where we found ourselves entranced by the huge fresco that, in one corner, shows Dante as a character among the virtuous people arriving in heaven. My 1965 poster is based on that image. Experts today are divided on whether it was actually painted by Giotto or by other artists in his workshop. But the power of Dante's visage—seemingly contemplating all he has learned about the human condition on his imagined voyage to the afterlife that inspired the *Divine Comedy*—remains gripping and profound. It was a deeply emotional experience, communing not only with my own youth, but with all of the philosophy, history, politics, and art I have learned about since.

The action of Dan Brown's *Inferno* takes place in Florence, Venice, and Istanbul, as well as New York and a few other locales. But the first two-thirds of the book are rooted in Florence, especially in venues that were known to Dante before he went into exile in 1302, never to return again to his native Florence.

Florence is, of course, one of Europe's most beloved tourist destinations. There is so much history and art to see and learn about, it can be truly overwhelming. Indeed, the French writer Stendhal was so overcome with the city's dazzling beauty that he started having heart palpitations. "Stendhal Syndrome" is a known medical problem, based on tourists becoming overstimulated by the artistic bounty of this fabled city.

For us, it was a new approach to Florence to zero in on Dante and to contemplate what aspects Dan Brown would find most interesting for his new novel. Here is a small sampling of the many highlights from our explorations:

Dante's "Neighborhood"

We are standing in front of the Badia, a tenth century abbey that was one of the city's most prominent landmarks in Dante's time. Brown opens his book here, with the "shade"—the character we will later learn is Zobrist—ascending to the top of the Badia and jumping from there to his death in order to preserve his secret. ("I climb the final stairs and arrive at the top," Zobrist narrates. "Dizzyingly far beneath me, the red tile roofs spread out like a sea of fire in the countryside, illuminating the fair land upon which giants once roamed...Giotto, Donatello, Brunelleschi, Michelangelo, Botticelli...")

Dante himself grew up and lived just a block or two from here, at least as far as historians can determine. It was in the Badia that the great fourteenth century writer, Boccaccio (author of the *Decameron*), read Dante's *Commedia* out loud to a large public audience, as part of his efforts to rehabilitate Dante fifty years after his death, and to claim him as the great poet-philosopher-citizen of Florence that he was. It was Boccaccio who dubbed Dante's *Commedia* "Divine," a sobriquet that has stayed in the book's title for the last seven centuries. Dante, once exiled by Florence, accused of trumped up crimes, and threatened with being burnt at the stake if he ever returned, is now the most cherished figure in the city's history.

We walk these millennium-old streets in the company of Alexandra Lawrence, an American living in Florence. She is the editor-at-large of *The Florentine*, the go-to source for local English language information. (*The Florentine* is referenced specifically in Dan Brown's *Inferno*). Alexandra gives walking tours relevant to the city's art, history, and culture. She loves to do Dante tours and has been doing them for years. Undoubtedly, she will be doing many more of them as the "Dan Brown tourists" begin to flock to Florence to see the locales of *Inferno*, just as they did to Rome for *Angels & Demons* and to Paris in the wake of *The Da Vinci Code*.

Alexandra leads us to what is called the Casa di Dante ("Dante's House"), a museum about Dante and medieval Florence. As we approach, a Dante impersonator in fourteenth century regalia is reciting passages from the *Divine Comedy*.

"Bear in mind that almost everything we think we know about Dante's life is basically speculation," Alexandra warns. This spot may not be the location of Dante's actual house. Researchers in the early twentieth century took their best guess at where Dante's house would have been located, and this tall, tower-style house was established here as a center to teach about Dante.

Inside, the exhibits and artifacts remind me that, as deeply humanistic as Dante's literary work is, he lived well before the Renaissance. His life experience is rooted in the Middle Ages—a generally dark time of Crusades, as well as bloody wars among the Italian city-states, and frequent violent power struggles between those pledged to the Pope and those to the Holy Roman Emperor. The brilliance of Dante's work was a factor that helped spark the Renaissance, but he himself had to endure the pain and disappointments that went with being a Renaissance humanist in a medieval world.

One of the best displays in the museum is a detailed presentation of the Battle of Campaldino, in which Dante fought on the side of the faction known as the Guelphs against the

Ghibellines. These civil wars were the dominant battles wreaking havoc throughout northern Italy in the thirteenth century. Dante would ultimately denounce this internecine fighting throughout the *Commedia*. The Casa di Dante gets a brief cameo in Brown's *Inferno*, when Robert Langdon and Sienna Brooks, desperate for a copy of the *Divine Comedy* in order to decode a clue, race to the bookshop there, only to find it closed. In fact, the bookshop is an excellent source of Dante books and souvenirs, including a version of the entire 14,000-line *Commedia* in small type on a single sheet of poster paper.

The renovated building is a "tower-style" house that was common in Dante's day. Several families shared this type of building— six or seven stories, with one family group to a floor, and a shared kitchen usually at the top to prevent fires from starting below. The families living here were often members of a common business organization known as a *Consorteria*—i.e., a Consortium—a word Dan Brown appropriated as the name of the provost's group that, in the novel, has been secretly helping Zobrist conceal his work on the Inferno virus. In addition to creating economies of scale and lowering the average cost of real estate for prosperous Florentines, the top of the tower could be effectively used to spot enemies before they arrived and to spy on the comings and goings of people in the neighborhood.

These houses arose in the context of a factionalized society where kidnapping, murder, bribery, conspiracies, and civil wars were relatively common occurrences—or at least constant threats. Over the course of the thirteenth century, fundamental control of Florence changed several times between Ghibellines and Guelphs. Once the Guelphs consolidated their power, another civil war began between the Black and White Guelph factions. (Dante is associated with the White Guelphs).

Even Machiavelli, who literally wrote the book on power politics, called it the worst time in any city's history. From the internecine divisions in Florence in that period, Machiavelli wrote, "came as many dead, as many exiles, and as many families destroyed as ever occurred in any city in memory."

Close by the Dante House is the palace of the Portinari family. Beatrice Portinari, the daughter of the prominent and politically powerful Folco Portinari, becomes the great—and apparently unconsummated—love of Dante's life. According to Dante's notes, poems, and other historical sources, Beatrice and Dante actually met just a few times in life (the first time when they were eight-and nine-year-old children, the second time a numerologically significant nine years later).

Although Dante was obsessed with Beatrice, she was never a likely marriage partner for him, owing to class distinctions. She married a prominent banker in 1287, and then died at only twenty-four years old in 1290. Yet Beatrice (properly pronounced by Italians as "Bay-A-Tree-Chay," usually while letting her name roll off their tongues slowly with a loving and lofty look in their eyes) was immortalized by Dante as his spiritual guide in the *Divine Comedy*. It is the great Roman poet Virgil who is Dante's guide to the Inferno, but it is Beatrice, the paragon of beauty and grace, who takes him through Paradiso.

We stop in for a brief visit at the Chiesa di Santa Margherita dei Cerchi, more popularly known as the "Church of Dante," where it is presumed that Dante and Beatrice saw each other, first as children and later as young adults. A key scene in Dan Brown's *Inferno* is set in this church. Some say Beatrice is buried here, although many historians dispute that. Even so, the church is treated as a kind of shrine to her. Dozens of people from all over the world leave letters every day to Beatrice in a basket near her "tomb," asking her for advice in matters of love or help on more practical life issues. Dan Brown visited the church while writing *Inferno* and left a letter beseeching Beatrice for inspiration in writing his book. Invoking the words of Homer, Brown says his note read, "Sing in me muse, and through me, tell a story of a man versed in symbols." The original Homer quote ("Sing in me muse...") is an invocation from Homer to his muse to inspire within him the strength to tell the story of the *Odyssey*. Brown adapted these famous lines for his plea to the spirit of Beatrice to guide him through his *Inferno*.

A very short walk from the Casa di Dante is a curious small building, the Congregazione dei Buonomini di San Martino (The Company of Good Men of San Martino). The small chapel you encounter on entering contains several amazing Renaissance art pieces. The building is so little known to tourists that you can be almost assured of a few minutes of personal time and space to commune with masterpieces every bit as delicate and rich as many in the ultra-crowded Uffizi Museum. Beginning six centuries ago, political opponents of Medici rule in Florence began gathering here trying to figure out ways to help the men (and their families) who had been sentenced, often unfairly and without due process, to prison, exile, death, or "only" to bankrupting fines that took them from being on top of society to a state of personal ruination. The Buonomini di San Martino was a charitable organization specifically devoted to helping "good men" who, for whatever reason, had ended up on the wrong side of the powerful Medici clan and their successors. Dante, no doubt, could have used their help in his day, since his wife and children were left in Florence without much of an income after his exile. According to those I talked with in Florence, the Company of Good Men of San Martino has been helping exiles all over Italy and Europe for hundreds of years. They maintain secret files on every case and everyone they have ever helped. When I heard this, I felt sure the odd little building in Piazza di San Martino would show up in *Inferno*, but maybe Dan Brown is saving it for a future book.

Palazzo Vecchio

> I pass behind the palazzo with its crenellated tower and one-handed clock . . . snaking through the early morning vendors in Piazza di San Firenze with their hoarse voices smelling of lampredotto and roasted olives...
> —from Zobrist's self-narration of the moments leading up to his suicide in Dan Brown's *Inferno*

The "palazzo with its crenellated tower and one-handed clock" in this quote refers to the Palazzo Vecchio (Old Palace), Florence's town hall, whose construction began during Dante's youth. Dante would not have recognized the current edifice, most of which was constructed long after his death. But when Duke Cosimo I de' Medici moved his operations here in 1540, this building became the seat of power from which the Medici family—bankers to Europe, political wizards of Florence, patrons of Renaissance artists including Michelangelo and Leonardo da Vinci—would invent modern capitalism and control Florence for the next century. Today, in addition to housing the Town Hall, the Palazzo Vecchio is open to the public as a museum.

Michelangelo's famous seventeen-foot-tall statue of David stood outside the Palazzo for almost 400 years, from the time he sculpted it in the first years of the sixteenth century to 1873, when it was moved indoors to the Accademia Gallery in another part of town. Today a replica stands guard at the front of the Palazzo, along with several other giant marble statues of Renaissance origin. The actual David statue is one of only a few of Florence's top tourist attractions that doesn't get much play in *Inferno*. Robert Langdon bemoans the fact that, while he has always made it a point to go see the David statue in the Accademia before he leaves Florence, he won't even have time for that visit on this fast-paced trip, where he is racing against the clock to save the world from a terrible bioterrorist plague. We made the visit Robert Langdon couldn't and spent an hour in absolute awe of this work of Michelangelo's staggering genius. Seeing David in person is a chance to meditate on our own humanity and to renew our belief in art, beauty, and the ability of the Davids of the world to overcome the Goliaths. (Dan Brown told *The New York Times* in June, 2013 that one of the books he is most looking forward to is Malcolm Gladwell's new book on the many "Davids" in history, and their high success rate in defeating "Goliaths").

A good portion of the action in Brown's *Inferno* is set in the labyrinthine spaces of the Palazzo Vecchio. For example, Dante's death mask is on display here, although it is obscure and easy to miss. The mask, which becomes one of the McGuffins central to

Brown's plot, is presumably a re-creation made well after Dante's death. In the novel, Zobrist is said to have purchased the death mask and then loaned it to the Palazzo Vecchio. It's easy to see where Dan Brown got this idea of a private donor of Dante's mask: The display indicates that Dante's death mask was donated by a certain Senator d'Ancona. (Unlike US museums, very few objects in Italian museums indicate private citizens as donors). A bit of internet sleuthing by Julie, my wife, suggests that this refers to one Alessandro d'Ancona, born in Pisa in the nineteenth century in a Jewish family, and who served as mayor of Pisa and senator from his region. He was also a prolific writer on Italian literary history, especially on themes relating to Dante.

For sixty-five pages, Brown's characters, Robert Langdon and Sienna Brooks, are hunting for clues or being pursued by their adversaries in various rooms, secret passageways, and attic areas of the Palazzo Vecchio. There is a standard "Secret Passageways" tour of the Palazzo. Dan Brown took the tour and he milks it for all it is worth in *Inferno*. The Studiolo, for example, is one of the rooms you can see on the Secret Passageways tour. Personally, I could have spent all day there and in its even smaller sister chamber, the Tesoretto room. Here, the Medici family kept valuable, mysterious and magical objects they had collected from the four corners of the world (and their secret document files as well). These rooms were designed by the great Renaissance painter and architect, Giorgio Vasari, at the direction of Francesco I, who was the alchemist in the Medici family. Almost every inch of the walls and ceilings of the Studiolo is covered by paintings, many of which contain alchemical symbols, codes, and clues to deciphering hidden mean-ings worked into the imagery. Most of the paintings, in turn, are actually cabinet doors, which once concealed secret objects of magical and alchemical significance.

The Studiolo is just off Palazzo Vecchio's main hall, the Salone dei Cinquecento, or "Salon of the Five Hundred." Vasari presided over renovation of this vast hall, one of the most magnificent—and theatrical—spaces in Italy. Since the Salon was used by the Medici family to convene important meetings and hold major celebrations, Vasari decorated it with massive murals depicting victorious moments in Florentine and Medici military history. Fifty-foot-high tableaus of battles rise up to meet a ceiling completely covered in additional painted scenes of the glories of Florence.

Hidden in the vast scale of one of these murals—Vasari's *Battle of Marciano*—are tiny white letters, one inch high on a small green flag carried by a soldier, that spell out CERCA TROVA (Latin for "Seek and you will find"). "CERCA TROVA" and "seek and find" are mentioned over and over again in Brown's *Inferno*. In the first chapter, these words are spoken to Langdon in his post-traumatic amnesiac delirium by a mystical character, a veiled woman who turns out to be a composite made up of parts derived from Dante's Beatrice, Greek mythic figures, and Dr. Sinskey. These words, echoing throughout the novel, continuously prompt him to continue on his mission to "seek and find" each of the clues that will lead him to ground zero for Zobrist's Inferno plague.

In the Salon of the Five Hundred, Langdon tells Sienna correctly that the CERCA TROVA insignia is "almost impossible to see from down here without binoculars." Yet Sienna, in one of the rare moments when her alleged super powers of perception pays off, is able to spot it anyway. (On the day I was there, I found it impossible to see CERCA TROVA with the naked eye, and even the guards in that room could only point me to the general vicinity at the top of this giant mural. I was able to find the inscription only with the zoom feature of Julie's camera. But this was before Brown's *Inferno* was published, and I imagine today that any guard will be able to point you to it).

CERCA TROVA is the watchword of *Inferno*, much as Brown emphasized the use of "hidden in plain sight" in *The Da Vinci Code* a decade ago. In *Inferno*, Brown also brings back for a small cameo one of the few real-life contemporary characters mentioned in *The Da Vinci Code*: Maurizio Seracini, the now well-known forensic art researcher. For three decades, Seracini has been hunting in the Palazzo for Leonardo da Vinci's lost masterpiece, the *Battle of Anghiari*. Many of those who saw it while it was still visible in the early sixteenth century believed it to be Leonardo's most powerful work.

The historical record shows that both Michelangelo and Leonardo were invited to develop important large-scale art works for the Palazzo Vecchio. It was the only time these two Renaissance masters worked on the same project. Machiavelli personally signed Leonardo's contract. Michelangelo never finished his piece, because he was called away to work on the tomb of Pope Julius II in Rome. Leonardo never finished his *Battle of Anghiari*, for a variety of technical and artistic reasons.

A few decades later, Giorgio Vasari was asked by the reigning Medici monarch, Grand Duke Cosimo I, to enlarge and completely redesign the space that is now the Salon of the Five Hundred. In order to do that, Vasari had to cover over Leonardo's earlier work, which Vasari himself esteemed highly. Half a millennium later, Seracini hypothesized that Leonardo's masterpiece may still be visible in a hidden space behind the Vasari mural and that Vasari intentionally preserved it. According to Seracini, Vasari left the words CERCA TROVA as a clue to future generations as to where to look for the concealed Leonardo. Several tests conducted by Seracini have been promising—one indicated the existence of a concealed space behind the wall, and the other turned up some evidence of pigment. But after a brief period when Seracini was allowed to conduct his forensic investigations, the powers-that-be in Florence have now shut further mildly invasive research down. (One important footnote: Not everyone agrees with Seracini, of course. Two of his critics, Alfonso Musci and Alessandro Savorelli, published an article in an Italian Renaissance studies publication in 2012 arguing that Vasari's CERCA TROVA had nothing at all to do with covering up the Leonardo painting, but was derived instead from a literary passage from ... drum rolls, please ... Dante's *Divine Comedy*.)

Prior to publication of *Inferno*, I had thought the hunt for Leonardo's *Battle of Anghiari* would be one of the book's important sub-themes. After all, Dan Brown had introduced Seracini to millions of readers in *The Da Vinci Code*. Brown loves the theme of hidden art works and secret passages, and Vasari and the CERCA TROVA phrase are key to *Inferno*. I also thought the real facts of the Medici family covering up the Leonardo painting five hundred years ago, combined with the town fathers of Florence preventing further research today, would lend themselves to a truly "Dan Brownian" conspiracy theory. In the end, Brown did not go in this direction. But the traveler to Florence can still have a great time searching for the CERCA TROVA inscription, walking through the Vasari Corridor and discovering the other treasures on the Secret Passageways tour.

Fans of Dan Brown's fiction will find other allusions in *Inferno* to multiple scenes in his prior books. The center of the ceiling in the Salon of the Five Hundred is Vasari's *Apotheosis of Cosimo*. It is this image through which Vayentha falls to her death after Sienna's quick martial arts moves take her down. Vayentha, who hoped to capture Langdon and redeem herself in the eyes of the provost, ends up creating a "jagged dark tear" in the center of the "massive circular canvas depicting Cosimo I encircled by cherubs on a heavenly cloud." (Don't worry: This is fiction. Vasari's *Apotheosis of Cosimo* is fine, and you can see it intact on your visit to the Salon of the Five Hundred).

Vasari's image of a heavenly Cosimo is similar in style and content to the *Apotheosis of Washington* painted three hundred years later by Constantino Brumidi. An American artist of Italian origins, Brumidi painted the scene of George Washington going up to heaven as the centerpiece of the interior of the U.S. Capitol building dome. The symbolism of this work figures prominently in Dan Brown's *The Lost Symbol*.

Other cases of throwbacks to plot points in prior Dan Brown books include his use in *Inferno* of the Vasari Corridor and the Duke of Athens stairway as secret routes through Florence. These episodes recall his use of the Passetto between St. Peter's and the Castel Sant'Angelo in Rome in *Angels & Demons*, as well as

Langdon and Katherine's scheme to elude the CIA men chasing them in *The Lost Symbol* by escaping on the Library of Congress book conveyor system.

I was expecting Brown to do more with the giant globe in the center of the Palazzo Vecchio's map room. In the sixteenth century this was the world's largest globe, and Vasari had called for it to be designed with the ability to exhibit a certain amount of motion and to be used dramatically to show off the "cosmological" interests of Cosimo. Although Brown did not dwell on the globe, the visitor to this room should.

The Duomo, the Baptistery, and the Ponte Vecchio

The Ponte Vecchio, a tenth century bridge over the Arno, today dotted with gold and jewelry stores and crammed full of tourists at all hours, comes in for some of the action in *Inferno* and a few history lessons from Brown. I never understood that running along the top of the Ponte Vecchio was the Vasari Corridor, constructed for Medici family members to come and go in secret from the Palazzo Vecchio and their nearby "offices" (*uffizi* is the Italian word for "offices," thus the name of the Uffizi Museum) and deposit them on the other side of town in the Boboli Gardens of the Pitti Palace. Langdon and Sienna travel the opposite way of the Vasari Corridor tour, starting in the Boboli Gardens and ending up in the Palazzo Vecchio. Many of Florence's other top tourist attractions figure in *Inferno*. The cathedral today known as the Duomo, the most prominent landmark in Florence, was under construction in Dante's time, but the great Dome for which it has been known for the last five hundred years did not come into being until Brunelleschi figured out how to engineer it a century after Dante's death. (Ross King's brilliant book, *Brunelleschi's Dome*, one of the best books to read about the history of Florence, is briefly referenced by Brown in *Inferno*).

Immediately adjacent to the Duomo lies the Baptistery, where Dante himself was baptized. This is the venue for several important plot developments in Brown's *Inferno*. He reminds us that

Ghiberti's famous carved bronze doors for the Baptistery have been traded out for replicas, but never mind. Even the replicas are still worth a good long look to see Ghiberti's genius for design.

***

It is our last dawn in Florence. We are gazing out at the Arno from our hotel, soaking in our last looks at the Ponte Vecchio and the Florentine "skyline"—the Duomo, the Campanile, the Badia, and the one-handed clock on the tower of the Palazzo Vecchio. A dragon boat from a local rowing club skims the water and speeds by. After a busy week in Florence, we are experiencing a mild case of Stendhal Syndrome. So much beauty, so much art, so much we have seen...and yet so much still to be seen.

When Dante returns from his ecstatic experience in *Paradiso* coming face to face with the essence of God, he can neither remember his experiences fully nor put them into words properly. Even the great Poet feels that his effort to describe what he has seen comes out as mere baby talk.

I feel the same way about my ability to describe Florence...The best thing you can do is go see it for yourself.

The Firenze Folio

BY JULIE O'CONNOR
Fine art photographer and photojournalist

Poster for the 700th Anniversary of Dante Alighieri's birth in Florence brought home by Dan Burstein's parents from a trip to Florence in 1965.

A view of the skyline of Florence that includes the Giotto bell tower (Campanile di Giotto), the Duomo, and the Badia church tower.

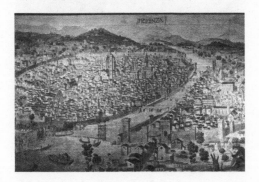

A map of Florence c. 1490 labeled, "The Pianta della Catena," by the Florentine miniature painter and engraver Francesco di Lorenzo Rosselli. It is among the first known examples of a detailed, complete representation of a city.

The open air courtyard of the Bargello National Museum. The Bargello was built in the mid-thirteenth century. The museum holds a remarkable collection of masterpieces dating back to Dante's time, as well as important Renaissance sculpture by Donatello, Michelangelo, and others, and a significant portion of the Medici collection.

Dante is depicted in this famous fresco of the Last Judgment found in the St. Mary Magdalene Chapel in the Bargello Museum. It is attributed by some experts to Giotto, or at least his workshop, and was painted after Dante's death, subsequently obscured, and partly restored in 1840. Giotto and Dante were friends in life and here stand side by side in Paradiso for eternity.

A close up detail of Dante (from the Bargello fresco), painted by Giotto
or another artist in his circle, standing among those in Paradiso at the
Last Judgment was discovered underneath centuries of plaster in 1840.
The frescoed walls had previously been covered over when the Bargello
Palace was converted into a prison.

The Badia Fiorentina is the oldest monastery in Florence. It was created by Willa, Countess of Tuscany, in honor of her late husband in 978. Dante, who is thought to have lived very close by, would have heard the monks singing the Mass and Vespers here in Latin.

Dante had already been exiled from Florence when the Badia's spire was constructed from 1310 to 1330. In the Prologue to Dan Brown's *Inferno*, the character Zobrist leaps to his death from this tower.

The actor Alessio Cinotti, known as Farfarello, performs the
the *Divine Comedy* from memory in the Piazza outside Casa
di Dante (the museum in Florence devoted to Dante). In
Inferno, Langdon and Brooks look for a copy of the *Divine
Comedy* at the bookstore here to help decode a clue, but find
the Casa di Dante is closed.

Near Casa di Dante, an example of a medieval tower-house. The
Torre della Castagna stood as early as 1038, when it was given to
the Badia Fiorentina for defense of the monastery. These tower
houses were often occupied by multiple families bound by common business interests and were called Consorteria. Dan Brown
uses the term "Consortium" to label the group that helps Zobrist
conceal his Inferno virus.

The Palazzo Portinari-Salviati was built in the 1470s on the site of Beatrice's family home on the Via Corso. It is now owned by the oldest surviving bank from Sienna.

Interior of "Dante's Church" (Chiesa di Santa Margherita dei Cerchi), where it is said that Beatrice, Dante's muse, is buried (although this is disputed). The basket is a collection point for letters to Beatrice. Those seeking counsel in love and in life leave notes addressed to her.

The Chapel of Company of Good Men of San Martino (Congregazioine dei Buonomini di San Martino) holds Renaissance masterpieces and aids individuals unjustly wronged. It is in Dante's "neighborhood."

The Palazzo Vecchio or "Old Palace" is the town hall of Florence as well as an art museum open to the public.

The recreated Dante Death Mask inside the Palazzo Vecchio. In the Dan Brown novel, Zobrist is said to own the mask and he loans it to the Palazzo Vecchio. Zobrist's inscription on the mask becomes the source for key clues for Robert Langdon.

Inside the Studiolo of Francesco I, a side room off of the Hall of Five Hundred. Among many paintings in this room designed by Vasari, this image is a portrait of Eleonora of Toledo by Bronzino.

Hall of the Five Hundred ("Salone dei Cinquecento") within the Palazzo Vecchio was built in 1494-5 and later enlarged and redesigned by Giorgio Vasari. The ceiling consists of thirty-nine panels constructed and painted by Vasari and his assistants in the mid-sixteenth century. These represent great episodes from the life of Cosimo I, scenes from great victories won by Florence, and other important moments in history. In the center of the ceiling is the painting, "Apotheosis of Cosimo I," through which Vayentha falls after a struggle with Sienna Brooks in Brown's *Inferno*.

The panoramic "Battle of Marciano" in the Hall of the Five Hundred is where Langdon sees the clue "Cerca Trova" (seek and you shall find) written on a minute battle flag in the battle scene.

View looking out from the Vasari Corridor, a secret passageway built in 1565 by Giorgio Vasari for Grand Duke Cosimo I de' Medici who wished to travel unobserved between the court and his residence. It runs above the Ponte Vecchio, connecting the Palazzo Vecchio to the Pitti Palace and the Boboli Gardens, and is part of Langdon and Sienna's escape route in Dan Brown's *Inferno*.

The Hall of Geographical Maps in the Palazzo Vecchio is where Robert Langdon escapes into a secret passage behind a map of Armenia that opens on hinges from the wall. In the center of the room stands the "Mappa Mundi" globe.

The Ponte Vecchio is the oldest standing bridge in Florence and the only one that was not damaged during World War II.

The main characters in *Inferno* are chased into the Boboli Gardens. This image shows the wildly decorative facade at the entrance to the grotto used by Langdon and Sienna to escape detection and ultimately to enter the Vasari Corridor.

View of the Duomo from inside the Palazzo Vecchio. The great dome was engineered by master goldsmith, Filippo Brunelleschi, and remains the largest brick dome ever constructed. The cathedral was built over a period of 150 years, beginning in 1296. Completion was delayed by wars and the outbreak of the Black Death among other reasons.

Brunelleschi was awarded the commission to build the dome in 1420. It was completed to the Oculus in 1436. The beauty of his plan was in the proposal to construct two domes with interlocking bridgework that made the dome self-supporting.

Dante was baptized in the octagonal Florence Baptistery, which stands across from the Duomo and the Campanile. It is thought to be the oldest building in the city dating to the sixth or seventh century.

The Props of Dan Brown:
Three Churches of World Significance

BY WILLIAM COOK
Distinguished Teaching Professor of History (Emeritus),
State University of New York, Geneseo

Dan Brown prominently features three churches in *Inferno*—the cathedral complex in Florence; the cathedral of Venice; and Hagia Sofia in Istanbul, the cathedral of Constantinople until the Turkish conquest of 1453 and now a museum after having been a mosque for almost 500 years. Like everything else in Brown's *Inferno*, they serve to push the plot forward. These are among the grandest churches in the world, but they are largely just props for Dan Brown.

Here are a few salient details about these three important building complexes in these three great cities that readers of Dan Brown's *Inferno* may wish to know:

Venice

There is evidence that Dante visited Venice. This is likely both because of his living rather close to Venice during most of the twenty years of his exile and because Dante describes the city's shipyards in great detail in *Inferno* 21. The Cathedral of Venice, dedicated to St. Mark (San Marco), was a prominent feature of Venice at the time; however, it did not become the Cathedral until the early nineteenth century. In Dante's time, it was the chapel of the Doge (head of state). It is extremely unlikely that Dante would have entered it. Although Dante uses imagery derived from mosaic art in *Paradiso*, it is clear that the mosaics he was citing were those of Ravenna, where he lived while writing the third canticle of his *Commedia*.

Constantinople

Constantinople was a shadow of its historic imperial self during Dante's lifetime. It had come under Latin rule in 1204 when the Fourth Crusade was diverted here from the original plan to re-take Jerusalem. After more than a half century of Latin rule, the Greeks recaptured the city four years before Dante's birth, though hardly all the Empire that it had ruled. For me, Hagia Sofia is the greatest building in the world, but Dante never saw it and made no mention of it in his *Commedia*.

Dan Brown is right in placing the tomb of Doge Enrico Dandolo in Hagia Sofia, for he was one of the leaders of the Fourth Crusade and died in Constantinople. That Robert Langdon does not know this and has to spend much time cogitating over the clues about where a "treacherous Doge" is buried strikes me as unlikely for a person of his expertise. Dandolo's tomb is in every guidebook and is a stop for just about everyone taking a tour or following a guidebook on their own. Similarly, the nearby sixth century cistern in which some of the book's critical action takes place is a major tourist site. People who have had a lot less experience than me in Constantinople easily figured out where Robert Langdon had to visit long before he did.

Florence

Florence's Cathedral was not standing at the time Dante lived in Florence. Five years before his exile, the city decided to build a grand new one. The plan for doing this was unusual. Instead of tearing down the old Cathedral, dedicated to Santa Reparata, a rather obscure early martyr, the idea was to build the new cathedral around the old one, eventually tearing Santa Reparata down and hauling its parts away. Dante saw none of this happening, and its trademark dome by Brunelleschi was built about 125 years after Dante was exiled from Florence.

The most important ecclesiastical building in Dan Brown's book, at least for Dante and his *Commedia*, is the much smaller and older octagonal building that stands directly in front of the cathedral. This is the Baptistery, dedicated unsurprisingly to St. John the Baptist, who is also the patron saint of Florence (San Giovanni). This wonderful building is not only important as the place where Florentines were baptized and thus entered the Church, but it was also a civic building where people became citizens of Florence as well as citizens of the City of God.

This building is now known principally for its fifteenth century doors of Lorenzo Ghiberti, which Michelangelo dubbed, "The Gates of Paradise" (those in place are copies, as Brown correctly points out, and the recently restored originals will be on display in the cathedral's museum when it reopens in 2015). The Baptistery was already an aged edifice in Dante's day, and he mentions it by name in both *Inferno* and *Paradiso*. In fact, he calls it "mi bel San Giovanni" in *Inferno* 19. No other edifice in Dante's Florence receives such praise from the poet, although several great churches, such as Santa Maria Novella, the Dominican church where Dante probably received part of his education, were essentially complete before his exile.

Dante had several reasons to think of this building as his beautiful Baptistery of St. John. He certainly appreciated its history, although his understanding of the building's origins are quite different from that of scholars today. While there *may* have been a pagan temple on this spot, Dante believed that the building was at least in part of Roman work and symbolized the change from paganism, where Mars was worshiped as the special god of Florence, to the building of Christian initiation.

Dante tells us in the *Commedia* that he was baptized in this great building, and his great-great-grandfather Cacciaguida tells Dante in *Paradiso* that he too was baptized in that same font. Cacciaguida is in Heaven, literally a saint; Dante can find continuity with his sainted ancestor through their common initiation into the Church. Moreover, Cacciaguida became a martyr through his death as a member of the Second Crusade and Dante becomes a crusader as well—in his case, a crusader against ecclesiastical corruption with his pen.

In *Inferrno* 19, Dante tells of an incident in his life that took place in the Baptistery. He saw that there was a malfunction in the baptismal font and that a baby would die unless he did something drastic. So Dante broke the font, presumably with some sort of tool, and rescued the baby. He explains that there may have been witnesses who regarded him as blaspheming by taking an implement of destruction to this piece of holy furniture. Dante defends his action by suggesting that since the device was malfunctioning and producing the opposite of what it is supposed to be producing—death instead of life—his attack was a pious act that "reformed" the font. This is a kind of prologue to the main part of *Inferno* 19, in which Dante has a discussion with a pope in Hell and hears a prophecy that the then current pontiff, Boniface VIII, would spend eternity there as well. Some readers might have thought it blasphemous for Dante to put a pope in Hell, but he is respectful to the office and is trying to call for reform of the Church he so loves. There is no evidence other than Dante's telling of this Baptistery story that it ever happened, and many scholars see it as a literary device rather than the recall of an actual event in his earlier life. Dan Brown recalls this story as he and Sienna search for Dante's death mask, but I think he somewhat misreads the beginning of *Inferno* 19.

We know from the chronicle of Dino Compagni, a contemporary of Dante and a political ally as a White Guelph, that in 1300, the year of Dante's fictional trip to the afterlife, people of all factions were called to a meeting at the Baptistery. Surely here, where presumably all became Christians and citizens of Florence, an oath they swore on the font itself would bind them. Yet their oath for peace and reconciliation was almost immediately abandoned. For Dino and probably for Dante, this abandonment of the oath meant that there was no peaceful solution to Florence's factional madness. In the next year, Dante would go into exile for the last twenty years of his life, never again seeing his beautiful San Giovanni.

Dante was probably an observer of the completion of the mosaic that covers the interior of the dome of the Baptistery. It contains four bands of narrative, two from the Old Testament (creation and stories of Joseph, both from *Genesis*, plus the lives of John the Baptist and Jesus). While these occupy five of the eight segments of the dome, the other three are a stunning Last Judgment. Brown describes the Judgment without recognizing that it is only 3/8 of the whole. As Brown points out, this mosaic can still inspire and scare visitors today, and some of its imagery finds its way into Dante's *Inferno*. In Heaven we find not only apostles and the usual crowd of saints but also two new saints of the time— Saints Francis and Dominic, both of whose lives are told to Dante in *Paradiso* by distinguished members of their orders: respectively, Saints Thomas Aquinas and Bonaventure.

Brown is a good storyteller and uses these buildings effectively to move his plot along. I do not want to be needlessly picky about details, since, after all, Brown's book is fiction. Still, he could have found ways to plant in his readers' heads the notion that they are worth visiting, just as I have expressed my wish elsewhere in this book that he had done more to encourage people to seek out and read Dante's *Commedia*.

Dolci:
Musings and Meditations on
Dante and Dan Brown

BY DAN BURSTEIN
Creator, author, and coeditor of the *Secrets* series

THE EPIGRAPH AND THE EPILOGUE, FIRE AND ICE,
DANTE, JFK, AND THE PERILS OF MORAL NEUTRALITY

The epigraph that opens Dan Brown's *Inferno* reads as follows: "The darkest places in hell are reserved for those who maintain their neutrality in times of moral crisis." The quote is not attributed to anyone. The exact same words are italicized and repeated in the Epilogue, where they are interpreted by Robert Langdon to mean that, "In dangerous times, there is no sin greater than inaction."

In between Epigraph and Epilogue, Sinskey hears Zobrist intone the exact same words about neutrality and the darkest places in Hell as she watches the frightening video message Zobrist recorded before his suicide. Watching the video, Sinskey feels goose bumps on her neck, because this is the "same quotation that Zobrist had left for her at the airline counter when she had eluded him in New York a year ago."

Indeed, we read those exact words once again in chapter 38 when Sinskey is handed a message from Zobrist at the airport as she is checking in for her flight from New York to Geneva, after having just alerted the "CIA, the CDC, the ECDC, and all of their sister organizations around the world," to Zobrist's potential bioterror threat she has just learned of as a result of his meeting with her at the Council on Foreign Relations. The three other times the quote is used it is unattributed. But in the JFK Airport scene, Dan Brown calls it a "famous quote *derived* (emphasis added) from the work of Dante Alighieri."

The quote is, in fact, derivative, but not exactly from Dante. The Poet was indeed critical of those who stayed neutral in times of moral crisis. But Dante did not consign the neutrals to the "darkest places in hell." In the *Divine Comedy*, he reserves the true "darkest places in hell" for the likes of Judas, Brutus, and Cassius, who betrayed Jesus and Caesar and caused their murders. For the neutrals, there is a different kind of punishment: Dante deems their lives to be so lacking in consequence that they are forgotten completely. They are not even worth the condemnation of Hell. They have no chance at redemption in purgatory, let alone heaven. No one wants them, and so they remain dead souls outside the gates of Hell, forever forgotten for the crime of having failed to choose sides at an important juncture.

The quote is not really "derived" from Dante. It is derived instead from President John F. Kennedy, who in turn derived it, with a few mistakes along the way, from his reading of Dante. The John F. Kennedy Library website notes:

> One of President Kennedy's favorite quotations was based upon an interpretation of Dante's *Inferno*. As Robert Kennedy explained in 1964, "President Kennedy's favorite quote was really from Dante: 'The hottest places in Hell are reserved for those who in time of moral crisis preserve their neutrality.'"

> This supposed quotation is not actually in Dante's work, but is based upon a similar one. In the *Inferno*, Dante and his guide Virgil, on their way to Hell, pass by a group of dead souls outside the entrance to Hell. These individuals, when alive, remained neutral at a time of great moral decision. Virgil explains to Dante that these

souls cannot enter either Heaven or Hell because
they did not choose one side or another. They are
therefore worse than the greatest sinners in Hell
because they are repugnant to both God and
Satan alike, and have been left to mourn their
fate as insignificant beings neither hailed nor
cursed in life or death, endlessly travailing below
Heaven but outside of Hell. This scene occurs in
the third canto of the *Inferno*.

It appears that JFK made this remark multiple times, but there
is a particularly good documentary trail citing this quote (using
the formulation of the "hottest places in Hell," not the "darkest
places in Hell") in remarks in Bonn, Germany, in June of 1963,
at the height of the Cold War and just a few months before JFK's
assassination. Dan Brown knows Dante well enough to know that
Dante's vision of the worst part of Hell where Satan resides is
characterized by brutally cold and frozen ice, not by the heat of
fire that has become more commonly associated with Hell in the
last several hundred years. So Brown changed "hottest" to "darkest"
and says the quote is "derived" from Dante, although this may have
been a last-minute correction, since in the Italian edition, the epigraph still uses the phrase *piu caldi*—meaning hottest, not darkest.

In any event, "The darkest places in Hell are reserved for those
who maintain their neutrality in times of moral crisis" has become
the most quoted sentence in Dan Brown's *Inferno*. Several of our
academic experts comment on it in their essays in this book. You
can find plenty of web discussion of this quote.

JFK can be forgiven for misremembering Dante's words and
thinking that the great Poet imagined Hell as fiery rather than icy.
It is an exercise in nostalgia to contemplate a time in our American
public discourse (a mere fifty years ago) when a President could
invoke Dante to discuss great moral issues and how we should
confront them.

But Dan Brown is playing a different kind of game here. He repeats this quote four times, strongly suggests that it comes from Dante, and asks both his characters and his readers to avoid condemnation to the darkest places in hell in their own lives by taking urgent action against the population explosion. By the end of the book, he has revealed that Sienna has never wavered in her support for Zobrist's mad scheme, and that Sinskey and even Langdon have become convinced that Zobrist is basically correct. The characters have all fallen in place. Now he wants the readers to do the same. But the readers haven't even heard a good argument against the population explosion thesis in the entire book, nor have they been offered any meaningful action alternatives besides Zobrist's madman's ability to determine the fate of the planet and the fertility rates of its several billion of its people.

The questions about how to make the earth's resources and population trends more sustainable and better harmonized are *not* the moral equivalent s of JFK's urgent appeals of that era for federal action to integrate the University of Mississippi or to check the spread of Soviet totalitarian power in the world. Nor are they the equivalents of Dante's call to get religion out of the earthly money and power business and restore it to its spiritual essence. Brown has many clever tricks up his sleeve in his *Inferno*. But the trick of creating a false equivalency between an issue he has identified as critical and the moral and philosophical wisdom of Dante falls flat. It does not work and does not even make sense.

GREEN EYES, BEAK-LIKE NOSE, MALE AND FEMALE

Dan Brown has endowed Bertrand Zobrist with green eyes and a beak-like nose. Three references in *Inferno* point to his green eyes, and more than ten references to his beaked nose—or to the Venetian plague mask's beaked nose that is a symbol for Zobrist. Interestingly, these notable traits allude separately to Dante and Beatrice. Several of the most notable portraits of Dante show him with a very pronounced beaked nose, or what in history was called an aquiline nose (referring to the Latin word for eagle). In *Purgatorio* 31, Dante suggests that Beatrice has emerald eyes. A few paintings depict Beatrice with green eyes. Green may here be a metaphor more than a physical attribute: the *Divine Comedy* has a variety of references to green, red, and white (and to emeralds, rubies, and diamonds) with each corresponding to a particular Christian virtue (hope, charity, and faith). Today's Italian flag incorporates these colors.

The integration of male and female is a signature theme with Dan Brown, who made many references to the metaphor of "chalice and blade" in *The Da Vinci Code*, which also stressed the importance of the female in early religions and specifically in early Christianity. Mary Magdalene figured prominently in *DVC* as the partner and wife of Jesus; Brown's Robert Langdon character seemed to believe in the theory that Mary was seated next to Jesus in the *Last Supper* painting, and that Leonardo da Vinci had integrated chalice and blade spaces into the image to illustrate the unity of male and female. Langdon is always paired with a beautiful, brainy female counterpart: Sophie Neveu in *DVC*, Vittoria Vetra in *A&D*, Katherine Solomon in *TLS,* and now Sienna Brooks in *Inferno*. Even before the Robert Langdon novels, Brown used the same formula of a male-female partnership to try to save the world from some outsized impending disaster in *Digital Fortress* and *Deception Point*.

Inferno provides a direct moment of sexual fusion for Langdon and Sienna when Langdon dons Sienna's blond wig (she is bald because of her medical condition, which is given as *telogen effluvium*, a stress-related kind of hair loss). Although her stated intent is to make him look like an aging rock-and-roll singer, the fact is they are sharing the same wig and the same blond hair that the reader believes makes her particularly feminine and attractive.

Many of Brown's books dissect images of sexuality in art and the role of gender in the history of religion. Examples abound in his fiction of his efforts to show the process by which the Mother Goddess, typical of archaic religions as well as the respect given to the "sacred feminine," was superseded by the male-oriented focus of modern Western religions. Yet despite his intellectual interest in sex and gender, Brown almost never writes sex scenes. Indeed, his work features an extremely rare *absence* of sex for bestselling fiction and especially for the action/adventure/thriller genres in which he works.

Neither Langdon nor his beautiful female partner are married in any of the books. Even though they are typically pressed together in incredibly intimate circumstances and share deep insights about themselves and life—and even though they are almost always attracted to each other—Brown studiously avoids showing his characters coupling sexually. *Angels & Demons*, the first of the Robert Langdon novels, written in the 1990s and published in 2000, ends on a note of sexual promise. After a moonlit balcony feast in which Langdon refuses to respond to Vittoria pressing her bare legs against his beneath the table, Langdon returns to the bed to study Illuminati symbolism further. After some rom-com repartee about neutrinos, Vittoria finally straddles the reluctant gentleman and slips off her robe. When Langdon tells her he has never had a rapturous, religious experience in his life and does not expect to have one, she shoots back, "You've never been to bed with a yoga master, have you?" No details are supplied of what happens next. There, the book ends.

What sex there is in the Brown novels seems to be there more for symbological and anthropological (and eventual cinematic) reasons, such as the scene in *DVC* where Sophie recounts her memory of coming upon her grandfather and his friends engaged in a sacred sexual ritual that was part of the Priory of Sion's worship of the sacred feminine.

In the anticlimax at the end of *DVC* (published in 2003), Langdon invites Sophie to meet him a month later in Florence, where he will be delivering a lecture at a conference. He promises her the elegant luxury of the Hotel Brunelleschi. She agrees, but only on one condition: "No museums, no churches, no tombs, no art, no relics."

Langdon presumably will spend the next month after this romantic moment (when Venus, "the ancient goddess," was shining down on them and Sophie kissed him on the lips) wrestling with how one makes love to the last known living descendant of Jesus Christ.

But it apparently took Langdon not a month but a decade to get back to the Hotel Brunelleschi, where he is staying in Florence for the plot of 2013's *Inferno*. There's no news of Sophie in *Inferno*, and, in any event, the plot action (in *Inferno*) is in complete violation of her request to spend their time together in bed, not in museums and churches. On his current trip to Florence, Langdon starts all over again with Sienna in the next installment of Brown's formula: Boy meets girl . . . boy and girl race together against a twenty-four-hour clock to save the world . . . boy and girl grow attracted to each other . . . nothing happens between boy and girl . . . boy and girl separate with vague plans to meet again someday.

Inferno provides an interesting exception to Brown's rules, however. There is a sex scene that occurs more than halfway through the book, beginning on p. 287. The scene runs for less than three pages, and while most of the verbiage is devoted to a discussion of transhumanism, there are a couple of paragraphs of indicated sex: "In that moment all the awkward sexual fears and frustrations of my childhood disappear...evaporating into the snowy night... For the first time ever, I feel a yearning unfettered by shame. I want him...Ten minutes later, we are in Zobrist's hotel room, naked in each other's arms..."

As most readers come upon this passage, their instinct is to fall into the trap Brown has carefully set for them and to understand the scene in the Chicago hotel room as a homosexual encounter between Ferris and Zobrist. Brown uses clever storytelling craftsmanship to create this illusion. Indeed, at least one major newspaper reviewer and one author of an e-book decoding *Inferno* fell publicly for the trap.

But on p. 354, the exact words of the same sex scene in snowy Chicago from p. 287 are repeated. Now we understand that the incident in the hotel room six years ago was not an encounter between Ferris and Zobrist, nor was it homosexual in nature. It is Sienna's memory of her heterosexual encounter with Zobrist. Until three-quarters of the way through the story, Sienna has been hiding from Langdon, and from the reader, that she is Zobrist's lover, muse, devoted disciple, and double-agent, who was there at the moment of his suicide, and whose interest in stopping the plague from unfolding is completely different than Langdon and Sinskey's.

Brown is having some fun with his readers here. He is fusing and confusing homosexual and heterosexual encounters and using these moments to shape reader perceptions of the characters and to introduce a major red herring. He causes the reader to assume that Ferris, who already seems creepy and suspicious, is the lover/disciple of Zobrist and a traitor to Sinskey and Langdon. Meanwhile, he conceals for another sixty pages the fact that Ferris is an OK guy who suffers only from allergies, not from exposure to the Inferno plague, and that it is Sienna who is the double-agent.

The repetition is itself somewhat Dantesque, in that the *Divine Comedy* is filled with discussions of issues—such as politics and poetry—that are visited repeatedly but with different meanings in each book of the *Commedia*. Dante's writing also uses father/son, king/prince, ancestor/descendant scenes in which one member of the pairing has ended up in Hell and another in Heaven to illustrate his parents.

A lack of interest in sex is in evidence throughout *Inferno*. Although Langdon is one of the most eligible bachelors in Cambridge (we learned this in *DVC*), his idea of a good time on a Saturday night is attending a lecture alone at Harvard. When faced with frightening and life-threatening circumstances in Florence, he finds it comforting to imagine himself back home, falling asleep in his chair after emptying a martini glass of gin and reading Gogol (more about that passage shortly). Langdon is so prudish that he even seems embarrassed by the overt sexuality of Renaissance statuary: "Normally, Langdon's visits to the Palazzo Vecchio had begun here on the Piazza della Signoria, which *despite its over-abundance of phalluses* (emphasis added), had always been one of his favorite plazas in all of Europe."

Sienna apparently never had sex before her first encounter with Zobrist six years ago, making her a beautiful twenty-six-year-old virgin at the time. Sinskey is sterile, and her sterility is used primarily to foreshadow the nature of Zobrist's virus he has unleashed on the world. But her inability to bear a child, confessed to her fiancé many years ago when she was last in Venice, drove him away and caused the relationship to end. It seems that she never married after that, and even though she is a world class doctor and head of the World Health Organization, never considered *in vitro* fertilization or any other new or old techniques (including adoption) to have a child.

Is there a larger purpose to this genre-defying disinterest in sex that runs throughout *Inferno*? Perhaps yes, and in three different ways.

First, Brown is rebelling against what he perceives (no doubt correctly) as our oversexed culture and, in particular, how much explicit and often kinky and over-the-edge sex you have to put into a novel (or movie or TV show) to qualify for popular entertainment. If you want to write a novel of ideas—and there's no doubt Brown wants to be a novelist of ideas, despite the pop culture format of his books and despite the critics' bashing of him—why do you also have to write about sex at every turn? (One also suspects from his prose style that Brown would only detract from his readership were he to attempt to augment his stories with more sexually explicit scenes).

Two, Dante himself makes significant use of metaphors and allusions regarding fertility and sterility. In Dante's *Inferno*, sexual sinners encounter the metaphoric punishment of wandering permanently in a *barren* desert with hot flames engulfing them. Later in the *Commedia*, Dante will have a dream that involves the two wives of Jacob, Leah and Rachel. One is extremely fertile and one appears sterile until later in life when she produces Jacob's two favorites sons. In Dante, most people would read reproductive fertility as a reward and metaphor for a virtuous life, while sterility is a punishment and a metaphor for going against God's injunction to "be fruitful and multiply." In Dan Brown's *Inferno*, on the other hand, where all the women (Sinskey, Sienna, etc.) are sterile or childless (except Marta, the pregnant curator who gives birth at the end of the story) and the men (Langdon, Zobrist, Ferris, the provost, etc.) are presumably unmarried and childless as well, these elements are spun in different directions in accord with Brown's plot about suggesting sterilization as a cure for overpopulation.

Three, there is a metaphor buried in *Inferno*'s sexlessness that pertains to Dante and Beatrice. If we are to believe Dante (which is not to say we should), Beatrice was his platonic ideal of the perfect woman, not his sexual fantasy of the perfect woman. They met only a few times, and his love for her was unconsummated physically. Yet he spent his whole life dreaming of her. For Dante, Beatrice is the embodiment of spiritual, not physical love. Dante's creation of Beatrice-as-muse is more in keeping with the chivalrous songs and romances of French medieval troubadours and storytellers who devote artistic works to a duchess, queen, or lady who is their muse, not necessarily their personal lover. A number of scholars agree this French cultural vernacular tradition was a major influence on Dante's creative development. Dante devotes two decades to writing the *Commedia*, and, in the end of the story, while he sees Beatrice in *Paradiso* and she guides him through Heaven, Dante, like Langdon, does not "get the girl."

The *Commedia* has a happy ending (qualifying it for the Italian meaning of a "comedy" in Dante's era, in addition to being written in the vernacular and focused on characters other than the nobility), but Dante and Beatrice do not live happily ever after together. Instead, they live on separately. After Dante's journey to the afterlife (which accounts for exactly as much elapsed time as the plot of Dan Brown's *Inferno*), Beatrice will remain in *Paradiso*. Dante, having learned from all that she and others have shown him, will return to the real world to try to live a more moral and spiritual life on earth. Exit, in separate directions, Robert Langdon and Sienna Brooks, just like Dante and Beatrice.

A 208 IQ? REALLY?

We are supposed to be impressed with how brilliant Sienna is when we learn she had an IQ of 208 as a child. It is good that Dan Brown tells us this, because we would not otherwise know from her dialogue lines, or her contribution to solving any of the clues, that she is particularly brilliant at all. In fact, of all the brainy, beautiful partners for Robert Langdon that Dan Brown has created, Sienna is the least obviously off-the-charts. An IQ of 208 is extremely unlikely and would make her among the highest IQ people since the advent of the test. By comparison, Steven Hawking weighs in at "only" 200, Einstein at 160. Kim Ung-Yong, a Korean former child prodigy, was once listed in the Guinness Book of World Records under "Highest IQ"; the book estimated the boy's score at about 210.

Of Marilyn vos Savant, one of the best-known high-IQ prodigies, Wikipedia tells us: "In 1985, *Guinness Book of World Records* accepted vos Savant's IQ score of 190 and gave her the record for Highest IQ (Women)." She was listed in that category from 1986 to 1989. She was inducted into the *Guinness Book of World Records Hall of Fame* in 1988. Guinness retired the category of "Highest IQ" in 1990, after concluding that IQ tests are not reliable enough to designate a single world-record holder." The Wikipedia article also notes that as a child, she tested at about 228, but that there are a number of controversies surrounding this test and the calculation of the result.

Where Sienna is clearly off-the-charts is in her martial arts skills, which come in handy in several situations. Dan Brown tells us that she has mastered the art of *dim mak*, a relatively obscure Chinese martial art whose name means "touch of death" or "death-point striking."

When you look into *dim mak* , you come across this interesting nugget: John Timothy Keehan, referred to as "a controversial martial artist figure during the 1960s and 1970s," was the best known American practitioner of *dim mak*. And what was Keehan's stage and performing name? *Count Dante!*

BOMBAY SAPPHIRE AND GOGOL SHOULD NEVER BE MIXED . . . A STRANGE SENTENCE OR A SERIES OF CLUES?

Dan Brown's books are full of carefully chosen words and phrases that work on more than one level. As in the example above, Brown could have endowed Sienna with any type of martial arts skill, but he chose *dim mak* partially because it is obscure, but probably also because its leading exponent was someone named Count Dante.

When one comes across a phrase or sentence in Dan Brown's writing that seems particularly artless or nonsensical, it is often trying—perhaps too hard—to convey something else. Dan Brown loves codes, symbols, anagrams, "ambigrams" (words that can be read right side up and upside down; these designs figure in the plot of *A&D*), and other verbal and printed pyrotechnics. So if you want to be in on the fun of a Dan Brown novel, you should look deeper when you come across a sentence like this one in *Inferno*:

"As Langdon stared into his own weary eyes, he half wondered if he might at any moment wake up in his reading chair at home clutching an empty martini glass and a copy of *Dead Souls*, only to remind himself that Bombay Sapphire and Gogol should never be mixed."

On the surface, this sounds like just a silly sentence; a poorly constructed, cliché of an image. Indeed, Tom Chivers, an editor at *The Telegraph*, selected this as one of his "Eight worst sentences in Dan Brown's *Inferno*."

But consider this:

> • *Dead Souls*, by the nineteenth century Russian novelist Nikolai Gogol, was deliberately intended to replicate Dante's *Inferno* and apply its imagery to the conditions of Russia. Gogol planned a three volume work that would draw on all three parts of Dante's *Commedia*. Dantesque ideas appear in several of Gogol's books.

• Bombay Sapphire, while it is a well-known brand of gin, has other connotations. Dante opens *Purgatorio* with a reference to the "sweet hue of Oriental sapphire," which signals the start of a new day and the beginning of his climb out of the Inferno. Sapphire in Dante's alchemical time was believed to have many properties: the blue color is associated with bright early morning light; exposure to this color is supposed to make the individual more pious and devoted to God and faith. In *Paradiso*, the Virgin Mary is said to be a "sapphire who enjewels Heaven."

• Bombay (Mumbai) is mentioned most likely because Dan Brown heard this story: "Kept in the basement of the Asiatic Society library, a colonnaded marble building in Mumbai's colonial heart, is perhaps the Indian financial capital's least heralded relic: one of the two oldest surviving manuscripts of Italian poet Dante Alighieri's *Divine Comedy*. Its some 450 richly illustrated pages, dating from the 1350s, are bound and wrapped in red silk..." (This particular account is from *Time*, January 2, 2009, when Brown was working on *Inferno*.)

SIENNA BROOKS AND SIENA, ITALY

There are always multiple layers and levels in Dan Brown's choices of names for his major characters (and frequently anagrams as well). A variety of commentaries in this book address some of the interesting nuances in character names (in particular, see Glenn Erickson's essay, "Letting the Genre out of the Bottle: Dan Brown's *Inferno* as Modern Parody").

When it came to naming the brilliant, beautiful woman at Robert Langdon's side (all four Langdon books feature a brilliant, beautiful female partner for the adventure), "Sienna" is an interesting choice. In Dante's day, the city of Siena, with one "n", was a Ghibelline stronghold and a frequent rival in bloody conflicts with Dante's Guelph-held Florence. Florence tended to look down on Siena, which was the young upstart in the rivalry, but Dante comments at several points in the *Commedia* that Siena actually does many things better than Florence.

In choosing the name Sienna, and introducing her very early in the story, Dan Brown is giving us an early warning that she will turn out to be a double agent with a different agenda. The *Commedia* is filled with discussions of treachery, an issue that Dante was very concerned with. There is a special place and special punishments in the *Inferno* for those who committed acts of treachery during their lifetimes. Although we don't learn that Sienna is Zobrist's lover/disciple/helpmate until we are three-quarters of the way through the book, Brown has actually tipped us off from the very beginning with his use of the name of Florence's greatest rival in Dante's time. And, since Dante is two-sided about the city of Siena, Brown has also conveyed something of the ambiguity of the Sienna character.

Earlier, we saw how Dan Brown weaves together the genders in search of a kind of philosophical/spiritual androgyny he believes lay at the heart of ancient religions. Although Robert Langdon remains Brown's primary incarnation of himself, he didn't select Sienna for the second lead character without an awareness that her name represents a shade of Brown, and therefore has at least a suggestion of himself.

As for the surname, Brooks, this may allude to the multiple rivers taken from Greek mythology and reworked by Dante into the landscape of the *Inferno* in order to serve different psychological and literary purposes. For example, Cocytus, a Greek mythological river in Hades, becomes a frozen lake that is home to the most treacherous sinners in Dante's *Inferno*. These sinners have committed four different kinds of treachery in their lifetimes, having betrayed relatives, country, guests, and benefactors/masters. All the rivers are important, but the other one with particular resonance for the relationship between Langdon and our Miss Brooks is the Lethe, another allusion to the Greeks. Toward the end of *Purgatorio*, Dante is bathed in this river, which induces amnesia just like Sienna and her colleagues have induced amnesia in Langdon. Shortly thereafter, Beatrice (partially analogous to Sienna), chides Dante for his amnesia and not realizing what a sinner he is, much as Sienna will later chide Langdon for not seeing the urgency and importance of Zobrist's plan to "save" the world.

WHAT'S UP WITH ALL THE "TALL" PEOPLE?

In Dan Brown's *Inferno*, protagonist Robert Langdon has changed in several important respects since his earlier adventures. For one thing, he seems a lot taller than he used to be. In both *The Lost Symbol* and in *Angels & Demons*, Langdon is said to be six feet tall. That squares with Dan Brown's general mid-century sensibilities—an important American midcentury male should be six feet tall (several inches taller than Brown himself). Six feet is a good height, but it would not be routinely referred to as "tall" by contemporary American standards.

In *Inferno*, Langdon is described many times as being "tall," although no height is given. (Langdon shifted his "tall frame," Langdon's "tall frame" materialized in the doorway, etc.) There are at least ten references to how tall Langdon is.

What is a bit odd is that everyone else is tall, too. Sienna Brooks is "tall and lissome."

Zobrist is also "exceptionally tall." When he meets Sinskey, Brown says that "a very tall and lanky silhouette faced her." And when he moves toward her, he seems "to grow taller with every step." "He is tall...so very tall..."

Sometimes Langdon is referred to simply as the "tall man." Sometimes Zobrist is referred to exactly the same way.

Sienna is not only "tall and lissome," she is also "tall and fair-skinned." But maybe Brown forgot how tall he had made her when, toward the end of the story, she has to "stand on her tiptoes" to kiss Langdon "full on the lips." (If she is "tall" she should be at least 5' 9".... A 5'9" woman, let alone an even taller woman, doesn't need to "stand on tiptoes" to kiss a man unless that man is over six feet).

So what's up with all the tall people? And why is Sienna tall throughout the book and then short when she wants to kiss Langdon?

THE SOLUBLON® BAG

Watching Zobrist's creepy video made before his death, Langdon and Sinskey discuss the specifics of the plastic bag that appears to contain the Inferno virus. They zoom in on the registered trademark for Solublon and Sinskey tells Langdon, "We've been in touch with the manufacturer...they make dozens of different grades of this plastic, dissolving in anywhere from ten minutes to ten weeks...Decay rates vary slightly based on water type and temperature...This bag, we believe, will dissolve by—" and then the provost adds the word Langdon is dreading: "tomorrow."

So it is the dissolution rate of this water soluble sac containing the virus that ostensibly becomes the ticking time bomb driving the final race to discover the location and get to the virus before it is released. (Of course, as it turns out, the virus appears to have been released several days earlier—and the rest of the actions of Langdon and the other characters will turn out to be pyrrhic in retrospect).

Solublon is a real name brand in the field of water soluble films for packaging and medical applications. The parent company is Aicello, a Japanese firm that declares on its web site that it has "developed a diverse range of cold and hot water soluble PVA films to meet the specific industry requirements by listening to our clients. Each grade of our lineup was developed to address specific customer needs." Presumably, they have not, in real life, worked with any mad scientist customers to develop a specific packaging film that will dissolve in a specified period in a cistern in Turkey and release the most virulent virus ever documented into the air and water.

One of the many, many flaws with Zobrist's plan is the lack of redundancy. No serious technologist would allow for a single point of failure in a plan like this. If anyone had found the Solublon bag before it released its contents into the water, if the Solublon did not dissolve at the specified rate, if the virus could not be kept alive in a Solublon bag in the water for several days, if....if....if.... dozens of other variables had not worked out perfectly, Zobrist would have killed himself in vain and everything he had worked for would have been aborted.

MONTAGUES AND CAPULETS

Dante achieved many firsts in the *Divine Comedy*. If you made a full list of these firsts, one interesting bit of trivia you would find is that he was the first to mention in book form the feuding families of Verona that the English-speaking world would later come to know by way of Shakespeare's *Romeo and Juliet* as the Montagues and the Capulets. (Romeo is the Montague and Juliet is the Capulet in this pair of starcrossed lovers whose lives end in tragedy.)

Dante refers to these two families by their Italian names—the Montecchi and the Cappelletti. These bold face names appear in a passage in *Purgatorio* where Dante laments the collapse of civil order in the Italian lands of the former Roman Empire. He cites warring factions and dysfunctional families as indicators of the moral and spiritual malaise in which Italy finds itself in the thirteenth and fourteenth centuries.

Some scholars believe that the Montecchi and the Cappelletti were not just feuding families but were also caught up in the Ghibelline versus Guelph factionalism that soaked northern Italian city-states in blood and conflict during the same time period. Indeed, it is possible that the tragedy of these two families is that they have fought each other for political control of their cities for so long that they have brought ruin to both sides. It may be a theatrical device several hundred years after the fact to humanize a bitter political rivalry by turning the story into one of a tragic romance between the young offspring of the Montagues and the Capulets.

Shakespeare wrote his version of the story in the 1590s. He apparently based it on a mix of several early and mid-sixteenth century English versions of the tale, English translations of popular Italian stories of the era, and similar stories that come from Greek and Roman classics. Curiously, despite the number of plays Shakespeare set in Italy, and his affinity for well-known Italian stories, he appears to have had no knowledge of Dante or the *Divine Comedy*.

This is especially curious, because Chaucer, who was born more than two centuries before Shakespeare, was already an admirer of Dante's (like Dante, Chaucer is the most important writer of his era and country chose to write in his vernacular, Old English). Chaucer is so familiar with *Divine Comedy* that he quoted from it and adapted a number of its stories and scenes in *Canterbury Tales*. Chaucer even referred specifically to Dante as "the grete poete of Ytaille, That highte Dant." Milton, born only a few decades after Shakespeare, was also highly influenced by Dante.

Shakespeare, however, seems to have missed the Dante boat, even though one of his most famous plays draws on families whose names appear to be first recorded in publishing history by Dante.

INTO THE WOODS: TUSCANY VS. NEW ENGLAND

What's the difference between Florence in the Middle Ages on the cusp of the Renaissance and New England in the early twentieth century on the cusp of modernism? It is interesting to look at the different ways that Dante and Robert Frost sense the issues in arriving in very different dark forests. They are each prototypical travelers of their time periods who find themselves lost in the prototypical woods of their geography and era. But each states their poetic predicament differently:

Midway in our life's journey, I went astray
from the straight road and woke to find myself
alone in a dark wood...
—Dante Alighieri, from the *Divine Comedy* (early
fourteenth century)

Two roads diverged in a wood, and I—
I took the one less traveled by,
And that has made all the difference.
—Robert Frost, from *The Road Not Taken* (1920)

JEFFREY SCHNAPP, A REAL-LIFE HARVARD PROFESSOR WHO DECODES DANTE

With the publication of *Inferno, Boston Magazine* interviewed Professor Jeffrey Schnapp, a real life Harvard Dante scholar, about ways in which the historic world of Dante might compare to Dan Brown's depiction. Among the highlights of Schnapp's comments:

> The manuscripts of Dante's own era are mul-
> timedia works of art that weave together lan-
> guage-based forms of artistic practice with many
> layers of visual crafting. Medieval authors and
> scribes were fascinated by the notion of magic
> words or anagrams and frequently integrated
> visual tricks and techniques into forms of literary
> expression. Dante is no exception and makes use
> of anagrams, acrostics, and other embedded visu-
> al codes in his *Comedy*...

Schnapp then goes on to cite key examples. One is an extend-ed acrostic in Canto XIX of the Paradiso, which corresponds to a prophecy about the decline and fall of the monarchies of Europe. In another case, a series of nine (Dante was fascinated by numerol-ogy and threes and nines in particular) tercets begin with the letters of the word lue (or lve in Roman letters), which suggests plague in Latin. Schnapp says that, "Dante (lived in) an era during which actual plagues were relatively frequent." Direct experience of the bubonic plague caused deep fears in the population, and Dante's acrostic may be referencing this as well as foreshadowing the Black Plague of 1348 that he would not live to see. But Schnapp cautions, "What dominates in Dante's poetic universe, rather than any naturalistic medical notion of the plague, is a moral understanding of the plague. It is moral plagues that plague Dante."

DAN BROWN ON BOOKS AND PUBLISHING

In *Inferno*, Dan Brown makes numerous references to the state of book publishing. Despite his personal success, he is clearly concerned about the future of the book. Brown makes several references to contemporary pop culture and to the handful of authors who have had publishing successes similar to his.

In the scene where Langdon is pleading with his editor, Jonas Faukman (a character based on Brown's real life editor, Jason Kaufman) to procure a NetJet for him, Faukman is reluctant to go to the expense needed to do this favor for Langdon. "If you want to write *Fifty Shades of Iconography*, we can talk," Faukman tells Langdon, making a word salad sentence out of Langdon's alleged expertise in iconography as a symbologist and a reference to the *Fifty Shades of Gray* phenomenon (books of erotica that dominated the bestseller lists in between Dan Brown's *Lost Symbol* and *Inferno*).

As he thinks over whether he is going to be helpful to Langdon or not, Faukman recalls the fact that Langdon missed his last deadline by three years. This is an allusion to *The Lost Symbol*, which was widely expected to appear in 2006-7 after Dan Brown's great success with *The Da Vinci Code* in 2003—but was not actually published until 2009, despite frequent rumors that it would be published in each of the years in between.

Stieg Larsson's *Girl with the Dragon Tattoo* (and the other books in his trilogy) also dominated global bestseller lists in the years between *Lost Symbol* and *Inferno*. Brown may be paying homage to the Larsson books with the character of Vayentha, whose spiked hair and motorcycle posture are reminiscent of Lisbeth Salander, Larsson's girl with the dragon tattoo.

Brown also references e-publishing and e-books.

An important plot device for Langdon's theories about Dante is a flashback to a lecture he had given at the Societa Dante Alighieri in Vienna. In a packed 2,000-seat hall, Langdon explains the culture and context of Dante's life and times. At one point, "after listing the vast array of famous composers, artists, and authors who had created works based on Dante's epic poem," Langdon asks the audience how many of them are authors. When a third of the hands go up, Langdon thinks to himself: "Wow, either this is the most accomplished audience on earth, or this e-publishing thing is really taking off."

In interviews, Brown has described *Inferno* as his first story in which Langdon's cultural treasure hunt passes mainly through a literary work. The visual arts have provided more of the cultural clues in the prior books—examples being Leonardo's *Last Supper* in *DVC*, Bernini's sculptures in *A&D*, and Durer's *Melencolia I* in *TLS*. But in fact all Brown's books are about books as much as they are about anything else. *Da Vinci Code* brought the Gnostic gospels to the attention of many readers for the first time, including referencing important real books, like Princeton scholar Elaine Pagels' book, *The Gnostic Gospels*. Brown drew on many real books that had never received much public interest prior to 2003 when *DVC* called attention to them. Indeed, his use of other authors' books even triggered a completely baseless but nevertheless prominent UK "plagiarism" suit brought against Brown by some of those associated with the book, *Holy Blood, Holy Grail*. His thanks for giving publicity to this book and even naming *DVC* character Leigh Teabing based on an anagram of one of the book's principal authors, was a lawsuit that tested whether a fiction writer was entitled to adapt ideas and theories found in a nonfiction book, or whether nonfiction authors had some kind of copyrightable control over not just their words but their ideas. Brown prevailed handily in the case.

Angels & Demons, written before Brown really hit his stride with *Da Vinci Code* has a fictional book by Galileo as the McGuffin.

The Lost Symbol emphasizes Freemasonry's love of books. It treats the Library of Congress in Washington, DC, as a temple to the book, which it is. Langdon and Katherine Solomon actually come to personify books as they escape from the Library of Congress by means of the book conveyor belt.

Throughout *TLS*, the characters are in a hunt to track down and understand the occult secrets known as the "ancient mysteries." In the end, this will turn out to be Dan Brown's metaphor for the wisdom of the ages, including the Judeo-Christian Bible, but also including all the other works of wisdom from ancient societies to modern science. Peter Solomon tries to explain to Robert Langdon that the sum total of all the wisdom of all these books is captured in the line from the Hermetic tradition: "Know ye not that ye are gods?" (This sentence, like "Cerca Trova" in *Inferno*, is the watchword of *TLS*). This idea of attributing God-like powers to mortal men is not just a proverb from an ancient mystery cult, but reflected in the books at the heart of all religions, including the *Book of Psalms*. Indeed, Psalm 82 says "I have said, Ye *are* gods; and all of you *are* children of the most High."

In *Inferno*, we will revisit this theme that Dan Brown is very focused on—that humans, made in the image of God, have God-like powers of knowledge and creativity. Thus, Zobrist has no problem "playing God" and taking the future of the species into his own hands, and transhumanists more broadly tend to believe there is nothing wrong with humans taking a technological or scientific hand in their own evolution.

Toward the end of *TLS*, there is a long meditation on the importance of the book as a container of wisdom: "Books. Every culture on earth had its own sacred book..." This discussion continues with the wise Dean Galloway contemplating the words said to be from his Masonic Bible: "Time is a river...and books are boats.

Many volumes start down that stream, only to be wrecked and lost beyond recall in its sands. Only a few, a very few, endure the testings of time and live to bless the ages following."

Clearly, Dante's *Divine Comedy* is one of those. Whether Dan Brown's books will stand that test of time is another matter altogether.

MICHELANGELO AND DANTE

Today it is easy to look back at Dante and see the origins of Renaissance thinking, art, and literature in the *Divine Comedy*. But how cognizant were the actual Renaissance geniuses of their debt to Dante? Dan Brown helps answer that question in *Inferno* by having Professor Langdon call our attention to one of Michelangelo's lesser known roles—as a poet, in addition to his better known roles as a painter and sculptor—and to one of his lesser known poems. This poem is titled "Dante" and it says of him: "Ne'er walked the earth a greater man than he." Langdon calls this a virtual "blurb" from Michelangelo encouraging Renaissance Italians to read Dante.

Langdon goes on to discuss ways that Michelangelo's Sistine Chapel paintings drew from Dante's vision of hell, even when that vision was at odds with certain details in the Bible.

A small but interesting footnote to Brown's use of Michelangelo: Michelangelo's ode to Dante, as translated by the leading American nineteenth century poet, Henry Wadsworth Longfellow, refers to Florence as an "ungrateful land." Longfellow was a great champion of Dante's and spent several years creating the first American translation of *The Divine Comedy*, which was published in 1867.

But Dante himself, while bitter about his exile from Florence, never called his native city-state an "ungrateful land." That particular phraseology is derived from Michelangelo via Longfellow. Yet Dan Brown uses it on the first page of *Inferno*, putting that very phrase into Zobrist's stream-of-consciousness rant as he climbs the Badia tower to jump to his death. The reader may assume it is a quote from Dante, but it is actually from the partnership of Michelangelo and Longfellow.

BROWN'S *INFERNO* IS NOT THE FIRST SUSPENSE NOVEL TO BASE ITSELF ON DANTE–OR ON POPULATION CONTROL ISSUES, FOR THAT MATTER

Speaking of Longfellow, as we were just above, and if you enjoyed the Dante-related themes of Dan Brown's *Inferno*, you might want to check out Matthew Pearl's 2003 crime and suspense novel, *The Dante Club*. Pearl tells a mysterious tale of serial murders in the 1860s, where each death scene resembles a scene described by Dante. He creates fictionalized versions of the leading poets and men of letters in the Boston area of that time period: Longfellow (who is then at work on his first American translation of the *Divine Comedy*) enlists Oliver Wendell Holmes, James Russell Lowell, and J.T. Fields into a Dante Club. The club is, at first, working together on the translation, but it then morphs into a detective agency to try to solve the murders before they do damage to Dante's incipient reputation in America. The second part of the last sentence is Pearl's fiction; the first is fact: Longfellow did gather around him leading poets, professors, and publishers in Boston and Cambridge and formed a Dante Club designed not only to improve his translation taken up in his grief after the death of his wife, but to champion Dante and help familiarize American readers with the *Divine Comedy*. For many years afterward, American intellectuals developed a passion for Dante. Clubs and societies devoted to Dante were formed in many college communities, and Longfellow's translation became the American standard.

As for suspense thrillers with misguided madmen who want to take global population control into their own hands, Dan Brown also fails to break new ground. That plot was cleverly laid out by Lionel Shriver in her 1994 novel, *Game Control*. Even the plot twist of otherwise intelligent people coming under the sway of the madman's theories (as Sienna, Sinskey, and Langdon all eventually come to agree with Zobrist in one way or another) is foreshadowed by Shriver in her novel from two decades ago. As her publisher describes it, *Game Control* features:

> Eleanor Merritt, a do-gooding American family-planning worker, drawn to Kenya to improve the lot of the poor. Unnervingly, she finds herself falling in love with the beguiling Calvin Piper, despite, or perhaps because of, his misanthropic theories about population control and the future of the human race. Surely, Calvin whispers seductively in Eleanor's ear, if the poor are a responsibility they are also an imposition. Set against the vivid backdrop of shambolic modern-day Africa—a continent now primarily populated with wildlife of the two-legged sort—Lionel Shriver's *Game Control* is a wry, grimly comic tale of bad ideas and good intentions...Shriver highlights the hypocrisy of lofty intellectuals who would 'save' humanity but who don't like people.

THERE'S SOMETHING MISSING FROM THE CLIVE JAMES TRANSLATION OF *DIVINE COMEDY*

In that wonderful way the great wheels of cultural synchronicities turn, Clive James, one of the English language's most respected critics and essayists, not to mention novelist, poet, memoirist, and translator, published his new translation of the *Divine Comedy* about six weeks before Dan Brown's *Inferno* was published. James had spent a decade developing this new translation, which generally received positive reviews, although it has also had its detractors.

In a great instance of incredible compliment meets incredible putdown, James wrote a review called, "The heroic absurdity of Dan Brown," in which he said of Brown that "he makes you want to turn the pages even though every page you turn demonstrates abundantly his complete lack of talent as a writer."

But without saying a word, Brown's plot in *Inferno* had already laid bare one of James's glaring deficiencies as a translator. In one of Brown's infrequent decisions to opt for subtlety, he created a plot that involves the contemporary and very much real-life transhumanist movement. With all Robert Langdon's discourse on Dante, he never observes that it was Dante who coined the word "transhumanism." Brown obviously knows this fact and has opted to leave it unstated. In the *Paradiso* section of the *Divine Comedy*, Dante's exposure to the heavenly bodies and to God has allowed him to cross the boundary of normal human beings and to become transhumanized. "*Trasumanar*" is the Italian word he coins to describe this process. In his translation from the 1960s, John Ciardi phrases Dante's self-reported inability to describe his heavenly experiences in words in this way:

> How speak trans-human change to human sense?
> Let the example speak until God's grace
> Grants the purse spirit the experience.

By contrast, Clive James puts the same idea from Canto I of *Paradiso* this way:

> ...To pass beyond the curb of
> Of mere humanity is a step doomed
> Not to be put in words: Let it suffice
> That the example should be put to him
> Graced with that history...

James seems to have decided Dante's concept needed a different translation. So in English, he explains Dante's transhuman experience as passing "beyond the curb of mere humanity." That's adequate, and arguably more intelligible to a twenty-first century audience than Ciardi. But James ends up missing a key word-invention of Dante's that also turns out to be very important to understanding Dan Brown's *Inferno*.

DRONES, DAN BROWN, AND THE RENAISSANCE

Contemporary fiction continues to incorporate new technology into its plots, and Dan Brown is part of one of the latest trends of authors integrating the use of drones in their stories. The "toy helicopter" drone that appears in *Inferno* parallels a primitive late 1960s era drone that plays a major role in Kurt Andersen's *True Believers* (2012) and a fanciful animal-shaped balloon drone that reappears periodically in William Gibson's *Zero History* (2010). (Gibson actually had a drone-like mini-helicopter in his fiction as far back as *Mona Lisa Overdrive* in 1988).

Inferno's helicopter drone is a deliberate reference to the Renaissance era designs of Leonardo da Vinci, whose notebooks included designs for various flying machines, including something that approximates a helicopter. In case Dan Brown's readers miss the visual reference, he makes it explicit in the Boboli Gardens scene: "Langdon wondered how the original Renaissance visitors here would have reacted at the sight of a real-life helicopter—a fantastical dream of Italy's own Leonardo da Vinci—hovering outside the grotto."

WHO INVENTED DOUBLE-ENTRY BOOKKEEPING?

In introducing the powerful Medici family, which dominated Florentine business, politics, and culture for several hundred years during the Renaissance, Dan Brown tells us in *Inferno* that "During its three-century reign, the royal house of Medici amassed unfathomable wealth and influence, producing four popes, two queens of France, and the largest financial institution in all of Europe. To this day, modern banks use the accounting method invented by the Medici—the dual-entry system of credits and debits."

Not so fast, Mr. Brown. Jane Gleeson-White, in her 2011 book *Double Entry: How the Merchants of Venice Created Modern Finance*, credits the invention of double-entry bookkeeping to the Venetians, not the Florentine Medici. In particular, she attributes the most important work to develop this system to Luca Pacioli, a young man from a small hill town who was attracted to the big city—Venice—and learned bookkeeping from merchants there. Eventually, he would mix and match the then-prevailing Venetian system with what he learned from Greek and Arabic mathematical systems and some of his own ideas to create the overall architecture for what is generally known as double-entry bookkeeping today.

DANTE AMONG THE ASTRONAUTS

Dante and Dan Brown share a taste for bringing references to science and recent discoveries into their storytelling.

Like the ancient Greeks, Dante knows that the earth is round. (It is only in the two centuries between Dante and Columbus that Church-influenced public thinking will give retrograde currency to the notion of a flat earth). He is aware of the different time zones and that the earth is in a different position relative to the sun at the same moment in Jerusalem as compared to Florence. He knows there is a world beyond the Pillars of Hercules. He also knows there is a civilization in the Indus river valley and he worries philosophically that it cannot be just that the man of the Indus who has never heard of Jesus cannot be saved spiritually.

Dante pays a lot of attention to the stars and the constellations, ending each section of the *Commedia* on a reference to stars, just as Dan Brown ends his *Inferno* with the word "stars." (Dante: "Thence we came forth to re-behold the stars." Dan Brown: "The sky had become a glistening tapestry of stars".) In the wake of the publication of Dan Brown's novel, science writer Amir Aczel commented on Dante's advanced understanding of heavenly formations, noting his reference to what is known as the "Southern Cross" a century and a half before this constellation was documented by European explorers and navigators. In *Purgatorio*, Dante says:

> Then I turned to the right, setting my mind upon the other pole, and saw <u>four stars</u> <u>not seen before except by the first people.</u> Heaven appeared to revel in their flames: O northern hemisphere, because you were denied that sight, you are a widower!

Although it is not without dispute, many experts think that "four stars" is a reference to the Southern Cross. Dante knows he is describing something he expects most of his contemporaries—all of whom are northern-hemisphere dwellers—don't know about. Indeed, Dante claims he is the first to see this celestial formation since Adam and Eve ("the first people"). However, owing to the phenomenon of the *precession of the equinoxes*, the visibility of the Southern Cross in the northern hemisphere has changed considerably over a 26,000-year time cycle. It was visible to the Greeks 2,500 years ago, but by Dante's time, you could no longer see the Southern Cross as easily in most of Mediterranean Europe. It took Portuguese and Italian explorers traveling into the southern hemisphere in the fifteenth century to re-identify it, although Dante may have been aware of some sightings around 1300. Even today, the Southern Cross is visible at some times of the year in the northern hemisphere in the latitudes of North Africa, Egypt, and the Middle East. Dante could have come upon references to it from Greek, Roman, or Egyptian sources. There is evidence in his writings that he understood the *precession of the equinoxes* and was therefore not dependent on future generations of European explorers to re-find the Southern Cross. This kind of obscure, if not completely unknown detail, especially about astronomical and scientific facts that most intellectuals of 1300 did not know, fills Dante's encyclopedic mind and finds its way into the *Commedia* in a manner that modern scholars marvel at.

Dante is also realistic about earth's extremely modest place in the scheme of the universe. He is not afraid to draw the obvious— were it not for medieval religion—conclusion that earth is but a small speck in the cosmos.

It is instructive to compare the comments of twentieth century astronauts who looked back at earth from space with Dante's imagined visit to the celestial realm in *Paradiso*. Considering the gap of seven hundred years, and the fact that the astronauts actually went into space while Dante only imagined celestial travel, their view of earth is remarkably similar:

> It suddenly struck me that that tiny pea, pretty and blue, was the Earth. I put up my thumb and shut one eye, and my thumb blotted out the planet Earth. I didn't feel like a giant. I felt very, very small.
> —Neil Armstrong

> Then looked I downward through the seven spheres. How mean, how paltry our proud earth appears seen from that height! I must smile to see its meager aspect.
> —Dante Alighieri

THE STORY OF FRANCESCA AND PAOLO, "THE KISS," AND A NEW TALE OF ULYSSES

When Dante meets Francesca da Rimini (a.k.a. Francesca da Polenta) in the Inferno, he hears her story and he is obviously moved by the tragedy of it. Indeed, he is far more moved by Francesca's plight than he will be by most of the stories he hears from the Inferno's cast of famous sinners. Francesca had an affair with her brother-in-law, Paolo. When the lovers were discovered in bed together, Francesca's husband killed his wife and brother on the spot. Now, Francesca and Paolo, who could not control their lust and desire while on earth, are condemned forever to the Inferno, to be buffeted for all eternity by the hurricane wind of lust, while locked in a permanent embrace they cannot enjoy.

Dante plays an interesting game of subtle allusions and references in recounting this story that was gossiped about in his own lifetime. Francesca explains that she and Paolo used as a kind of stimulus to love a copy of a French romantic book about Lancelot and Guinevere, and the love affair that took place behind King Arthur's back. "That day we read no more," she says, implying that stimulated by the book, they closed it and submitted themselves to the power of love. But the line "That day we read no more," is a reference to another person reading another book: St. Augustine reading St. Paul. In telling his own story of youthful lust and passion almost a millennium earlier, Augustine, a major force in Dante's thinking, uses essentially the same line—that day I needed to read no more and closed the book—to explain how he understood the message of St. Paul's *Epistle to the Romans*, and there and then decided to change his ways, get his passions and desires under control, and turn toward God. There is also a name play on Paul and Paolo taking place here: Francesca is in bed with the "wrong" book and the "wrong" Paul, and as a result, her experience is the opposite of Augustine's. Of course, you can read Francesca's story in Dante's *Inferno* and get the meaning, power, and tragedy of it without understanding any of this. But the double meanings and the word play are there if you choose to look for them. (Cerca trova!)

Dan Brown has adopted this technique of cross-stitching allusions into a layer below the text of his *Inferno*, as we have seen above in the case of the references to Gogol, Sapphire, and Bombay. There are many other instances of this throughout Brown's novel, none of which need to be puzzled out to enjoy it.

The famous sculpture by Auguste Rodin, The Kiss, is based on the Francesca and Paolo story. Indeed, its original title was "Francesca da Rimini." Rodin was deeply interested in Dante and spent many years creating works that essentially put a nineteenth century sculptor's eye to the *Inferno*. His most famous sculpture, The Thinker, is actually believed by many to be Rodin's interpretation of Dante contemplating the Gates of Hell. One of dozens of the most prominent names in the Western cannon of literature, art, music, philosophy, and poetry to be fascinated/obsessed with Dante, Rodin spent thirty-seven years of his life working on a massive sculptural tableau of the Gates of Hell, peopled by many of the sinners and scenes from Dante's poem.

But returning to a most fundamental question: Why does Dante show so much pity for Francesca? Why do readers end up sympathizing with her? And why is she allowed to tell her story in a way that makes Dante and the reader think of her as a beautiful, gracious woman captured only by love? She shows almost no remorse and vents her anger at her murderous husband—in effect accusing him of being the real sinner. She predicts that he will end up in hell as well. Could it have anything to do with the fact that Dante's patron at the end of his life was Guido II Novello da Polenta, the nephew of Francesca? Guido, who was the most powerful person in Ravenna for a time, housed and hosted Dante there, paid him great respect as a poet and philosopher, even as he was still in exile from Florence, and sent Dante on diplomatic missions on his behalf. Although *Inferno* was presumably written before Dante took up residence in Ravenna, no definitive version was published until after his death. Might he have revised the Francesca story to make it a more humanistic tale rather than the sordid, gossipy version that surrounded the story of Guido's family at the time? Because of the *Divine Comedy*, Francesca today is remembered as one of the world's great lovers and as a tragic soul rather than merely a sinner.

Perhaps not surprisingly, Dan Brown has managed to work into his modern story several plugs and cameo roles for his friends and people who have helped him with his research. (See David Shugarts in this book on the Friesian horse troupe from New Hampshire that makes an appearance in Brown's novel).

But there is also another interpretation to be made about Dante's view of Francesca, and perhaps Ulysses as well. Fair warning: This one is a literary/philosophical thought provocation that will not be endorsed by mainstream Dante scholars. What if Dante himself is guilty of the sin of adultery just like Francesca? After all, we never really learn why Dante is in the midlife crisis represented by finding himself lost in the dark wood at the opening of the story. We know that Beatrice, when Dante finally meets up with her, scolds him for having forgotten her memory and perhaps implies very subtly that he devoted himself to other women (besides his wife Gemma) after Beatrice's death. So perhaps Francesca's story of being spurred on to passionate, adulterous love (by a French vernacular romance, written in a style Dante was known to have studied and learned from, no less), is actually Dante's story?

After Francesca, the other character in *Inferno* that we feel for similarly is Ulysses. With Odysseus/Ulysses (Dante apparently did not read Greek and relied on Latin versions of Homer's epic tales for his understanding of the character), Dante deploys a tactic he uses in several other key places in *Divine Comedy*: He freely reinvents and adapts the classic story, even in a book nominally imbued with deep reverence for the classics. (And Dan Brown, in turn, relies on the permission inherently granted by Dante's freewheeling attitude toward the classics to reinvent and adapt Dante himself to serve his own purposes in his twenty-first century *Inferno*!)

In the case of Ulysses, Dante invents an entirely new and penultimate chapter for the *Odyssey*. Ulysses himself was a swaggering hero to the Greeks, about as close to a god as a mortal man can get. If he were a god, he would be the god of leadership, cunning, and inventive intelligence. Whatever he did, whatever sins he committed during the long years after the Trojan War when he was away from home and family, he was always thinking of home and family and trying to return to his wife and son, Penelope and Telemachus. So much did he long for his home in Ithaca that the *Odyssey* is considered the original story of nostalgia.

The Romans had a more critical view of the man they called Ulysses, one that emphasized his guile and masterful deceptions. (Odysseus is generally believed to be the originator of the Trojan Horse stratagem that brought the Greeks victory). Although his sins of deception could be construed as a reason for him to be consigned to hell, Dante creates a whole other story—one unknown in the works of Homer or later Roman poets (unless Dante had come across one of the several lost books of Homer)—that causes Ulysses to end up in hell.

In the *Divine Comedy*, Dante will have Ulysses explain that he didn't really care so much for home and family once he made it back to Ithaca. Instead, he almost immediately raised his old crew and set out again to take on yet another adventure. This one, an attempt to sail beyond the Pillars of Hercules to discover "what lies beyond the sun" in the land they call unpeopled—i.e., in the direction of America and the New World—ends in disaster.

A terrible shipwreck claims the lives of Ulysses and all his men in Dante's telling. Now Ulysses is guilty of having conned his men into taking one more trip and is responsible for their deaths. He is also guilty of a multitude of other sins—daring to go too far, daring to break the boundaries of the known world, daring to believe that he could rely on his skill and cunning to overcome every obstacle. These are suitable medieval reasons for condemning this most famous of all Greek heroes. But one cannot read this section of Dante's *Inferno* without seeing a substantial touch of the poet himself in Ulysses' character. Ulysses, who has known every physical adventure imaginable, is drawn to this last trip because, like Dante, he is driven by the quest for knowledge and the desire to know what no one else knows. Dante, with this very poem, is trying to break the chains of the prevailing medieval worldview and sail to a new world. He shares the belief of his Ulysses that no knowledge should be forbidden.

We cannot easily conclude that Dante is Francesca, rather than merely sympathetic to her. But several important scholars see a very direct connection and even an identity between Dante and Ulysses.

Dan Brown has doubtless read these theories. The idea of Dante seeing himself as both Francesca and Ulysses would certainly resonate with Brown's investing part of his own persona in Langdon and another part in Sienna.

Acknowledgments

Special thanks are due to a number of people who helped make this book a reality. Lou Aronica and his team at The Story Plant embraced our vision and helped us move from idea to book in a matter of weeks. Danny Baror and Heather Baror continued their tradition of causing us to say that in Baror International, we have the best agent in the world.

It takes a village to make a *Secrets* book, and we are privileged to have assembled an unparalleled group of experts to contribute to *Secrets of Inferno*. Many thanks to: Teodolinda Barolini, Steven Botterill, Jamais Cascio, Joel E. Cohen, William Cook, Alison Cornish, Glenn W. Erickson, Paul Erlich, Laurie Garrett, Cheryl Helm, Giuseppe Mazzotta, David Orban, David A. Shugarts, Gregory Stock, and Natasha Vita-More.

Allison Cronk, Barbara Aronica-Buck, and Mick Spillane, and the team at Story Plant also deserve our thanks, as does Perseus, our book distributor.

We are deeply appreciative of the work of more than thirty international publishers who have placed so much faith in us through the last decade of publishing our *Secrets* titles in global markets, ever since *Secrets of the Code* in 2004. Sperling & Kupfer in Italy and Ta-Ke Shobo in Japan have been very special partners for us. *Grazie mille* and *domo arigato*.

Julie O'Connor provided the cover photo of Dante's death mask, as well as all the photography of Florence.

Special appreciation as well to: Adam Guha, Alexandra Lawrence, Cynthia O'Connor, Miguel Sal, Claudia Sala & Alberto Elli, Ettore Sobrero, Brian Weiss, and to those who looked after us in Italy, including the staff of the Hotel Lugarno in Florence and Barbara Ronchetti in Lake Como.

As always, our families have provided great ideas and insights, helped us think about the issues, and supported us at every step of the book process. Julie O'Connor and David Burstein, and Helen and Hannah de Keijzer, are partners in all we do.

Contributors

Dan Burstein is the creator, editor, and author of the *Secrets* series, which includes the world's bestselling guidebooks to the fiction of Dan Brown. Beginning with *Secrets of the Code* in 2004, Burstein has spearheaded six books of commentaries on Brown's fiction that today have over four million copies in print worldwide. The *Secrets* books have been translated into over thirty languages and have, in aggregate, appeared on more than a dozen bestseller lists, including twenty-eight weeks on the *New York Times* bestseller list. They have also been the basis for three documentary films and three collector's editions of *US News*. The author of fourteen books, Burstein has had a passionate interest in Dante Alighieri and the *Divine Comedy* since he was twelve years old. Burstein has won many journalism awards over his career, and he and coauthor Arne de Keijzer were nominated for a 2012 Edgar Award by the Mystery Writers of America for their book on Stieg Larsson and the *Girl with the Dragon Tattoo*. Burstein is cofounder and managing partner of Millennium Technology Value Partners, a New York City-based venture capital firm that has invested in some of the leading technology companies of our time.

Arne de Keijzer is cocreator and coeditor, with Dan Burstein, of the *Secrets* series. Over his writing career, de Keijzer has contributed to a wide variety of publications and authored books on topics ranging from international business to new technologies. For two decades, he ran his own business consultancy in the China trade, during which time he wrote the best selling *China Guidebook* and two editions of *China: Business Strategies for the 90s*. His collaboration with Dan Burstein began in 1998 with the publication of *Big Dragon*, an innovative look at China's economic and political future and its impact on the world. The team subsequently formed Squibnocket Partners LLC, a creative content development company that has now published ten books, including two *New York Times* bestsellers.

Teodolinda Barolini is Da Ponte Professor of Italian at Columbia University. She is the author of *Dante's Poets* (Princeton, 1984; Italian trans. Bollati Boringhieri, 1993), *The Undivine Comedy: Detheologizing Dante* (Princeton, 1992; Italian trans. Feltrinelli, 2003), *Dante and the Origins of Italian Literary Culture* (Fordham, 2006; Italian trans. Bompiani, 2012), and the editor and commentator on Dante's lyric poems, *Rime giovanili e della 'Vita Nuova'* (Rizzoli, 2009). She is currently working on the second volume of her commentary to Dante's lyric poems. Barolini is a Fellow of the American Academy of Arts and Sciences, the American Philosophical Society, and the Medieval Academy of America. She served as the fifteenth President of the Dante Society of America (1997-2003).

Steven Botterill is Associate Professor of Italian Studies and Director of the interdisciplinary doctoral program in Romance Languages and Literatures at the University of California, Berkeley. He is the author of two books and numerous articles on Dante, and a two-time elected member of the council of the Dante Society of America. His teaching covers the spectrum of Italian literature and culture from 1200 to 1500 CE, with occasional forays into the Romantic period and modern poetry. He is currently completing a book entitled *Dante and the Language of Community* and is researching one on Dante's theological ethics.

Jamais Cascio writes about the intersection of emerging technologies, environmental dilemmas, and cultural transformation, specializing in the design and creation of plausible scenarios of the future. In 2010 he was named a Distinguished Fellow at the Institute for the Future, where he is a primary contributor to the annual Ten Year Forecast program. Cascio is also a Senior Fellow at the Institute for Ethics and Emerging Technologies. In March 2006 he started Open the Future, his online home. Cascio has also applied his skills in the entertainment industry and designed several science fiction game settings. In 2009, he published his first book, *Hacking the Earth: Understanding the Consequences of Geoengineering.*

Joel E. Cohen is the Abby Rockefeller Mauzé Professor of Populations and head of the Laboratory of Populations at the Rockefeller University and Columbia University. At Columbia, he holds appointments in the Earth Institute and the Departments of International and Public Affairs, as well as Earth and Environmental Sciences and Ecology, Evolution, and Environmental Biology. Cohen was a MacArthur Fellow and elected to the American Academy of Arts and Sciences in evolutionary and population biology and ecology and the US National Academy of Sciences in applied mathematical sciences. He studies the demography, ecology, epidemiology, and social organization of human and nonhuman populations and mathematical concepts useful in these fields. His most recent book is *International Perspectives on the Goals of Universal and Secondary Education* (coedited with Martin Malin).

William R. Cook holds degrees from Wabash College (AB, LHD) and Cornell University (MA, PhD.). He taught medieval history at SUNY Geneseo for forty-two years, retiring in 2012. He was Visiting Professor of Religion and History at Wabash College 2008-2010 and 2013. He is the author of five books, including *The Medieval World View* (Oxford University Press, 3rd ed. 2012) with Ronald Herzman. Cook has made nine audio/video courses for The Teaching Company, including the bestselling *The Cathedral* and *Dante's Divine Comedy* (with Ronald Herzman). He has won many teaching awards, including New York State Professor of the Year from The Council for the Advancement and Support of Education in 1992.

Alison Cornish is Professor of Italian in the Department of Romance Languages and Literatures at the University of Michigan, Ann Arbor. She is the author of various articles on Dante and his culture in addition to two monographs: *Reading Dante's*

Stars (Yale, 2000) and *Vernacular Translation in Dante's Italy: Illiterate Literature* (Cambridge, 2011). She is on the editorial board of *Dante Studies*, *Italian Culture*, and the Devers Series in Dante Studies. She teaches courses on Boccaccio, Petrarch, Ariosto, Machiavelli, and Italian Through Opera, in addition to Dante's *Divine Comedy*.

Glenn W. Erickson is Professor of Philosophy at the Universidade Federal do Rio Grande do Norte in Brazil. He has written extensively in the areas of comparative literature and history of thought and on the intersticies of philosophy, mathematics, and the arts. He is also a regular contributor to the *Secrets* series.

Paul R. Ehrlich has pursued long-term studies of the structure, dynamics, and genetics of natural butterfly populations. He has also been a pioneer in raising issues of population, resources, and the environment as matters of public policy. Ehrlich, the Bing Professor of Population Studies at Stanford University, is a fellow of the American Association for the Advancement of Science, the American Academy of Arts and Sciences, and the American Philosophical Society. The winner of many prizes and awards in ecology and biological sciences, he is a widely published author whose most famous book is *The Population Bomb* (1968). Along with his wife Anne, he also wrote *The Population Explosion* (1990) and *Healing the Planet* (1991).

Laurie Garrett is Senior Fellow for Global Health at the Council on Foreign Relations. In 1992-1993, she was a Fellow at Harvard University, working closely with the emerging diseases group. During the 1990s, Garrett continued tracking outbreaks and epidemics worldwide, noting the insufficient responses from global public health institutions in Zaire, India, Russia, and most of the former USSR, Eastern Europe, and the United States. In 1994, she wrote her first bestselling book, *The Coming Plague: Newly Emerging Diseases in a World Out of Balance*. She joined the think-tank staff of the Council on Foreign Relations in 2004 where she regularly writes reports and articles on the intersection between global heath and public policy.

Cheryl Lynn Helm is the executive assistant for an Episcopal convent in upper Manhattan. She is a graduate of the University of Delaware with a major in music theory and a minor in medieval studies. In her spare time, she sings with the Canby Singers and composes choral music. Her skills as a Dan Brown puzzle solver have earned her a Cryptex, a signed illustrated *Da Vinci Code*, and a signed first edition of *The Lost Symbol*.

Giuseppe Mazzotta is Sterling Professor in the Humanities for Italian at Yale University, where he has been teaching since 1983 and where he also serves as Chairman of the Italian Department. He has published a number of books on Dante, including *Dante, Poet of the Desert* (Princeton, 1979) and *Dante's Vision and the Circle of Knowledge* (Princeton 1993). His two most recent books on Dante are *Reading Dante* (Yale, 2013) and *Confine quasi Orizzonte: Saggi su Dante* (Rome, 2013). He has received honorary degrees in Humane Letters from the Catholic University of America (2012) and in Sacred Letters from the University of Toronto (2012). He has also served as president of the Dante Society of America.

Julie O'Connor is the photo editor of this book and contributed significantly to the research process. She is an award-winning fine art photographer and photojoualist known for her "Doors of Tibet" series (www.JulieOConnor.com). She is also author/photographer of the book *Doors of Weston: 300 Years of Passageways in a Connecticut Town*. Her photographs for *Secrets of Inferno* were taken in Florence in 2013.

David Orban, a former chairman of Humanity+, is an entrepreneur, futurist, and CEO of Dotsub, a technology and services provider powering video viewing. David is also a member of the Faculty of and Advisor to the Singularity University, an interdisciplinary university whose mission is to assemble, educate, and inspire leaders who strive to understand and facilitate the development of exponentially advancing technologies in order to address humanity's grand challenges.

David A. Shugarts, a key contributor to *Secrets of Inferno,* has been a core member of the *Secrets* team since the publication of *Secrets of the Code* in 2004. He is also an award-winning journalist, investigative reporter, and editor. His profile of Dan Brown and the predictions he made about the content of *The Lost Symbol,* detailed in his book *Secrets of the Widow's Son* (2005), proved remarkably prescient and won him national acclaim.

Gregory Stock is a biotech entrepreneur, bioethicist, bestselling author, and a leading authority on the broad impacts of genomic and other advanced technologies in the life sciences. He founded the Program on Medicine, Technology and Society at UCLA's School of Medicine in 1997. Dr. Stock serves on the California Advisory Committee on Stem Cells and Reproductive Cloning and is the Associate Director of the Center for Life Science Policy Studies at the University of California at Berkeley. He is also the Chief Scientific Officer of Ecoes, a personal genomics company, and serves on the on the boards of Signum Biosciences and Napo Pharmaceuticals. Gregory Stock's books include *Redesigning Humans: Our Inevitable Genetic Future, Metaman: The Merging of Humans and Machine into a Global Superorganism,* and the bestselling *Book of Questions.*

Natasha Vita-More is a researcher in "the aesthetics of human enhancement and radical life extension, and hybridity, with a focus on nanotechnology, biotechnology, information technology, and cognitive and neurosciences." She has been called the first female philosopher of transhumanism and is well known for her "Transhumanist Manifesto" (written in 1983). She is chairman of the Board of Directors of Humanity+, past president of the Extropy Institute, the forerunner of Humanity+ (2000-2006), founder and director of Transhumanist Arts & Culture, and artistic director of the H+ laboratory. Her new book is *The Transhumanist Reader: Classical and Contemporary Essays on the Science, Technology, and Philosophy of the Human Future*, co-edited with Max More (2013).